Trading for Beginners

3 Books in 1:

Day Trading for Beginners

Forex Trading for Beginners

Options Trading Crash Course

indirect, which are incurred as a result of the use of information contained within this document, including, but not limited to, — errors, omissions, or inaccuracies.

Day Trading for Beginners

How to Day Trade for a Living: Proven Strategies, Tactics and Psychology to Create a Passive Income from Home with Trading Investing in Stocks, Options and Forex

Table of Contents

Develop a Trading Plan

Maintain Simplicity

Establish a Stop-Loss Level

Determine Your Position Size

Curb Your Emotions

Conduct Repeated Day Trading on the Same Stock

Conduct Generalized Daily Searches for Favorable Stock

Execute A Stock Screener Based on Preferential Criteria

Day Trading Tools and Services

Features of the Best Day Trading Platforms

Day Trading Charts

Technical Indicators

Types of Charts Used in Day Trading

Introduction to Candlesticks

Bullish Candlesticks

Bearish Candlesticks

Indecision Candle

Day Trading Risk Management

Price Action in Day Trading

Breakout Trading

Scalping

News Releases Trading

Introduction

Congratulations on purchasing *Day Trading for Beginners* and thank you for doing so. The following chapters will discuss everything a beginner would need to know concerning Day Trading and making a substantial passive income from home.

The first chapter is an introduction to Day Trading. The chapter begins with an explanation into the workings of Day Trading, it offers a breakdown into its basics and describes the meanings and importance of Volume, Price, and Technical Indicators to a Day Trader. The chapter concludes with an explanation of social trading and then a comparative mention of investments in Stocks, Options, and Forex trading.

The second chapter is a dive into the intricacies of risk management in Day Trading as well as the best Account Management strategies for traders in this line of business. The third chapter is a teaching on the strategies a beginner to Day Trading can begin his or her quest for stocks. The chapter covers the importance of conducting repeated Day Trading on the same stock, the process of conducting daily searches, and the process of executing a stock screener based on preferential criteria.

The fourth chapter is an in-depth study of the Day Trading tools and strategies. This chapter covers the tools and services available for Day Traders and then offers an explanation into the features of the Best Day Trading Platforms. The chapter concludes with a study of the charts available for Day Trading and an introduction to candlesticks. The fifth chapter is an explanation of the proper Day Trading risk management strategies and the meaning of Price Action in Day Trading.

The sixth chapter is an introduction and comprehensive study of some of the leading Day Trading strategies. Some of these include Scalping, breakout trading, range trading, and High-frequency trading, among others. A beginner will need to be familiar with these for he or she to start Day Trading in the best possible way.

The seventh chapter is about technical analysis, or in other words, the study of the price changes and trends of a stock or security. The chapter begins with a study of trendline analysis, and it continues to explain everything involved in volume analysis, and concludes with candlestick charting. Chapter eighth is about the mindset or psychology a day trader should have whenever he or she is trading. The chapter goes into detail to explain making trading decisions, keeping emotions at check, and exercising patience on every trade.

Every line of business has rules that all the players have to abide by, and people need to follow them to ensure a level playing field for everyone. The ninth chapter covers the various rules and regulations governing Day Trading, and it begins with the seven rules of Day Trading, other general rules, and concludes with an explanation of the workings of the Securities and Exchange Commission.

The tenth chapter begins with a step-by-step guide to making a successful trade, and then it provides a few examples of day trades. The eleventh chapter continues with the theme of success, since it begins with advice and methods that beginners should heed to, and concludes with the most common mistakes day traders make and a list of reasons people fail in Day Trading. The last chapter explains how an individual should expect an ROI and make a substantial passive income through Day Trading.

There are plenty of books on this subject on the market, thanks again for choosing this one! Every effort was made to ensure it is full of as much useful information as possible, please enjoy!

Chapter 1: Introduction to Day Trading

In order to understand Day Trading, it is important to know what it is not. Day Trading is not investing, which, in simple words, is the process of purchasing a stake in an asset with the hope of building a profit over time. Time, in this case, is subjective; however, investors can hold on to an asset for years or even decades.

Investors usually invest in organizations that pay off debts, make good profits, and have a good range of popular products and/or services. On the other hand, Day Trading is the process of purchasing and selling assets within the same day, often using borrowed funds to take advantage of small price shifts in highly liquid indexes or stocks.

How Day Trading Works

There was a time when the only people able to trade in financial markets were those working for trading houses, brokerages, and financial institutions. The rise of the internet, however, made things easier for individual traders to get in on the action. Day Trading, in particular, can be a very profitable career, as long as one goes about it in the right way.

However, it can be quite challenging for new traders, especially those who lack a good strategy. Furthermore, even the most experienced day traders hit rough patches occasionally. As stated earlier, Day Trading is the purchase and sale of an asset within a single trading day. It can happen in any marketplace, but it is more common in the stock and forex markets.

Day traders use short-term trading strategies and a high level of leverage to take advantage of small price movements in highly liquid currencies or stocks. Experienced day traders have their finger on events that lead to short-term price movements, such as the news, corporate earnings, economic statistics, and interest rates, which are subject to market psychology and market expectations.

When the market exceeds or fails to meet those expectations, it causes unexpected, significant moves that can benefit attuned day traders. However, venturing into this line of business is not a decision prospective day trader should take lightly. It is possible for day traders to make a comfortable living trading for a few hours each day.

However, for new traders, this kind of success takes time. Think like several months or more than a year. For most day traders, the first year is quite tough. It is full of numerous wins and losses, which can stretch anyone's nerves to the limit. Therefore, a day trader's first realistic goal should be to hold on to his/her trading capital.

Volatility is the name of the game when it comes to Day Trading. Traders rely on a market or stock's fluctuations to make money. They prefer stocks that bounce around several times a day, but do not care about the reason for those price fluctuations. Day traders will also go for stocks with high liquidity, which will allow them to enter and exit positions without affecting the price of the stock.

Day traders might short sell a stock if its price is decreasing or purchase if it is increasing. Actually, they might trade it several times in a day, purchasing it and short-selling it a number of times, based on the changing market sentiment. In spite of the trading strategy used, their wish is for the stock price to move.

Day Trading, however, is tricky for two main reasons. Firstly, day traders often compete with professionals, and secondly, they tend to have psychological biases that complicate the trading process.

Professional day traders understand the traps and tricks of this form of trading. In addition, they leverage personal connections, trading data subscriptions, and state-of-the-art technology to succeed. However, they still make losing trades. Some of these professionals are high-frequency traders whose aim is to skim pennies off every trade.

The Day Trading field is a crowded playground, which is why professional day traders love the participation of inexperienced traders. Essentially, it helps them make more money. In addition, retail traders tend to hold on to losing trades too long and sell winning trades too early.

Due to the urge to close a profitable trade to make some money, retail investors sort of pick the flowers and water the weeds. In other words, they have a strong aversion to making even a small loss. This tends to tie their hands behind their backs when it comes to purchasing a declining asset. This is due to the fear that it might decline further.

How to Start

People who want to start Day Trading should do several things to put themselves on the right path. Firstly, they need to step back and ask themselves whether this form of trading is really for them. Day Trading is not for the faint of heart. It requires a high level of focus and is not something people should risk their retirement plan to do.

Actually, beginners should consider opening a practice account before committing their hard-earned money. Reputable brokerage firms provide such accounts or stock market simulators to aspiring traders, through which they can make hypothetical trades and see the results.

In addition, aspiring day traders need to have a suitable brokerage account before they begin trading. Some brokers charge high transaction costs, which can erode the gains from winning trades. In addition, good brokers provide research resources that are invaluable to traders.

Aspiring traders who discover that Day Trading is not for them should do what smart investors do, which is engaging in long-term investing in a diversified fund or stock portfolio. They should regularly add more funds to their accounts and let the magic of growth expand their investment portfolio. This may not be as thrilling as Day Trading, but it is better than doing something that will clean out one's savings.

Consider Constraints and Goals

Before investing the time, energy, and effort in learning or creating and then practicing Day Trading, prospective day traders should consider their constraints and goals. For example:

1. Traders need to determine whether they have enough capital to engage in Day Trading. If they lack the capital, they should wait until they have it while they are learning about and practicing different trading strategies.
2. They should understand that achieving consistent gains takes several months to a year, even when practicing several hours each day. For those who practice intermittently, it will take longer to achieve success; therefore, prospective traders should put in the time and effort required to achieve their goals.
3. Once they start trading, they need to commit to trading for at least two hours a day, depending on their commitments.
4. Until their trading profits match or surpass their income, new day traders should not quit their day jobs. They also need to determine the ideal time of day to trade based on their other commitments. In addition, they should ensure that their trading strategy fits that time of day. Essentially, their trading strategy needs to fit their life.

5. People who want to venture into Day Trading need to determine whether they want to do it with the aim of quitting their regular jobs. To get to the point where they can replace their day jobs by Day Trading, prospective traders need to understand that they will probably need to practice and trade for a year or more, depending on their dedication.

Aspiring day traders should consider the factors above before investing their time and money in learning this line of trade.

Choose a Broker

While new traders are practicing and developing their trading strategies, they should set aside some time to choose a good and reputable broker. It may be the same broker they opened a demo or practice account with, or it may be another broker. Actually, choosing the right broker is one of the most important transactions day traders will make because they will entrust the broker with all of their capital.

Capital Needed to Start Day Trading

How much capital people need to start Day Trading depends on the market they trade, where they trade, and the style of trading they wish to do. There is a legal minimum capital requirement set by the stock market to day trade; however, based on the individual trading style, there is also a recommended minimum.

A day trader needs to have enough capital to have the flexibility to make a variety of trades and withstand a losing streak, which will inevitably happen. Traders also need to determine the amount of money they need, which requires them to address risk management. In addition, they should not risk more than 2% of their account on a single trade.

Capital is the most important component when it comes to Day Trading. By risking only 1% or 2%, even a long losing streak will keep most of the capital intact. For day traders in the United States, the legal minimum balance needed to day trade stocks is $25,000. Traders whose balance drops below this amount cannot engage in Day Trading until they make a deposit that brings their balance above $25,000.

To have a buffer, U.S. day traders should have at least $30,000 in their trading accounts. Stocks usually move in $0.01 increments and trade in lots of 100 shares; therefore, with at least $30,000 in their accounts, day traders will have some flexibility.

Day traders can usually get leverage up to four times the amount of their capital. A trader with $30,000 in his/her account, for example, can trade up to $120,000 worth of stock at any given time. Essentially, the trade price multiplied by the position size can equal more than the trader's account balance.

Day traders can trade fewer volatile stocks, which often require a bigger position size and a smaller stop loss, or stocks that are more volatile, with often require a smaller position size and a larger stop loss. Either way, the total risk on each trade should not be more than 2% of the trading account balance.

Day Trading Basics

Day Trading, on the surface, looks like it should be relatively easy. New day traders think it is all about making several simple trades as the price moves, making a little money, and repeating the whole process tomorrow. However, many dangers lurk in the Day Trading markets; unfortunately, a large percentage of new day traders are not aware of these dangers.

Some of the pitfalls for day traders include:

Lack of Risk Management

Often new day traders often lack risk management protocols, which is a huge danger. Sometimes, they have an incomplete strategy for managing risk. Nevertheless, they are usually optimistic about their Day Trading abilities, which often causes them to overlook critical risk management steps. Establishing a basic risk management strategy involves the following steps:

- **A Stop Loss**

Traders should place a stop-loss order in each trade they make to control their risk. People who are starting out on Day Trading should limit their risk on each trade to 1% of their trading account balance. The difference between their entry price and stop-loss price, multiplied by their position size, is their risk.

- **A Daily Limit**

A daily-stop loss limit can help day traders by limiting how much money they can lose in a day. If day traders suffer multiple losing trades each day, they may still find themselves down more than 10% in a single day. A typical daily-stop loss limit should not be more than about 3% of a trader's account.

Therefore, if the trader loses 3% on any given day, he/she will stop trading for that day. As day traders develop a profitable trading record and gain experience, they can adjust their daily-stop loss limit to be equal to their average profitable trading day. By placing this limit, a typical winning day will recoup the losses from a single day.

Improperly Tested or Untested Trading Strategies

New day traders are often so eager to start trading and make money that they start using untested or improperly tested trading

24

strategies with real money. Others, however, try out their strategies on demo accounts, and if they make a few successful trades, they immediately start trading with real money. Unfortunately, both of these approaches will probably lead to future disappointment.

Successful day traders, on the other hand, test their strategies on many different market conditions through demo trading to learn the pros and cons of their strategies before using them with real money. They demo trade for several months until they are comfortable with their Day Trading strategies before risking real capital with their strategies.

Broker

Choosing the right broker is one of the most important trades for a day trader. Day traders deposit their capital with their brokers, and yet some of them do not take the time to research their broker until a problem arises. Scam brokers, for example, can pop up anywhere.

Traders who find themselves working with such a broker will find it very difficult or even impossible to withdraw their money and any profits. Fortunately, scam brokers usually do not last long thanks to forum complaints. Therefore, a careful online search will reveal any problems with a broker.

A more subtle broker problem is constantly slow quotes. Day traders need direct and uninterrupted access to their broker, who then sends their orders to the appropriate exchange. They should test their broker's trading software because poor software will make it hard to execute trades in a timely manner.

Technology

No one is immune to technology problems. For example, computers can crash, power can go out, the internet can go down, and much more. Day traders cannot get out of a losing trade quickly if technology fails; therefore, they need to place a stop-loss order on every trade.

In addition, they need to program their broker's phone number into their cell phone and landline phone, so they can call them quickly in case of a problem. It is a good idea to have a mobile version of their trading platform on their internet-enabled mobile devices, which might still be operational if their computer crashes.

Order Types

The profits and losses day traders make come from the orders they place. Day traders should know their order types for getting in and out of a market order or a limit order. They also need to know how to set profit targets and stop-loss orders, both for going short and long.

For professional day traders, placing orders is automatic, like switching on a car's turn signal, when about to change lanes. Day traders who do not know their order types will have slow and clumsy trading or even place the wrong order type, which will cost them money.

It is normal for some trading mistakes to happen; however, compounding such mistakes with order-related trading mistakes is a recipe for disaster. Before they start trading, new day traders should know their order types.

Trader Personality and Tendencies

Another hidden danger for a new day trader is his/her personality and tendencies. In the beginning, Day Trading will be confusing, infuriating, and stressful in a way a new trader never thought it could. There are endless possibilities in the markets, and no one cares what anyone else is doing.

This freedom, however, can be unnerving and dangerous for many traders, which is why many of them lose money. When people are starting out, they do not know how they will react under different stresses and pressures. Some choose to quit, others to overtrade, and others still are too afraid to trade.

Many distractions keep people from staying focused and trading effectively. Traders should take a critical look at their personality to identify their shortcomings and then work to develop these six important Day Trading traits.

Volume, Price, Technical Indicators

Day traders can use technical indicators to provide trading signals and assess the current trade. Keltner Channels, a popular technical indicator, use average prices and volatility to plot lower, middle, and upper lines. These three lines move with the price to create the appearance of a channel.

Chester Keltner introduced these channels in the 1960s, but Linda Bradford Raschke updated them in the 1980s. Today, traders use the later version of the indicator, which is a combination of two different indicators, which are the average true range and the exponential moving average.

Created by J. Welles Wilder Jr. and introduced in 1978, the average true range is a measure of volatility. The moving average, on the other hand, is the average price for specific periods, with the exponential variation giving more weight to recent prices and less weight to less recent prices.

Keltner Channels are useful to day traders because they make trends more visible. When a certain asset or stock is trending higher, its price will frequently come close, touch, or even move past the upper band. In addition, the price will stay above the lower band and middle band, although it might occasionally barely dip below the middle band.

When an asset or stock is trending lower, on the other hand, its price will regularly come close to the lower band or reach it; however, sometimes it will move past the lower band. The price will stay below the upper band and often below the middle band.

Day traders should set up their indicators so that these guidelines hold true, at least most of the time. If the price of a stock is moving constantly higher but not reaching the upper band, the channel may be too wide, and the trader will need to decrease the multiplier. However, an asset that is trending higher but constantly touching the lower band shows that the channel is too tight, requiring an increase of the multiplier.

For their indicator to help them analyze the market, day traders need to adjust it correctly. If they fail to do this, then the guidelines for trading will not hold true, and the indicator will not serve its intended purpose. Once they set up the indicator correctly, day traders should purchase during an uptrend when the price of the asset pulls back to the middle band.

They should place a target price somewhere near the upper band and a stop-loss order halfway between the lower and middle bands. On the other hand, if the price of the asset is hitting the stop-loss too often, and the trader has already made the necessary adjustments, he/she should move the stop-loss a bit closer to the lower band.

This will give the trade more wiggle room and reduce the number of losing trades the trader has. During a downtrend, when the price of the asset rallies to the middle band, day traders should short sell, which means selling the asset with the hope of buying it back at a lower price.

It is also important to place a target near the lower band and a stop-loss order about halfway between the upper and middle bands. This trading strategy leverages the trending tendency and provides trades with a 0.5 risk to reward ratio. This is because the stop-loss point is approximately half the length of that of the target price.

However, traders should not trade all pullbacks to the middle line. If a trend is not present, this strategy will not work effectively. Sometimes, the price of the asset moves back and forth between hitting the lower and upper bands. This method will not be effective in such situations.

Therefore, day traders should ensure the market's pattern is following the trending guidelines. If it is not doing so, they should use a different strategy. The Keltner Channel strategy tries to capture big moves that may evade the trend-pullback strategy.

Day traders should use it near the opening of a major market when big movements happen.

The typical trading strategy is to purchase when the price breaks the upper band or sell short when it drops below the lower band within the first 30 minutes of the market opening. The middle band, however, acts as the exit point. This type of trade does not have a profit target. Traders simply exit the trade whenever the price touches the middle band, whether the trade is a winner or a loser.

Introduction to Investing in Stocks, Options, and Forex

When most people hear the term Day Trading, they think of the stock market. However, day traders also participate in the forex and futures markets. Some day traders, for example, trade options, but most traders who do so are more likely swing traders who can hold positions for weeks or days, but not fractions of a trading day.

People who want to be successful day traders should initially focus on a single market, such as the stock market. Once they master that market, they can try to learn and practice trading other markets if they choose.

Day Trading Stocks

Those who are thinking of Day Trading stocks should consider a few important factors. These are:

1. Under U.S. law, the minimum starting capital for Day Trading stocks is $25,000. However, they need to add a buffer above this amount and start with a capital of at least $30,000.

2. Market hours for Day Trading are from 9:30 am to 4 pm Eastern time. However, traders can still place trades one hour before the market opens.

3. The ideal periods to day trade stocks are from 8.30 to 10.30 am and 3 to 4 pm ET, when volatility and volume are high.

4. Day traders can trade a wide variety of stocks. They can also trade the same stock or a small number of stocks every day, or find new stocks to trade each week or even each day.

Based on these factors, prospective day traders will determine whether the stock market is a good option for their Day Trading. If they do not have the initial capital required, for example, they should consider the futures or forex markets, which require less starting capital.

In addition, if they cannot trade during the most ideal trading hours, their efforts will not produce as much fruit as they would have if they were available during those optimal hours.

Day Trading Futures

Some of the important things to consider about Day Trading futures include

1. There is no legal minimum starting capital required to begin Day Trading futures. Experts, however, recommend starting with $2,500 to $7,000 if one is trading the popular futures contract. The more money one starts with, the more flexible one will be when it comes to making trading decisions.
2. The official market hours for trading the S&P 500 and E-mini are from 9.30 am to 4 pm ET.
3. The optimal time to day trade ES futures is from 6.30 to 1030am and 3 to 4p Eastern time.
4. Commodities futures contracts also provide reliable Day Trading opportunities.
5. Most day traders who deal with futures often focus on one futures contract; however, others choose futures contracts seeing significant volume or movements on a particular day.

Day Trading Forex

Things to know about Day Trading forex include:

1. The minimum starting capital required is $500; however, experts recommend starting with $5,000 if one wants a decent monthly income stream.
2. Forex trades 24 hours a day; however, certain times are ideal for Day Trading than others.
3. Day traders can trade any different currency pairs, but beginners should stick to the GBP/USD or EUR/USD. These two currency pairs offer more than enough price movement and volume to generate a good income.

Based on these three factors, day traders will likely determine whether this market is appropriate for them to day trade. Those with limited capital should consider Day Trading the forex market, which is more flexible than other markets.

Social Trading

Social trading works somewhat like a social network. However, there is a big difference, which is that instead of sharing pet photos, dinner photos, and selfies, people use social trading networks to share trading ideas. Essentially, traders use this platform to interact, brainstorm and watch the trading results of other professionals in real-time.

Some of the benefits of social trading include:

1. Access to reliable and helpful trading information
2. Ability to earn while learning
3. Quick understanding of the trading market
4. Ability to build a trading community of investors

Since social trading networks cater for both professionals and beginners, they create a reliable trading community, which allows day traders and other types of market traders to generate an income as they learn.

The allure of this form of financial trading is undeniable. It is more exciting for a trader to earn a living working from the comfort of his/her home, rather than working a regular 9 am to 5 pm gig. However, inexperienced or careless day traders can destroy their portfolios within a few days.

Chapter 2: Risk Management and Account Management

Both account and risk management exercises are activities that coincide as you go through the Day Trading investment cycle. It is very important for you to ensure that you achieve your aims of making significant profits, while at the same time, mitigating losses from the capital in which you invested.

Managing your account and the risks associated with Day Trading involves the responsible handling of the available equity in your brokerage account. You can perform account management through further investment in profitable stocks, ingenious trade maneuverability, or exiting from trade deals that stagnate.

On the other hand, your risk management strategies involve responding appropriately to alleviate prospective losses in an uncertain future and limiting the degree of your exposure to financial risks. The following are some of the primary strategies that you can apply to your Day Trading to ensure active risk and account management:

Hire a Stockbroker

As a beginner or a new investor participating in Day Trading, it could turn challenging if you went at it alone. You need advice on the right stock opportunities in which to invest, guidelines on how to handle probable financial risk exposures, and knowledge of technical analysis to keep track of your capital progress.

A qualified and registered stockbroker typically offers these financial services at a commission or flat fee. You need to seek the assistance of such stockbrokers to tap into their experience and expertise in Day Trading. Besides, the chances of attaining your profitable goals increase when you employ the services of a stockbroker.

Account management and risk management are strategies that are innate to a stockbroker, especially when given access to the account. Therefore, you need to open a brokerage account from which all your Day Trading activities take place. Maintaining liquidity in this account is as essential as making the right trade deals.

Since you may not interact with the stock market all the time, running the trading account becomes the responsibility of your stockbroker. You need to give him or her freedom to make informed choices on long and short trades, however risky they might seem at first. Trust your broker to understand what he or she is doing with the account and hence the need to hire an honest stockbroker, preferably from a well-known brokerage firm.

In addition, it is usual for your stockbroker to have extensive experience with managing financial risks. Most of the strategies meant to combat potential financial threats such as spreads are somewhat complex to understand, let alone apply them effectively. The same levels of complications and fair sophistication apply to the tools used for technical analyses.

You need to follow these analytic tools to make informed choices based on their data. A stockbroker comes in handy at this point to assist in data interpretation. You also get to learn about the various management strategies of which you had no idea previously. Generally, account and risk management in Day

Trading is often all about making the correct decisions from technical analysis.

Develop a Trading Plan

This document is a crucial tool for you as a new investor in Day Trading. If you do not possess such a program, then it may be time to develop one that tailors to your specific trading. Creating a trading plan is an activity that you need to perform with the help of your stockbroker. The broker typically has experience in the Day Trading sector, and so he or she can offer you pointers on the trading opportunities that have the potential of being productive. Based on this vital tip, you can create a comprehensive trading plan that contains an overall objective that is set out. Besides, the program should have tactical or short-term goals set at regular intervals during the cycle. The primary purpose of these operational targets is to enable you to keep track of the progress of your Day Trading activities.

Once you complete the creation of a trading plan, you must stick to its guidelines at all times. You and your broker need to have a chance at Day Trading's success. Hence, you both have to adhere to the rules of the trading plan. It sets out instructions on how you should react and what measures to take with your capital under different situations. Since the future of Day Trading is often uncertain, it is essential for your plan to cover emergency financial responses. If you diligently adhere to your trading plan, your likelihood of attaining profitable returns eventually increases significantly. In addition, you will have a policy of intervention to potentially risky financial exposures.

Maintain Simplicity

In Day Trading, you may falsely believe that you need to overextend yourself on high-risk investments to make substantial amounts of return. This belief is a dangerous position for you to adopt when getting into Day Trading. Keep in mind the notion that the underlying stocks are often a more volatile type of security than other investments. Fluctuations in the value of the traded stock are frequent and typically occur over a relatively short period.

You must learn how to make small trade deals on the stock from the low-risk end of the trading spectrum. Beware of succumbing to the desire to stick your neck out for the riskier stocks. Greed and emotional influence are the leading causes of such irresponsible trading practices. In the case of a specific trade deal turning awful, you need to exercise restraint from the urge to make illogical trading decisions to try to cover your previous loss.

Besides, keep an eye out for volatile stocks and avoid trading in them as much as possible. If you can, distance yourself and your portfolio from such stocks. Ask your broker to let go of highly fluctuating stocks entirely due to their corresponding high levels of financial risk. All these missteps are easily avoidable when you stick to the simple trading practices laid out in your trading plan.

As a result, you will evade massive losses associated with complicated, high-risk trading that is subject to a high level of emotional influence. Proper and responsible account management demands that you avoid rash decisions that may lead to prospective losses and missing out on potential profits. Risk management also takes care of itself by minimizing your exposure to the high-risk end of the trading spectrum and keeping clear of volatile stocks.

Establish a Stop-Loss Level

To manage the amount of risk to which you are willing to expose your trading portfolio, you can issue orders that reverse potentially hurtful financial positions. A stop-loss order limits the amount of stock price that you can tolerate without taking a significant financial hit.

This order enables your stockbroker to cease all the Day Trading activities immediately. It allows him or her to instantly stop either buying or selling any further stocks based on the unfavorable prices. The order indicates the specific stock price beyond which you cannot risk either purchasing or offloading, respectively, because doing so would expose you to an apparent financial loss.

Getting into an apparent losing situation is an irresponsible practice on your part. Eventually, you will end up with a depleted brokerage account due to the mismanagement of the available capital that you previously had. Stop-loss orders are especially useful when conducting Day Trading on volatile stocks. It is advisable to set the stop-loss order to an amount that is as close as possible to your trading entry point.

Besides, close monitoring of the fluctuating price of your particular stock is a must to ensure the successful execution of the order when required. As you can realize, when used in this manner on the volatile stocks, such stop-loss orders act as risk management tools that mitigate the financial downside associated with rapidly fluctuating stocks.

Determine Your Position Size

Position sizing involves making decisions on the amount of capital with which you intend to take part in particular day trade. The size of your investment is directly proportional to the level of risk exposure. A high-volume trade will invariably expose you to more financial risks than a small number of trade deals.

Your brokerage account will often get caught in the crosshairs of high-risk transactions and Day Trading practices. Exhaustion of the amount of available capital in your trading account becomes even more likely. Therefore, an early determination of your trading position is essential before engaging in any form of transaction. Your position size divides into an account and trade risk based on the number of shares of stock that you acquire on a particular trade.

For you to minimize any potential financial downfall resulting from the degree of your account risk, you must set a limit on the amount of capital to trade in each deal or transaction. A fixed ratio or small percentage is often the recommended format for this account limit. Maintaining consistency is vital in setting these account restrictions.

Do not keep altering the allocated portion for different trading deals. You should pick one value and apply it to all of your transactions during the Day Trading. A preferable limit should be one percent of your available capital balance or less. Make sure to adhere to the strategy of simplicity by making only small amounts of capital allocations to the low-risk stocks.

In addition to the risks to your trading account, the other financial exposure from position sizing concerns the trade risk. The best strategy to counteract trade risk involves the use of stop-loss orders. The gap between the entry point to your Day Trading and the specific numerical amount set as the limit on the order constitutes your trade risk. As earlier mentioned, this order enables you or your stockbroker to exit from a trade deal upon reaching the set limit of loss. This action results in capping further loss of capital; hence, it contributes to managing financial risk in this manner.

Consequently, you should execute stop-loss orders close to your trading entry point to minimize the likelihood of potential losses spiraling out of control. Be careful not to set it excessively tight to inhibit your ability to carry out any trading. Position sizing is responsible for both account and risk management. The evasive maneuvers described usually contribute towards minimizing risk.

Remember to allow for some flexibility when setting the restriction value on a stop-loss order. You need this leeway to give your stocks a chance to increase in value without encountering an obstacle in the form of the stop-loss order. Such moves enable you to maintain a healthy trading account. As previously mentioned, the number of shares needed for a potentially profitable trade relates to your ideal position size, as shown below.

The ideal number of shares required (Position Size) = Account risk / Trade risk.

Curb Your Emotions

Emotional influence on Day Trading practices can turn counterproductive very fast if you are not careful. The primary emotions to look out for are self-confidence and fear. Excessive confidence can cause you to have a false sense of self-belief in your trading abilities. As a result, you may end up making illogical trading choices and decisions based on your cockiness.

You should understand that you become more prone to develop a false sense of overconfidence whenever you are on a winning streak. The successive trade deals that end up panning out give you an air of self-belief that could be subject to abuse. You get to trust your super abilities in trading and dare to engage in more risky transactions. It is at this point that you will experience a massive financial catastrophe, especially if you overextend yourself financially. Beware of situations that seem too good to be accurate as well.

The other emotional input of concern is the fear of experiencing losses. Overcoming this fear is possible as long as you trade in amounts of money that you can afford to lose in case the transaction goes wrong. In Day Trading, you are bound to have trouble due to market fluctuations, especially when dealing with volatile stocks.

Losses are part and parcel of Day Trading, and you must learn how to bounce back after a particularly nasty run of successive losses. You may experience crippling fear that could render you unable to continue trading if you do not have a coping mechanism for potential losses. In addition, the fear of further losses may discourage you from taking risks resulting in missing potentially profitable opportunities.

Fear is responsible for holding onto a stock position for too long, as well. Instead of selling your shares at a reasonable profit, you may decide to wait on much higher prices leading to a loss if the trend in stock price undergoes a reversal. Another critical factor to consider in risk and account management is the tendency to chase after quick profits to cover for a recent run of bad trade deals and accompanying losses.

You must adhere to your trading plan guidelines and instructions even during such tough times. Do not modify or alter your response and come up with stupid decisions that you usually would not make. Remember that for you to ensure responsible management of your capital, you need to start making choices based on logic. Emotional corruption can hamper your ability to make significant profits and expose you to unnecessary risks.

Chapter 3: How to Find Stocks for Trade

In Day Trading, you will need to deal in stocks and their fluctuations in prices. Buying and selling stocks depend on the number of shares of a particular stock that you have. When you conduct profitable trade deals, the chances are that you will have a healthy trading account. The available capital in your account is vital to enable you to continue investing in the Day Trading opportunities.

However, if you experience a run of losses and bad transactions, you are likely to run out of capital eventually. A series of successive losses tend to cause an emotional reaction from most traders. Beware of trying to recoup your losses by chasing profits based on rash decisions. It is also essential to trade only with an amount of capital that you can afford to lose. Remember to adhere to your trading plan for guidance and instructions on how to respond to financial losses.

You can also apply the strategies laid out for risk management. Stock markets tend to vary in their trends over time, and hence, you are bound to go through a couple of difficulties. The most crucial aspect of this emotional roller coaster is how you react to both returns and losses. Besides, in case you want to increase your profit margin, you should know how you would acquire more stock for your trade deals.

Since the availability of securities for Day Trading may not be an issue, you should try to focus and narrow down your stock selections. Identification of potentially profitable stocks can be a challenging affair. However, there are tactics, skills, and techniques that you can apply to ensure that you invest in the most productive kind of stock.

Conduct Repeated Day Trading on the Same Stock

This tactic involves carrying out your Day Trading under the same condition's multiple times. You need to identify your most profitable stocks and focus all your trading expertise and time on only these particular stocks. This move ensures that you always get some form of returns from your investment since you already know how it usually performs. Avoid trading in many different types of securities or stocks. The selection of a few stocks whose market trends are easily understandable should be your next step. You can narrow your possibilities to around three or four stocks in which you can become an expert.

Once you have identified the relevant stocks, you must dedicate your full attention and monitoring to their market trends. When choosing your preferred stocks, make sure to select those with sufficient volume in the market. This strategy allows for the adjustment of your calculated position size. When dealing with volatile stock, this flexibility enables you to apply for stop-loss orders with big margins to your corresponding small trading positions.

The opposite move is correct for a calm stock market. You will have the freedom to take an expansive trading position coupled with tight margined stop-loss orders. In addition, using this information, you will get to know the best periods to buy or sell specific stocks that would maximize your returns. The more you trade, the more you will be in a position to acquire more stock at a favorable market price. Eventually, you will end up with a lot of stock held as assets within your Day Trading portfolio.

Conduct Generalized Daily Searches for Favorable Stock

You can decide to perform your Day Trading activities in the old fashion way by looking for the volatile stocks that trend attractively. Volatile stocks are more likely to make significant movements in the course of your Day Trading. This technique requires a high degree of self-discipline to keep searching for productive stocks even during tough periods.

It is different from the repeated trading explained above. This trading exercise does not impose a recommended limit on the number of shares you can seek and does not involve Day Trading on the same stock repeatedly. As a result, you end up actively looking for favorable stocks from the vast online stock market to trade daily.

Ideally, you need to spend your time monitoring the market for the presence of stocks that are big movers and trending well. Consider researching the day before. You need to find out information about the stock availability and potential for returns.

This research may include looking into the institution or company. Besides, you can find out how the product performs with market consumers.

For you to maximize your likelihood of acquiring more stock, pay attention to relevant breaking news affecting the stock. Also, be on the lookout for the stocks that earnings are due and any new stocks flooding the market on the following day. All this information should give you an upper hand in your quest to purchase and hold more trading stocks.

Execute A Stock Screener Based on Preferential Criteria

This tool is a computer software program that looks for any available stocks upon its execution. You can search for stocks based on your customizable criteria. Ideally, you should seek a limited number of stock types that show excellent levels of volatility and raw volume. Restrict your search criteria to about three or four stocks as well. Such limitations will enable you to focus all your attention on the effective management of selected stocks and their trading accounts. A weekly stock screener search can occur for you to spend ample time trading on the stocks that meet your search criteria.

Beware of distractions from other commodities that are not on your search results. Succumbing to temptations from a seemingly attractive stock will result in a spiraling fall into your potential financial ruin. Also, note that if a particular stock maintains a regular rate of returns, do not switch stock types. You have to keep profitable returns, as well. When run correctly with the relevant criteria, a stock screener can supply you with a range of various profitable stocks from which you can choose. Depending on the filtration criteria, the following are some examples of online stock screeners:

1. StockFetcher.com
2. ChartMill.com
3. StockRover.com
4. Finviz.com

To avoid wasting time on endless searches for the biggest movers and the best stocks, try limiting your searches to a handful of stocks. This search should ideally take place once a week, preferably over a weekend. Once you have identified your small group of favorable stocks, spend the rest of the time involved in actual Day Trading. Focus your attention on only these listed stocks for at least the whole week until your next search is due. By following this technique, you will end up accumulating and Day Trading in the kinds of stock that you deeply understand and are customizable to you too.

Chapter 4: Day Trading Tools and Platforms

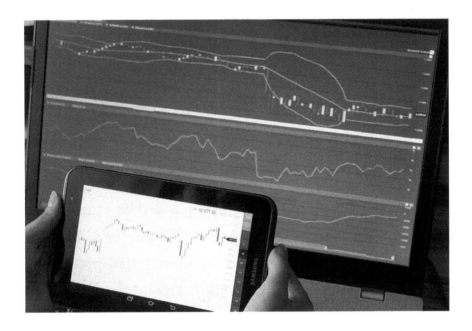

People develop and adopt various tools and platforms to enhance a trader's experience while trading. Initially, a beginner may view the whole process of a transaction as being too difficult due to how complex some markets appear to be. However, with the right information, a person can receive proper guidelines that will introduce him or her to the business and gradually propel him or her into expert traders. The knowledge will enable him or her to develop his or her technical and fundamental analysis that will inform his or her successful trading strategies.

Below is information that introduces a person to the tools and platforms that various traders utilize in their businesses. Moreover, there is also an introduction to some trading aspects like Day Trading, technical indicators, chart types, and candlesticks. Read on to learn more.

Day Trading Tools and Services

Day Trading or intraDay Trading takes place when a trader enters a trade and holds a particular market position for a short time before exiting. A day trader opens and closes that position in a single day. A trader undertakes Day Trading to avoid losses associated with overnight risks and, instead, aims to use volatility to his or her advantage. A trader needs to have some tools and services that are essential to accessing and succeeding in Day Trading. They include:

1. **Electronics** – A day trader needs a computer and a phone where the laptop or desktop has enough memory to run the trading software without crashing or lagging. Additionally, he or she needs a phone to make relevant communications to appropriate people, such as calling brokers.

2. **Direct Access Trading Brokerage** – An intraday trader should obtain the services of a suitable broker who fit his or her requirements in Day Trading. He or she needs to hire one who offers a low commission and allows for the use of customized Day Trading software.

3. **Software** – A trader needs to carry out research and find the Day Trading software that matches his or her needs and strategies well. He or she also should ensure that the computer is compatible with the software and that his or her broker can access it.

4. **Trading Platform** – The intraday trader must learn about various Day Trading platforms and their features and select to use the one that will fulfill his or her trading objectives. Besides, he or she should ensure that the platform matches his or her skills and knowledge concerning trading tools and analysis.

5. **Internet Connection** – A trader must ensure to have an excellent and stable internet connection to help him or her to avoid the errors that take place due to poor accessibility. He or she views old data rather than the current prices on the market since the unstable connectivity results in lagging and misinformation. Additionally, he or she can create backup internet access, such as having different internet providers for his or her mobile phone. In doing so, if one internet provider has issues, the trader can still access the other connection.

6. **Knowledge and Skills** – An intraday trader should continually learn and practice trading to improve his or her skills. He or she can learn individually and practice via online tutorials or use an expert as a guide to perfect his or her trading skills.

7. **Features of the Best** Day Trading Platforms

A Day Trading platform is essential because it helps a trader to transact efficiently and ensure to minimize risks and make profits. The following are some of the best Day Trading platforms and their features:

1. **Charles Schwab** – Provides the best premium features that are critical to a trader's success in the market and is the easiest to learn. It offers competitive rates and has a balance since it provides vital trading and functionality tools while lacking certain customization features.

2. **Tradespoon** – Has flexible rates and suits traders of all levels as it provides professional and widespread trading tools. It has a rich library of studies and historical information that a trader can use to gain further knowledge or customize his or her trading strategies.

3. **TD Ameritrade** – Offers a trader excellent trading tools and guidance to help both beginners and experienced traders to grow in the market. It also provides retirement resources for traders. It has expensive rates, as it is the

most resourceful platform that also provides traders with the chance to develop and undertake real-time stock scans and other advanced analysis.

4. **Interactive Brokers** – It provides the best rates and best suits the high-volume traders due to its professional features like programmable order types like algorithmic types. It does not allow for research, but its tools suit the hyperactive and active traders.

5. **E-Option** – Offers the best features for advanced traders as it enables them to access sophisticated and customized tools that they can use to undertake in-depth technical analysis and trade moves.

6. **Fidelity** – Contains several tools that enable a trader to transact efficiently, such as customized profiles, automatic identification of general patterns, chart trading, and drawing tools, among others. It also offers competitive rates due to its practicality.

Day Trading Charts

Day Trading refers to a trader entering and exiting a market position in a single day while charts use historical data to provide a trader with feedback regarding the conditions of a market. A trader using trading charts in his or her trades receives significant additional information that helps him or her to make appropriate decisions in Day Trading. They enable him or her to study the past price movements and patterns that assist him or her to understand the current market and even make some predictions on particular trades.

A day trader needs to understand the various aspects of Day Trading charts, which are technical indicators and the different chart types. Knowledge of these two features enables him or her to possess a comprehension of vital tools that help him or her to make a profit from the trading day's volatility.

Technical Indicators

An intraday trader utilizes technical indicators to carry out technical analysis of the market. They enable him or her to look at and understand the various meanings of chart patterns. The patterns provide him or her with a visual representation of the price movements and trends in the market that allow the trader to make sound and profitable decisions in the trade. Some of the commonly utilized indicators in Day Trading include:

1. Simple Moving Average (SMA)

An SMA indicator uses an average that consists of the total amount of the closing prices in a given period and dividing the sum by the number of days in that period. A day trader can make profits if he or she uses a fast-moving average since the slower ones can cause losses if there is a reversal or end of a trend. Many traders frequently use a 10-day moving average because it does not lag and indicates the direction and considerable moves of prices in the market.

2. Oscillators

These refer to indicators such as the Relative Strength Index (RSI) and the Moving Average Convergence Divergent (MACD) that reflect unclear price trends. The signals move between the upper bounds and lower ones, and the subsequent readings provide the day trader with feedback regarding the market conditions.

3. Volume Indicators

A volume indicator will signal to a day trader changes concerning the number of trades taking place. The trader will know when there is a considerable amount of transactions and indicate the area in the market where they occur. He or she can then quickly take up an appropriate position and make profitable moves in the Day Trading market.

4. Average True Range (ATR)

These indicators enable a day trader to evaluate the trades before entering it. As a result, he or she makes accurate and well-informed decisions because the ATR indicator utilizes the actual price of securities to provide a precise representation of volatility.

Types of Charts Used in Day Trading

Many traders use different charts to maneuver the Day Trading markets. Each trading chart contains various features that work to provide diverse and useful information to a trader. A trader looks at the graphs and utilizes those that best suit his or her trading aim and strategies. The following are some popular types of charts that a trader can use to interpret and understand the market conditions.

1. Candlestick Charts

Candlestick charts are easy to understand and use, and they provide a trader with the most feedback by signaling where a price travels in a given period. They also enable him or her to incorporate information concerning frames of time. In this case, he or she can identify the highest and lowest price points, along with the last closing price that takes place in that particular period.

Candlesticks assist a trader in getting precise visual readings of the market by presenting only relevant information, such as the Heikin-Ashi chart that shows trends and reversals. Different candlestick charts also show various aspects of the market, such as time, volume, and price movements.

Some candlestick charts only use the movements of the price to help a day trader to identify the resistance and support levels. The resistance levels indicate the highest highs of trade, whereas the support levels show the lowest lows. Renko is an example of such a candlestick chart that employs colored bricks to reflect the trends of a trade.

When there is a downward trend, the blocks visible will be black, while white ones will be visible when an upward trend takes place. The bricks also move in terms of the price movement whereby a new white or black block appears in the following column if the price respectively moves above or below the previous one.

Other candlestick charts help a day trader to find points of reversals and sets of swing highs and lows. These charts enable him or her to determine areas and conditions of bias in the market, which assist him or her in making appropriate moves that give him or her gains. An example here is a Kagi chart that uses changes in price directions to signal reversals.

The intraday trader sets a particular reversal amount, and the price direction will shift to the opposite side once it reaches that predetermined percentage. It also indicates swings concerning high and low line signals, in that, the lines become thinner as the market drops below the previous swing. Conversely, the line gets thicker as the stock increases above the prior swing.

2. Bar Charts

Bar charts provide a day trader with signals that are easy to read and interpret as they use color, horizontal, and vertical lines to reflect range or price in a given period. The horizontal lines show the closing and opening prices, whereas the vertical lines indicate the price range of a particular duration. Additionally, traders use them along with candlestick charts to reflect the trading actions in the market.

A bar with candlesticks uses the variation between the low and high to show the trading range. The top of the candle or wick represents the high state while the bottom of the candle signals the low one. Moreover, the chart uses different colors on the candlestick to indicate the opening and closing prices within a period of interest. A red candle could represent the closing price at the low end of a candle and have the opening price at the high end. Meanwhile, a green candle reflects its prices in reverse of the red candle.

3. Line Charts

Line charts indicate to an intraday trader the history of prices by showing a track of the closing prices in the market. The trader forms the lines when he or she links several closing costs in a given frame of time. He or she uses line charts along with other kinds of trading charts to get essential information for a successful Day Trading experience.

4. Charts Based on Time Frames

All the trading charts that a day trader utilizes contain frames of time that he or she set according to his or her aim or trading strategies. The trader can use intraday charts breaking down into 2-minute, 5-minute, 15-minute, and hourly charts. Each time interval indicates the price actions of trade of interest, and he or she can use the information represented to make relevant trading decisions and moves.

5. Free Charts

An intraday trader can use free charts that are available online and offer the trader not only with tools for technical analysis but also with advice, demonstrations, and guidelines about chart analysis. Different free charts provide various features such as delayed futures data, real-time data, and selection of frames of time and indicator accessibility. Furthermore, these charts enable a trader to participate in various markets like the forex, futures, stock exchanges, and equity markets. FreeStockCharts and the Technician are examples of free charts that an intraday can access and utilize without spending anything.

Introduction to Candlesticks

The Japanese merchants developed candlesticks to monitor daily momentum and prices in the rice market in the 18th Century. A candlestick is a kind of chart that shows the opening, closing, high, and low prices in a particular period. As a result, it helps a trader to identify the entry or exit points of a market since it signals how the investor's feelings influence the trades.

The broad section of a candlestick is the real body, which a trader uses to determine if the closing price of trade was lower or higher than the opening price. Additionally, they also employ colors to help him or her to identify the state of the closing price more quickly.

The real body of a candlestick is green or white when the stock closes higher and red or black when the stock closes lower. Hence, the colors assist the trader to quickly interpret the market conditions at a glance and make appropriate decisions without wasting time.

The candlesticks' different colors also represent the sentiments of the market by indicating the outlooks of the traders. They signal if the traders have a bearish, bullish, or indecisive approach to the market. A trader then makes a judgment and takes up relevant positions in the market that provide him or her with gains.

Bullish Candlesticks

A bullish sentiment takes place when traders do a lot of purchasing because they expect the price of an asset will increase in a given period. As a result, the bullish outlook will form an intense buying pressure in the market. The bullish candlesticks will have a long green or white real body to show that the stock prices closed at a higher place than the opening price. Furthermore, it helps a trader to determine significant price actions at a particular area and time if a long white candle appears at an appropriate support level of price.

If the price initially moves significantly lower after the open and then shifts to close in the high vicinity, the bullish candlestick forms a reversal pattern called a hammer. The sellers lower the prices in a trading session, and it results in an intense buying pressure, which leads to the trading session ending on a higher close.

Thus, a hammer creates an uptrend, and its real body is short with a lower and longer shadow since sellers are reducing the prices. An inverted hammer indicates a reverse of the hammer candlestick since it develops in a downtrend. Other bullish candlesticks that a trader can utilize in the market include the morning star, the piercing line, bullish engulfing pattern, and the three white soldiers.

Bearish Candlesticks

A bearish outlook refers to the situation where there is an intense pressure of selling in the trading markets. It occurs when traders carry out a lot of selling trades in a particular duration. The bearish candlesticks have a long red or black body that signifies that the stock prices closed at a lower position than the opening price. Therefore, as the day goes on, the stock price falls leading to the opening price is higher than the close of the previous day. It leads to the formation of a long black candlestick that does not have an upper shadow but only possesses a short lower shadow.

Traders also refer to the bearish candlesticks as the hanging man, and they utilize them to try to select a bottom or top in the market. Moreover, the patterns of a bearish candlestick tend to indicate a switch in the attitude of investors. The sentiment changes from bullish to bearish after a length of time. Examples of bearish candlesticks include the bearish harami and bearish engulfing candlesticks.

Indecision Candle

This candlestick differs from the bullish and bearish types in terms of its body shape. While the bullish and bearish candlesticks are long, the indecision candle has a small real body, in that, the open price and the close price are near each other. Additionally, there are long wicks that attach to each side of the body and are equal in their lengths. The candlestick's body also lies between the low and the high, resulting in it being at the center of the entire candle range.

This candle occurs at a trend's top and bottom and can indicate to a trader about price or trend reversals if it develops at significant places on the chart after undergoing long moves. The name of this candlestick comes from the indecisive conduct that it shows since it signals both bullish and bearish activities. The stock closes at around the same place as the opening price because the bears and bulls were both very active in the market.

This double price action leads to there being two long wicks on either side of the candle's body. Their presence and lengths indicate that the price attempted to shift both upwards and downwards in the trading session. Consequently, it signals that no one won in the market and that it failed to maintain higher and lower prices. The Doji candlestick is an example of an indecisive candle.

These features mentioned above provide descriptions and information concerning the various tools and platforms used in trading. A person needs to understand them to allow him or her to gain vital knowledge that will help him or her to trade in the markets successfully.

Chapter 5: Trade Management and Price Action for Day Trading

Day Trading Risk Management

In all forms of trading, traders have a specific level of risk that they may be willing to take. Since the ultimate aim of participating in any particular trade is to gain profits, your exposure to risk should be as minimal as possible. In Day Trading, the incidence of risk may not be as damaging to small-scale low-risk traders. However, failure to enforce risk management strategies may be financially catastrophic for large investors and companies. The following risk management strategies could be of use to new investors in Day Trading:

a. Employ stop-loss orders

b. Take favorable positions

c. Stick to your trading plan

d. Make low-risk trades

e. Seek expert assistance

1. Stop-Loss Orders

These orders provide a mechanism for you to minimize the extent of any potential losses. The stop-loss order mandates the trader or your stockbroker to cease a particular type of trade instantly upon meeting specific conditions. Ideally, these orders indicate the range of values beyond which a given trading action begins to become significantly unprofitable. It applies to both short and long trading positions. Falling prices are not ideal for stock sellers, and stock buyers frown on expensive costs.

For instance, you could set a particular limit for the range of losses that you may be willing to tolerate adequately. Beyond this limit, your damages would start affecting your bottom line significantly, hence the need for an immediate halt to the trade deal. For them to act as a risk management tool, you need to have your stop-loss orders in place long before taking part in Day Trading. In this manner, you will be covering a potential loss that is yet to occur as opposed to reacting to real-time unfavorable stock prices.

2. Position Sizing

Taking a favorable trading position is the essence of position sizing. Before jumping into any trade opportunity, you should acquire relevant information about that trade. This data should enable you to make the appropriate selection when choosing to take a position. Ideally, rising stock prices with the expectation of a corresponding upward trend in the price chart favor buying stocks. Hence, this Day Trading scenario warrants you to take a long position. Short positions are beneficial when the prices drop or when the trading chart shows a sustained downward trend in the stock price. Position sizing is more of an account management strategy but also applies to risk evasion techniques. If you grow accustomed to taking productive positions, your risk index decreases, and vice versa. Therefore, you should seek assistance with position sizing and how to take up profitable positions if the need arises.

3. Trading Plan

You need to keep track of the progress of your Day Trading investments. In this regard, you must stick to the guidelines set out in your trading plan. This plan provides you with instructions on how to react or respond to specific scenarios in the course of your Day Trading. These directives usually offer the best course of action in the event of most adverse financial situations. In addition, if you strictly stick to your plan from the beginning, you will have no risk to manage later. Besides, you could seek the help of your stockbroker when drawing up a new trading plan. Make sure to capture every probable adverse eventuality and how to mitigate the risks associated with it. Trading plans often discourage you from making decisions based on emotions, which would likely happen in the absence of a trading plan.

Simple Trades

Day Trading often has small margins for either profits or losses. Therefore, you must learn to conduct small but assured trade deals in this strategy. It is advisable to refrain from lusting over the promises of impractically significant returns. The greed resulting from chasing quick profits over short time intervals is counterproductive to your ultimate aim. When you conduct illogical trades using large amounts of money, you are likely to run out of your available capital sooner than you expect. A simple trade has to be low in its risk index, small in amount, and a value that you can afford to lose. Volatility and trade volume are factors that affect your type of trade, but if you stick to logic, your profits will outnumber your losses. Most financial risk exposures are the consequences of rash decisions and poor Day Trading habits. If you have challenges in trying to identify the viable trading opportunities, you could seek the help of other seasoned traders or a stockbroker.

4. Expert Assistance

Whenever you engage in an unfamiliar trading practice, it is advisable to know what you are doing. The same advice applies to investors who are new to Day Trading. Heeding to this counsel will spare you from financial ruin down the line. One way you could make use of available Day Trading expertise is by hiring a stockbroker. Trading blindly without any idea of the expectations is a risky proposition. Stockbrokers are often highly experienced traders in their own right. They know about all the potentially profitable trading opportunities and doomed trades that are bound to go bust.

Therefore, when you have a qualified and registered stockbroker by your side, you are less likely to get yourself into financially risky situations. It is essential that you can predict a wrong trade deal from a mile away, but since you cannot, a stockbroker may be the next best option. In addition to spotting potentially wacky trade deals, your stockbroker is typically responsible for managing your brokerage account. He or she participates in the different trading commitments and takes favorable trading positions on your behalf. As a result, the chances of making a fruitless trade decision are minimal.

Price Action in Day Trading

Price action is one of the strategies used by traders who take part in Day Trading. It relies on the movements in the price of the security under trade. Plotting the raw stock prices against the trading period on a chart is necessary, thereby showing the behavior of your stock value over a specified time. Indicators that are common to other strategies play an insignificant role when using price action.

As a price action trader, you will not bother to find out the conditions affecting particular price movements in either direction. You will take the pattern at its face value because you put more credence to the trends in the stock prices than their contributing factors. As per this reasoning, it could be an excellent time to sell your stock when the prices start rising due to its corresponding increase in value. A downward trend is suggestive of falling prices; hence, buying the stock at favorable prices is possible.

As an investor or trader, your point of entry into Day Trading is dependent on potential profitability and minimal risk exposure. Buying at the least reasonable price and selling at the highest stock price are the two main objectives in price action Day Trading. Besides, technical analysis comes from the price action of a particular stock over a specified period. Price action mainly deals with the ongoing, real-time stock price fluctuations. It is an instant form of Day Trading strategy without the lagging period or delays experienced in waiting for the relevant indicators.

You can modify your stock price chart to show distinct price movements in different colors. This color transition alerts you to a trading opportunity due to the obvious and easy to spot a change in price direction. Once again, you will only concentrate on the upward or downward trend in the price and if that particular pattern will hold. The following concepts describe some everyday experiences attributed to price action Day Trading:

a. Price Breakouts
b. Candlestick Charts
c. Optional Indicators
d. Support and Resistance
e. Technical Analysis

1. Price Breakouts

A primary concept for you to understand is the Day Trading event of a breakout. It is common in almost all cases of price action trading. A breakout is a sudden jump in stock value in either direction from an extended hovering position. This spike in your stock price is readily visible on a price action chart. A breakout is an indicator that alerts you to a possible trading opportunity. However, it could also be a false breakout, in which case, the prices would soon rebound in the opposite direction.

For instance, if the price of a particular stock keeps fluctuating between $25 and $27 for about a month, you would not think much of the security. Yet, if the stock price goes up to $29 in one day after the month, your curiosity and alertness would peak. This sudden upward spike in the stock price is the breakout. Ideally, you would assume that the price is about to keep rising and continue on this trajectory for the foreseeable future. Therefore, as a price action trader, you would take a long position on the same stock hoping for a significant profit from the increasing value. However, the breakout could turn out to be false, and the spike to $29 was only a one-day occurrence.

In this case, the rebound effect would cause the stock value to start dropping. A possible explanation could be that the upward spike caused many other price action traders to buy the stock, which in turn led to more investors who previously held shares to sell. Based on the mechanism of economies of scale, this influx of stock security into the market causes its price to start falling. The price could decrease by a considerable margin past the initial low of $25 to the horror of the traders who took an initial buy position. If you bought plenty of shares based on the initial upswing in the breakout ($27 to $29), you would experience a massive loss afterward.

This uncertainty is part of the characteristics of price action trading, i.e., you can only know the previous behavior of a particular stock, but you cannot predict its future action. Learn to accept the possibility of losing some capital in such price action trades that do not go according to your expectations. Price action trading is akin to speculative trading. Hence, the best mentality you can have is to try to increase your profit margins on the good days more than your losing margins.

2. Candlestick Charts

Another mechanism that is useful in price action trading is the use of candlestick charts. These charts provide more information about the stock price that may assist you in making a more informed decision. The candlestick chart contains details such as the opening and closing prices of a specific stock; hence, you get to know the range of this value within a day. In addition, the candlestick charts show both the maximum and minimum amount of the stock in a single day of trading. In this case, you can estimate the real value of the stock by averaging these particular values.

Due to this additional data, more accomplished day traders often use a combination of candlestick charts and breakouts in their price action strategies for a detailed source of information. They both eliminate the confusion caused by multiple interpretations of the same price action chart. You may see a downward trend and think that the stock value is decreasing, while another person might conclude that a turnaround or price reversal may be imminent. In the end, you both take contrasting positions on a single trade that are equally justifiable. This need for an overall complete picture enables you as a trader to come up with a trading resolution based on the whole trading status of a given stock price. For instance, a particular stock may show multiple drops in its intraday price while keeping with an overall upward trend on a week over week basis. As a result, such dreaded incidents as the rebounds associated with the stand-alone price action breakouts will not catch you off guard again.

3. Optional Indicators

In addition to candlestick charts, you may incorporate a group of specific indicators depending on your objective. However, due to lag delay, trade indicators are not essential to price action trading. In case you need them, trade indicators can easily fit on a price action chart. Examples of such commonly applied indexes include:

- **Moving average**

This indicator enables you to pick out the mean price movement of your particular stock over a specified time frame. In its purest form, this indicator centers on the average value of your security or commodity under trade based on the most recent behavior of that particular stock.

- **MACD indicator**

The acronym for this indicator stands for Moving Average Convergence Divergence. It depicts momentum by relating the previously mentioned moving average to a specific point on the price chart. This point indicates the price level at which you may decide to purchase stock, thereby making it subjective. Taking a particular position depends on this interaction. A possibly long trading position is considerable if the MACD indicator goes above your level or price point.

• Stochastic Oscillator

Just like the MACD, this indicator is descriptive of momentum, as well. First, based on your trading hunch, you decide on an appropriate trend that your stock price will take. This hopeful trend will enable you to estimate the expected value in the stock price at a particular time in the future. Next, sit back and wait for the trading to reach your estimated time. Finally, use the stochastic oscillator to verify whether the current stock price and pattern at this new time match with your earlier speculated expectation.

• RSI indicator

This indicator is suggestive of a market that is either overbought or oversold on a particular security or stock. This description is a measure of the strength of that specific stock within the stock market. Hence, the acronym for this indicator stands for Relative Strength Indicator. It enables you to make an informed judgment on the viability or risks of trading in a certain way and on a particular stock.

• Fibonacci Retracement

This indicator is useful for testing the level of support or resistance when subjected to the trends in the price action chart. You can obtain a detailed perspective of the stock market based on the patterns formed by this indicator. This information guides you on when and how to trade as well as on which particular stocks to trade.

• Bollinger Bands

Whenever you want to find out the usual trading price range of a particular stock, you should use this indicator. Bollinger bands typically show you the stock price limits beyond which breakouts occur. A brief consolidation of the stock price typically occurs within such Bollinger bands. A breached Bollinger band is usually indicative of a breakout, thereby requiring you to alter your taken position.

4. Support and Resistance

These terms describe the behavior of the price action trend. Ideally, you often encounter an oscillating pattern in an ordinary stock trading session. Some uptrends typically alternate with their corresponding downtrends. The highest point or level of the stock price that the stock can reach, as depicted by the price action chart, is the resistance. All trends past this point either hold position or reverse their direction downwards. A rise in the price of a particular stock often means that buying securities is the predominant trade activity.

At first, the buyers in the stock market outnumber the available security in circulation, leading to an increase in the price. The price chart, therefore, registers the uptrend. With high stock prices, investors who hold a lot of stock will take up short positions. More stockholders follow suit resulting in a stock market overflowing with that same stock. This time, the particular security outnumbers the buyers, and its price stabilizes, but if this imbalance continues, the stock prices will begin to drop. Therefore, the point at which the stock prices stop their upward trend is the resistance.

Support, on the other hand, is the exact opposite of resistance. It is the lowest price that a given stock reaches beyond which the only further direction becomes upwards. In the above scenario, the high stock prices begin to fall in a saturated market. The fall is due to the concept of economies of scale. More buyers purchase increased amounts of stock at progressively cheaper costs hence the downtrend on the price action chart. This downward direction in the price of commodities would scare any more stockholders away from selling.

Therefore, the market soon runs into a deficiency of available stock. At this stage, once again, the stock buyers outnumber the insufficient stock in circulation. The trend holds steady for a while as per the price action chart. A prolonged state of a low volume of securities in circulation triggers an increase in its price. This outcome is valid because of the more demand from buyers outnumbering the circulating stock supply. This change in the trend of the stock price signals the point of support.

5. Technical Analysis

In the case of technical analysis, data from price action trading charts are essential for such indicators as the patterns of ascending triangles. These triangles are useful in predicting an imminent major breakout. This prediction is due to previous attempts at a series of multiple minor breakouts by periods of a rising price trend. The pattern caused by the efforts of these bull trends is typically indicative of a gain of momentum with each attempt. From this informative data analysis, you can expect an overall breakout shortly.

Along with the technical analysis, trend and swing traders use price action as a source of data for their indicators or tools as well. Concurrently, they can obtain information on the levels of resistance and support for the specific trade deals in which they participate. For this data to become productive to them, the swing traders need to have the skills required for price action interpretation. Of more use to such external traders, is the ability to derive relevant predictions of the corresponding breakouts or consolidation from the price action charts. Beware of applying technical analysis to raw price action data. For technical analysis to make sense, you need additional information such as the trading volume, market factors, and investor influence.

In the absence of accompanying technical analysis, the psychological and emotional weight might creep into your decisions. As a result, your mental faculties experience clouded judgment, thereby rendering your incapable of making logical choices. Price action trading is beneficial to small traders looking for low-risk opportunities to invest their small amounts of capital. They are usually in search of a quick profit over a brief period so that a single breakout event may suffice. Complex and in-depth analysis is probably more applicable in large-scale settings, for example, corporations, companies, financial institutions, and wealthy private investors. This category of investors is typically long-term and is often on the hook for massive capital loans over an extended period.

Chapter 6: Day Trading Strategies

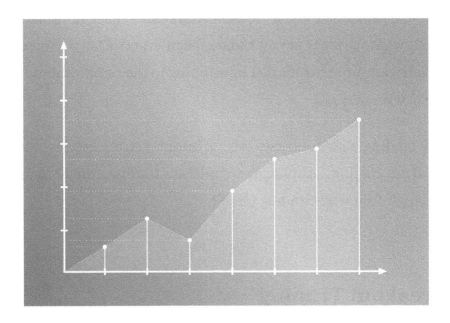

Day Trading is the buying or selling of an asset or security, within the course of a single trading day. A trading day refers to the span of time when a particular forex or stock exchange is open. Trading days are usually seven to eight hours long, from Mondays to Fridays.

Day Trading uses various techniques and strategies to make a profit from price changes for a specific asset. It involves adjusting to events that bring about short-term market fluctuations.

News releases and announcements such as corporate earnings, interest rates, and other economic statistics give information about what the forex or stock market can expect. Day traders can then benefit from the market by attuning to the significant moves the market makes.

Day Trading, therefore, uses several intraday strategies, including breakout trading, scalping, news releases trading, range trading, and high-frequency trading (HFT).

Breakout Trading

A breakout happens when the price of a stock moves beyond the Support or resistance level. The Support or resistance level is the point at which the increase in the price of security stops because of an increase in the number of sellers who want to sell at that price. Day traders use breakout trading to take a position within the early stages of a trend.

A day trader buys an asset when the price of the asset breaks above the resistance level, or the trader sells an asset when the price of the asset goes below the resistance level.

Day Trading uses breakouts because breakout set-ups mark the begging point for significant price trends, significant price swings, and an increase in the unpredictability of the market or volatility. Such breakout set-ups include pullback-consolidation Breakout, reversal-consolidation breakout, reversal at support or resistance level, strong area breakout, and finally, false breakouts or fake-outs.

Pullback-consolidation breakout takes place within the first five to at most twenty minutes as soon as the forex or the stock market opens. The term pullback refers to the price drops that are comparatively short before the prices go back up.

A pullback is usually a few consecutive sessions. Consolidation refers to the case when there is a longer pause before the prices go back up. Pullbacks provide entry points for day traders who want to enter a position when there is a significant upward price movement of a commodity.

Reversal-consolidation breakout happens when a significant move in one direction is followed immediately by a more substantial step in the opposite direction. That is then followed by a long pause or consolidation. After the consolidation, day traders push the price in the reverse direction, assuming that the initial trend was wrong.

Reversal at Support or resistance level is a stage where the stock price has reversed frequently before. When this happens, day traders are not able to push the price of a security in a specific direction.

Strong Breakout happens when a breakout was so strong that it brought about a price gap. Day traders use strong breakouts to buy assets while avoiding selling any commodities in the market. That is to avoid making losses when the price continues to move upwards, following the Breakout. Traders place stop-loss orders when buying assets at this point, to reduce loss.

False Breakouts or fake-outs take place when a price breaks past the Support or resistance level but does not continue moving upward in that direction. When this happens, traders plan their exit by canceling out orders to reduce potential losses. Alternatively, traders avoid taking the first Breakout they see.

Generally, day traders wait until the price moves back to the original breakout level before they trade breakouts. The traders expect to see whether the price will move back to generate either an upward or a downward trend, depending on the direction the traders are trading.

Scalping

Scalping is a Day Trading strategy that day traders use to try to generate small profits on small price changes throughout the day.

When scalping, day traders assume that most assets or stocks will complete the initial stage of a movement. However, traders do not know the direction the stock prices will move. That is because, after that first movement, some stocks may stop advancing, while others may continue to develop.

As a result, day traders aim to take as many small profits as they can, while maintaining a higher ratio of winning trades compared to the losing trades. That strategy helps the traders to keep benefits that are equal or somewhat more significant than losses.

Day traders use three types of scalping. The first type is market-making. In market making, the trader attempts to make profits on the gap between the bid and the asking price of a security. The traders achieve this by issuing out a request and an offer for a particular stock. However, a trader makes extremely small profits because he or she must compete with the other market makers for the shares on both bids and offers.

The second type is more traditional, where traders buy large numbers of shares, which they later sell for a profit when there are small price movements. In this case, traders enter into positions for a couple of thousand shares and wait for small price movements measured in cents.

The third type is much closer to the old method of trading. In this type of scalping, a trader puts up a certain number of shares on any set-up from his or her system and exits the position as soon as the first exit signal develops near the 1:1 risk-reward ratio.

News Releases Trading

Day traders trade news events that are worth trading because news events have the capacity to increase volatility in the short-term. Therefore, traders look for financial information that will cause price movements in the currency market. The currency market mostly responds to economic news from the United States (U.S), and to other financial news from around the world.

Traders mostly follow economic news from the eight major currencies. Such currencies include the U.S. dollar (USD), the British pound (GBP), the Euro (EUR), the Swiss franc (CHF), the Japanese yen (JPY), the Australian dollar (AUD), the New Zealand dollar (NZD), and finally the Canadian dollar (CAD).

Generally, the most significant news releases from any country include information on inflation, trade balance, manufacturing industries surveys, interest rate decisions, retail sales, business sentiment surveys, consumer confidence surveys, industrial production, natural disasters, political unrest, and unemployment. Therefore, because the relevance of these releases may change, traders keep an eye on the focus of the market at all times.

Traders trade news releases by looking for consolidation periods ahead of big numbers and trade the breakouts that are on the back of the numbers.

Range Trading

In range trading, day traders employ support and resistant levels to make their trade decisions. In other words, traders take note of overbought (resistance), oversold (support) areas, buy at the oversold area, and sell at the overbought area.

Day traders use this strategy in markets that are constantly fluctuating, with no visible long-term trend. The goal of a trader is to identify points at which stock prices have gone above or below the regular prices but will likely move back to the original value, or points where support or resistance has formed and is expected to hold again.

As such, range trading uses the Support and resistance strategy, and the breakouts and breakdowns strategy. In using the

Support and resistance strategy, traders buy when the price is close to the support level, and sell when the price reaches resistance. Traders use technical indicators such as the relative strength index (RSI), the stochastic oscillator, and the commodity channel index (CCI). Traders use the indicators to confirm the oversold and overbought situations when the price oscillates or fluctuates within a trading range.

For example, a trader can buy a stock when the stock price is trading at Support, and the RSI showing an oversold reading below 20, and sell when the RSI gives an overbought reading above 60. To reduce the chances of making losses, a trader can place a stop-loss order outside the trading range.

In using the breakouts and breakdowns strategy, traders enter in the direction of a breakout or a breakdown from a trading range. Traders make use of indicators such as price action and volume, to check whether a price movement is in force.

High-Frequency Trading (HFT)

The high-frequency trading strategy makes use of algorithms to capitalize on short-term market inadequacies.

HFT uses dynamic computer programs to manage a large number of orders within seconds. High-frequency traders achieve this by making use of complex algorithms to analyze various markets and to complete market orders depending on market conditions. Therefore, traders with fast delivery speed profit more than those with slower delivery speeds are.

HFT brings in liquidity to the markets and does away with small bid-ask spreads. The liquidity that HFT produces disappears within seconds, and therefore only traders with quick execution speeds can benefit from it. Additionally, HFT removes small bid-ask spreads, which bring in minimal profits.

Major investment banks, hedge funds, and institutional traders or investors use HFT to handle a significant number of orders at super high speeds. The HFT platforms allow traders to manage millions or orders and evaluate multiple markets and trades within seconds, thus giving the traders a considerable advantage in the open market.

HFT has become popular in the open market following the introduction of incentives that high-frequency trading offers so that institutions can add liquidity to the open market. By giving small incentives, trades acquire more liquidity, and the institutions involved reap benefits from every trade they make, in addition to their high execution speeds.

Day Trading is, therefore, a career that requires traders to understand the basics of the marketplace. Individuals who try to take part in Day Trading without any knowledge and experience often lose their investments. A day trader should, therefore, be skilled in technical analysis and chart reading, to understand the ins and outs of the products or services that he or she trades.

Additionally, day traders should only invest capital, which they can afford to lose. That will help the traders leave out their emotions when trading while protecting them from financial devastation. In addition, a trader needs to have an execution plan in order to have an edge over the rest of the market.

Various strategies that a day trader can capitalize on include swing trading, trading news, and exploiting price differences of identical financial instruments on different forms. These strategies will help the trader to make consistent profits with minimal losses.

However, a profit-making strategy is ineffective without discipline. Lack of discipline can make traders make huge losses because they fail to initiate trades that meet their own standards.

Day traders mostly depend on volatility in the market to make profits. That is to say, a commodity may get the attention of the trader when the price of the commodity continually fluctuates during the day.

In addition, day traders rely on securities that are profoundly liquid because the liquidity gives the traders the opportunity to change their positions without interfering with the price of the security. When the cost of the underlying security moves up, a trader may enter a long position or a buy position, and sell the security when the price moves down so that he or she can profit when the price falls.

Day Trading consequently requires access to some of the most sophisticated financial services and instruments in the open market. Hence, day traders need access to various news sources and competent analytical software. In addition to these instruments, the traders will need to have a competitive edge in the market that will help them to acquire more profits than losses.

A trader can become more competent by taking time to understand how the market works, coming up with an execution strategy, having enough capital to start, and finally, by taking on trading opportunities that are within his or her trading limits. Day Trading requires sound methods that will give a person a statistical edge in every trade he or she makes.

Chapter 7: Technical Analysis

Technical analysis is the study of the price changes and trends of a stock or security. The study involves traders inspecting a stock's trading history through technical indicators and charts in order to determine the future direction of the stock price.

Statistical trends, such as price movement and volume identified from the past, determine future trading opportunities. Technical analysts, therefore, focus on price fluctuations, trading signals, and analytical charting tools to examine the strength or weakness of a specific security.

Technical analysis is more dominant in forex and stock markets where traders limit their attention to short-term price movements. Technical analysts aim to comprehend the market emotion behind the price patterns by looking for trends rather than evaluating the basic qualities of a stock.

Technical analysts assume that markets are resourceful with values representing influences that impact the price of a stock or security. However, the analysts acknowledge that price fluctuations are not entirely haphazard but move in recognizable trends that have a tendency to reoccur in the course of time.

There are two different approaches to technical analysis: the top-down approach and the bottom-up approach. The top-down approach involves evaluating securities that fit into a certain standard. For example, a trader may want securities that moved away from their 50-day moving average as a buying prospect.

The bottom-up approach deals with assessing stocks that appear primarily interesting for potential entry and exit points. For example, a trader may discover undervalued security in a downward trend and use technical analysis to find a particular entry point when the security price stops decreasing.

Different types of traders use different types of technical analysis. While position traders may use analytical charts and technical indicators, day trades may use simple trend lines and volume indicators to arrive at trade decisions. Similarly, traders coming up with computerized algorithms may use a combination of technical and volume indicators in their decision-making processes.

Trendline Analysis

Day traders study trends to forecast the future price changes of stock. Historical trends in the price movement give day traders an idea of what the price movements will be in the future.

Day traders carry out trend analysis on short-term, medium, and long-term time frames. In that way, the traders can determine when the price of a security will rise or fall. Along with that, traders can also predict when the market will rise or fall.

By being able to determine price movements, traders aim to time the market so that the traders can enter long positions or buy when the stock prices are at their lowest and sell when the shares are at their highest buying price.

As such, day traders pay attention to an economic institution's financial information and general economic conditions in order to forecast accurately, the future trend of an investment in the marketplace.

For instance, a trader's trend analysis shows that company X's security is at a low price, and according to past price action, the security's price tends to rise once it hits that low price. Consequently, the trader may take that as an indication that he or she should buy the company's security in order to make a profit when the security price moves up.

However, when the trader miss's information that the company laid off 30 percent of its workforce, in an effort to refinance its debt due to payment problems, then the trader may be setting himself or herself up for a loss.

Therefore, although technical analysts may use large amounts of data to carry out an analysis, there is no guarantee that the analysts' predictions will be accurate.

Volume Analysis

Volume analysis involves the evaluation of the number of shares or contracts that a particular stock or security has traded within a specified period.

Day traders use volume analysis to examine patterns in volumes in relation to price movements. As a result, the traders are able to know the importance of changes in the price of an asset or security.

Like any other technical indicator in the market place, the volume presents buy and sell signals to traders. Traders can know which signal to take by studying the pattern of the price movement. Are the trends strong in one direction? In addition, the traders can look at the moving average at the point of a breakout to determine whether the price movement captures the sentiments of significant investors.

When the demand for an underlying stock is high, it means that many traders have an interest in the underlying stock and are therefore prepared to pay more for it. The volume gives an indication to day traders of how many investors want certain security.

Day traders use two types of volume indicators; the positive volume index (PVI) and the negative volume index (NVI). Both indicators operate based on the previous day's trading volume and the market price of a commodity. Consequently, when the trading volume goes up from the previous day, the traders fine-tune the PVI. When the trading volume goes down from the previous day, the traders adjust the NVI accordingly.

Traders use the PVI and the NVI to evaluate how volume affects price movement. An increase or a decrease in the PVI implies that the volume drives the price movement. Contrariwise, an increase or a reduction in the NVI suggests that the volume has a minimal effect on the price changes.

Candlestick Charting

Day traders use candlestick charting to trace price fluctuations. The traders utilize the candlestick charts to show the price changes during a single time period for any time frame. For instance, each candlestick on a 4-hour chart shows the price movement within four hours.

The peak point of a candlestick displays the highest price a stock traded during the set period, whereas the lowermost position indicates the lowest prices of the stock during that time period. The part in between the highest and the weakest points in the candlestick shows the opening and closing stock prices for that period.

Traders choose the colors to use in the candlestick charts as a way to follow the price movements at a glance. As a result, traders get more visual cues and trends as they carry out technical analysis.

Chapter 8: Psychology and Mindset

Day Trading, like any other form of investment, is subject to influence from human emotion and psychological impact. Whenever money or capital is in play, people tend to take matters rather personally because of the inevitable consequence of the hope that comes along with the promise of significant returns. People will strive to make money while at the same time, avoid circumstances that may cause them to lose their capital. It is from this zero-sum mentality that the influence of psychology or emotions may creep into a sensible mindset. Such control takes over every aspect of the Day Trading instincts that you learned over time.

Your knowledge goes out of the window when a situation that triggers your psychological response arises. A high degree of counter-productivity thus ensues. It, eventually, leads to the dismissal of logical decisions in favor of hunches as well as the need to chase after fleeting profits and cover your previous losses. For you to manage your Day Trading expertise through challenging scenarios, you need to look out for emotions that alter your reasoning capability adversely. Try to improve and nurture a productive mindset, while at the same time, avoid promoting a mental culture that justifies negativity falsely. The following few behaviors and traits are central to your particular mindset whenever you decide to participate in Day Trading:

Do Not Rationalize Your Trading Errors

This mindset t is one of the leading obstacles to the progress and eventual success of your Day Trading endeavors. You are often prone to justify any trading mistakes that you make to the detriment of moving forward. For instance, you get an entry into a particularly promising trade deal later than necessary in spite of your much earlier knowledge of its potential for profitability. The delay causes you to miss an excellent opportunity at the previous entry point. However, you decide to justify this misstep by convincing yourself of your preference for trading late over missing the same deal entirely.

The downside to such delays is often a faulty sense of size estimation in taking your trading position. Hence, the resulting increased exposure to financial risk you become disadvantaged by. Beware of your procrastination when it comes to productive openings that are currently available in Day Trading. If you possess this tendency, consider getting rid of it as soon as possible before it costs you a lot more capital in the long run. In case you are not prone to the frequent postponement of your responsibilities to a later date, be alert for the development of this mentality with the trading company that you keep. You can quickly become influenced by the kind of traders from whom you seek advice on more complex trading strategies. When present, stockbrokers affect your trading ethos, as well.

Poor trading etiquette from these external sources will rub off on you and vice versa. Try to keep the company of well-known responsible trading partners and stockbrokers when the need arises. Another rationalization scenario involves a run of profitable results. Based on a series of trade deals that made you successive returns, you begin to convince your brain of your seemingly high intelligence. This false belief in your skills may lead you to overestimate your trading expertise. Before long, you may start engaging in Day Trading on a hunch rather than apply logic to your decisions. You stop referring to your trusted trading plan and jump into many trading opportunities haphazardly. After a while, these instances of carelessness and trading arrogance will catch up with you because they always inevitably do. Your chances of plunging into a financial disaster go up.

With your eventual financial ruin come the cases of psychological meltdown leading to a negative feedback loop. A wrong decision from your misplaced sense of conceitedness will invariably lead to high-risk exposure. As a result, you suffer significant losses eventually, and consequently, your emotional health suffers, causing you to spiral into a state of depression. This loop is often self-propagating, meaning that it feeds onto itself. Bad decisions lead to adverse outcomes and a fragile mindset, which, in turn, is prone to make more bad decisions, and the loop goes on and on. Keep in mind that in Day Trading, such a feedback loop is often disastrous. All these adverse effects arise from your initial false sense of justification for a wrong deed.

Beware of Your Trading Decisions

This advice is so apparent that it sounds redundant when mentioned. However, decisions are typically the product of your reasoning and judgment at a particular moment. When it comes to decisions on Day Trading, psychological influence is often a determining factor in the process. Keeping your wits about you is very crucial, especially when everything seems to be out of control. You need to realize that every trade has its ups and downs and how you deal with the challenging times is often more consequential. Try to maintain a logical mindset when making Day Trading choices from a variety of bad options. When it seems that an imminent financial downturn is inevitable, the extent of your loss becomes essential. In this case, you will need to make a sensible decision on the degree of losing margins that you can tolerate adequately.

At this point, you are probably in a state of so many overwhelming emotions that your foggy mental faculties become clouded. An expected human response is to run away from danger, naturally, but in certain situations, fleeing may not be an option. A reflex in a trading scenario often leads to an impulsive decision. Such a choice is, in turn, typically not well thought or deliberative. You should confront your unfavorable circumstances head-on and attempt to fix the situation, however hopeless. This sense of perseverance is usually the essence of most trading excursions, especially when the times become financially rough. Going through the loss of some capital and other Day Trading challenges is often a painful experience that can lead to illogical decisions.

Always remember to uphold vigilance and adhere strictly to the guidelines in your trading plan when confronted with obstacles during your trades. The trading plan usually has instructions on how to handle these seemingly desperate situations. In addition, the prior preparation of any trading guide is generally free of emotional or psychological influence; hence, you can rely on it to maintain neutrality. Also, beware of making trading resolutions when going through a phase with a foul mood. Such conclusions are bound to lead you into a financial catastrophe, especially if you are not careful. Learn to put off the verdict to a time when you can resume logical thinking. When you make any rash decision, it can only result in your further exposure to even more risk.

Keep Your Emotions in Check

Learn to stick to a Day Trading system and method that you trust. Such a strategy may be one that has a history of always making significant returns. Once you master and fully grasp how to apply a specific approach to your trading deals, try to fine-tune it to your preference based on your ultimate objectives. Afterward, stick to this tried, practiced, and tested system in all your searches for valid trade deals. On some days, the stock market may be slow with a low volume of trade. The volatility in such a case is often negligible. However, due to an unchecked emotional influence, you develop a sense of greed or lust for profits.

The desire for benefits on a slow day is common. It leads to the urge to trade on anything to make a small profit. In this situation, you will move from Day Trading into gambling. Trading requires a logical mindset on your part with a lack of psychological attachment whatsoever. Gambling is a consequence of emotional and mental factors running amok in your Day Trading system. If a particular trading style worked on multiple times in the past, teach your brain to consider it. Your trusted trading system will indicate a lack of valid trade opportunities on a specific slow market day. In this case, curb your emotions, desires, and urges to chase a quick profit; however strong they seem.

You should never allow yourself to resort to gambling under any circumstances. Gambling is detrimental to healthy and responsible Day Trading behavior. The risk exposure exponentially rises when you grow accustomed to the desire for profits. If a given day of trading is unfavorable, you should not take part in invalid and unworthy deals. In addition, you should only trade on verifiable opportunities. At certain times, you may experience a series of successive returns in a relatively short period. Learn to know when to stop and how to curb your lust for wanting more returns. Trust your system to trade only on valid deals; however, multiple opportunities are available. An emotion that goes unmonitored in such situations is the greed for more profit.

You convince yourself psychologically that the various deals could be a sign of your lucky day. This mentality in a false belief is wrong, and you need to be aware of it. Your psychology can play deceitful tricks on your logical mind leading to high-risk trading deals. You must realize that in Day Trading, it is almost impossible to get more returns out of a system than what the stock market offers. Emotional corruption also comes into play in a scenario where you bite off more than you can chew.

The greed for substantial amounts of returns may cause you to take high-risk trading positions for a chance at quick profits. However, you must remember that profits and losses are both possible outcomes from a Day Trading session. Therefore, you need to learn to trade in amounts that you can afford to lose. After all, Day Trading involves taking a chance based on a speculative position. You should practice trading in small amounts of money within the confines of low-risk deals. In this case, a potential loss may not be as damaging as the earlier high-risk trading position driven by greed. Eliminate the role of emotions in Day Trading and learn to accept the uncertainty of an unknown future outcome.

Be Patient When Trading

Patience is a crucial trait to have when you take part in Day Trading due to the upswings and downward trends in stock prices. It can become challenging to identify the right entry or exit point for a particular trading opportunity, given the fluctuating nature of a volatile market. However, when you master the art of being patient and studying the trade intently, you can come up with a winning strategy. Having a planned approach is essential, and you should prepare one before engaging in any Day Trading. Often, most seasoned traders include trading strategies for different market conditions in their trading plans. Hence, when making your trading plan, consider incorporating a trading strategy within it.

If unsure of how to proceed, you can always seek the assistance of qualified stockbrokers. They have the experience of encountering various Day Trading scenarios in the real world. If trustworthy, they could provide you with invaluable insights on coming up with a proper strategy. Now it is up to you to stick to the plan in every session in which you participate. Patience demands that you pay attention to the planned strategy and ignore any attractive distractions when trading. For instance, a brief upswing from a potential price action breakout may be misleading. It might cause you to falsely believe that the stock price is about to pick momentum and keep rising on the chart.

However, as attractive as this scenario might be, a sense of diligent patience demands that you ignore it and refer to your strategy. Upon referral to your trading plan strategy, you may encounter the concept of false breakouts. You also learn that these false upswings in trend usually follow a prolonged period of price consolidated. As a result, your patience allows you to evade a potentially wrong entry point to a trading position. You are also able to pick the right exit point from a particular trading session based on strategic patience. The price action chart acts merely as a guide for your trading actions and not the determining factor.

Chapter 9: Day Trading Rules

Day Trading is the ability to buy and sell financial instruments within the same trading day. There is a group of day traders called the pattern day traders (PDT) these are just traders who make more than four trades within five days and who use a margin account to trade. Day Trading has rules, and failure to adhere to certain rules can be costly. Rules also vary depending on location and the volume you trade.

7 Rules of Day Trading

The following rules of Day Trading, if used correctly, can help traders make profits and avoid huge losses.

How to Enter and Exit A Market

Day traders should have a predetermined plan in place of when to enter and exit a market. A trader can quickly find yourself out of the game as soon as you press the enter key if they do not have a plan. As a day trader, you have to accept the fact that you do not control the market. Therefore, one of the key factors to succeeding in Day Trading is usually determined by your ability to enter and exit your trading positions. Knowing the prices at which you wish to enter and exit can help make profits or save you from losing out on more.

When making the plan:
- Use indicators
- Set a target price before you enter the market.
- Know how much stock you plan to trade
- Plan for when to exit the market - when the market is going against your expectations, do you exit your position to avoid bigger losses?

Trading Rush Hours

Another important Day Trading rule is to avoid the first hour after the market opens and the last hour before it closes. It is wise to wait and observe during those times. Do not be eager to jump in as soon as the market opens. The first and last hours are the most volatile times in the market. This is because the stock is likely reacting to some overnight news releases, and this is when the big investors and trading experts compete. In the last hour, traders are also rushing to close out their positions.

Be Cautious of Margin Trading

Another important rule is to trade with the money you have, not borrowed money. It is important to be cautious of margin trading. Trading on margin means that you are borrowing money from a brokerage firm to trade; Money you will have to pay back. A margin account increases your purchasing power and allows you to use borrowed money to increase financial leverage; however, not all trades are profitable. Therefore, you risk losing the small bit of your capital as well as the borrowed money. Margin trading should be used in trades that you are sure will be profitable.

Be Realistic

Another important Day Trading rule is to avoid greed. It is very easy to be carried away by greed when trading, do not lose out on small profits because you think you can make more. It is very important to remain realistic about profits. The market is always changing; sometimes, it is better to settle on a small profit than to make big losses.

Be Knowledgeable

Do not day trade if you do have no sufficient knowledge of what is happening in the markets. Not everyone can trade in the market. Most traders start with paper trading and intense training. You need to be aware of information about the stocks you plan to trade, basic trading procedures, and always be on the lookout for anything that can affect your stocks. You can start by practicing using a demo account; this is a trial and error account, where you do not use real money. This account enables traders to experiment with trading before they can set up a real funded account.

Cut Your Losses

This is the number one rule in trading; cut your losses. Placing a trade is taking a risk; every trader, even the best in the world, has had bad trading days. Losing is part of trading. Traders need to accept their losses when the market starts going against them instead of hoping for a turnaround. This can be a lethal mistake. Have an exit strategy and react accordingly. Accepting your loss reduces the chance of it happening again. By cutting your losses, you learn from it and make the necessary changes to avoid a repetition.

Risk Management Plan

Risk management plans help cut down losses. The idea is to avoid risking more than you can afford to lose. With a risk management plan, even when a trade goes wrong, they still have money to trade tomorrow. Traders follow the 1% rule, which allows them to trade only 1% of their capital on any single trade. This ensures that only 1% of their money is at risk on any single trade.

Other General Day Trading rules

These rules are not binding but can be helpful when making trading decisions:

Keep A Trading Journal

The process of Day Trading can be nerve-wracking, and in most cases, traders do not remember with clarity and context all the moves they made at the end of the day, so as a rule, it is important to journal while you are trading. It does not have to be detailed, and you can write in bullet points and edit later. Journaling gives you the ability to track your trades, gains, and losses. You can also use the information to analyze your overall market performance and tweak your strategies.

Tax Rules

There is no one size fits all when it comes to tax rules. Taxes depend on the country where you are trading. Each country has different tax obligations, and the consequences of not meeting them can be extremely costly. It is important to research on taxes before you start trading.

Manage Number of Trades

A good rule of thumb is to avoid making more than three trades a week. It is more difficult to keep an eye on multiple trades at once, especially if you luck experience. If a trader makes four or more-day trades within five days, the account moves from cash account to a pattern day trade account, also known as a margin account, which has certain limitations like:

• Minimum Account Balance

Day traders who use margin accounts must maintain a minimum balance of $25,000. This does not apply to day traders who use cash brokerage accounts. If the account balance falls below this amount, the owner loses any buying power. This minimum balance can be maintained in the form of cash and securities. Pattern day traders are not allowed to cross guarantee to meet the minimum balance.

- ## When the minimum capital is not reached

When a pattern day trader account goes below $25,000, they are issued with an equity call. The balance must be restored using cash or other marginal equities. Traders should deposit the funds within five business days, and they are not allowed to make a withdrawal on the amount for at least two working days.

- ## Increased leverage

Pattern day trade accounts have increased access to margin and, therefore, leverage. They may have access to twice the standard margin amount when trading stocks. The amount is usually decided every morning.

Have A Trading Plan

Another important trading rule is to always have a trading plan and stick to it when trading. One of the worst habits' traders have is trading impulsively without any guidelines. Traders should assess their success or failure on a trade based on how they stuck to their trading plan and not whether they made a profit or a loss. Ensure that your trading plan works for you and stick to it.

Don't Chase Trades

Another rule is to avoid is chasing trades. Sometimes traders decide to chase fast-moving stocks when the market makes large and quick moves in prices instead of focusing on their trading plan. Even though the move can lead to more profits, sometimes trading decisions made in a rash can be costly. Most traders learn the importance of this rule when their poor trading decisions cost them.

Emotions

Another rule of Day Trading is not to let your emotions affect your trading decisions. Emotions have a way of influencing a trader's performance. The two common ones are fear and greed. These emotions can make a trader miss desirable gains or miss opportunities. This is why traders have to follow the rules and stick to the trading plans they made when their mind was rational. Traders should learn to be self-aware of moments when emotions are taking over and counter the response.

A Positive Mindset

A trader should always start his or her trades with a positive mindset. Avoid letting any negative thoughts or situations hinder your judgment abilities. In trading, it is important to focus on your actions, your strategies, and tools to be a success; all this requires a positive mindset.

Be Patient

Day Trading takes years of experience to master. It takes time to develop successful strategies; therefore, patience is key. You might experience losses after losses, which can make you lose hope, but with time, it gets better. Part of being patient is to plan when to buy stock and wait for the best time to sell

Always Use A Stop Loss Order

A stop-loss order is issued when a trader places an order with a broker to buy or sell the stock once it reaches a certain price. Stop-loss orders are ideally used to limit loss. When you have a stop-loss order, you do not have to monitor stock all the time. Sometimes, frequent fluctuations can activate the stop-loss order; therefore, it is advisable to select a stock-loss percentage that allows for such fluctuations.

Embracing Technology

Technology has proven to be very successful in helping day traders view and analyze the market. Technology has made it possible for more and more people to access trading, traders can practice light-speed trading, have a virtual trading platform for 24 hours a day. Traders need to embrace technology while trading, gone are the day one had limited time to trade, now, when one market closes, another opens.

Follow The 80/20 Rule

The 80/20 rules suggest that 80% of your profits should be generated by 20% of your trades. 20% of your work should generate 80% success. This rule can be used to analyze four key areas when trading

- **Trading performance**

This rule can be used to improve trading performance and analyze relationships like which tools, indicators, and strategies are causing the most wins and losses. What day of the month do you make wins and losses?

- **Individual performance**

This rule can also be used to improve efficiency. How much time do you spend on a task, and why? What do you do that reduces or increases your focus on trading? By analyzing such questions, you can know what areas need improvement

- **Market Understanding**

80/20 rule can help one improve their understanding of the market. For example, the market usually does not trend 80% of the time and trends 20% of the time.

- **Strategy performance**

The rule is useful in analyzing the efficiency a trader's strategy is. Are the majority of the wins the result of a specific strategy? Do the tools and indicators influence the strategies positively or negatively?

Use Limit Orders, Not Market Orders

Market orders are used to inform brokers to buy and sell an asset at the best available price at the time of execution. However, the best is not always profitable. Instead, traders should use limit orders. Limited orders have a controlled minimum price and maximum price for buying and selling, and therefore traders can ensure they remain profitable.

Avoid Penny Stocks

Penny stocks are small capital company stocks that are purchased cheaply per share. As the name suggests, these were stocks that traded for less than $1 per share. However, nowadays, penny stock is stocking that trade for $5 per share. So, why should we avoid penny stock?

- They are not traded on public exchanges like regular stocks. Therefore, there is not enough financial information about them to determine if they are good investments. Companies that sell this penny stock are also not subject to certain disclosures, and therefore can mismanage their financials.
- Companies offering the penny stocks are usually new in the market, and therefore it is hard to predict their performance
- Penny stocks are not as liquid as most people would think; people buy and sell them over the counter, and do not trade them on a public exchange. Therefore, it becomes hard to find a buyer if you wish to sell.

- Since penny stocks have low asset value, they have high risk. The company can go bankrupt, making you lose money.

You are better off buying reputable stocks from solid companies.

Number of Stocks

If you are a beginner, as a rule, only buy one or two stocks during a Day Trading session. You can increase the number as you learn the game, but as a newbie, it is advisable to focus on one or two stocks to be able to track and find opportunities. You can easily miss good opportunities if you have too much going on.

Importance of Leverage in Day Trading

Leveraging in trading is the ability to use borrowed funds from brokerage firms to increase one's trading position. It is considered high risk because it increases the amount of profit or loss a trader makes. Leverage is usually given a fixed amount that varies depending on the brokerage firm. Forex trading offers very high leverage ratios. Ratios can be as high a 400:1, and this means a trader with $1,000 in their account can trade up to $400,000 in value. This is because if the accounts are managed properly, the risk becomes manageable.

Leverage is important in Day Trading because:

- It reduces the amount of capital a trader needs to trade, which gives them room to take on other trades
- It allows traders to get greater returns for small up-front investment
- Leverage does not affect any profit or loss that a trader makes.
- Leverage can reduce the risk of certain types of trades.
- Leverage makes the market exciting.
- When you use leverage and make a profit, you can pay back the borrowed amount and still have more money left than if you had just invested your capital
- In some countries, it offers favorable tax treatment.

Generally, a trader should not use their entire available margin. Leverage should only be used when the advantage is on one's side. Most experienced traders usually trade with very low leverage to protect their capital against any trading mistakes they make. Experienced traders should not be afraid of leverage, especially when they learn how to manage it.

How the Securities and Exchange Commission Works

The security and exchange commission (SEC) is a government agency in charge of overseeing the security markets. It also protects investors and facilitates capital formation. The SEC maintains efficient, transparent, and effective markets.

History

Before SEC was formed, the blue-sky laws were enacted and enforced at the state level to protect the public against fraudsters. Although the laws varied across states, all companies offering securities to the public as well as stockbrokers and brokerage firms had to register themselves. These blue-sky laws were found to be ineffective as companies like the Investment Bankers Association ignored them. The congress then created the SEC through the Security Exchange Act of 1934, which was passed after the stock market crashed in 1929. It was created to restore the public's confidence in financial markets.

SEC was to address two notions:

- Companies that sell securities to the public should be honest and release any information to the public that may affect their securities.
- Investors should be treated fairly.

The SEC is made up of three organizational structures:

1. The Commission Members

The commission is made up of five commissioners carefully selected by the president, who all belong to different political parties. They retain their seats for five years, and one is designated as chairperson. They may serve for an extended 18 months past their five-year term if there is no immediate replacement.

2. Divisions

SEC consists of five divisions:

- Trading and Markets- this division monitors how the industry operates, interprets any proposed changes, and oversees self-regulatory organizations like all broker-dealer firms, investment houses, the Financial Industry Regulatory Authority (FINRA). The SEC has delegated the tasks of making rules and enforcing them to FINRA.

- Corporation Finance - this division oversees public companies' disclosures and ensures investors get relevant information so that they can make informed investment decisions for the companies.

- Enforcement-together with three other divisions, enforcement investigates privately any SEC law violations and takes action on violators. The SEC only prosecutes civil suits; the justice department handles criminal cases.

- Investment Management-this division supervises registered investment companies as well as registered investment advisors. The division also administers various federal security laws. Other responsibilities include

  - Interpreting laws and regulations for the public
  - Responding to no-action requests
  - Enforce any matters involving investment firms.

- Economic and Risk Analysis- this division integrates economics and data analytics into the core mission of the SEC. The division uses a variety of academic work and market knowledge to help commissions solve complex matters.

When handling civil suits, the SEC can only perform two actions:

- Injunction-this an authoritative warning or order, any violations can lead to fines or imprisonment
- Issue civil money penalties and the disgorgement of illegal profits

3. Regional Offices

US SEC has 11 regional offices throughout the country. The regional offices have the following offices:

- The Office of General Counsel-which gives legal advice to the commission as well as represent the agency in court
- The Office of Compliance, Inspection, and Examinations-this office is in charge of inspecting stock exchanges, broker-dealers, mutual funds, and credit rating agencies.
- The Office of the Chief Accountant- ensure any auditing and accounting policies set by the SEC are enforced
- The Office of Information Technology-oversees the IT department

- The Office of internal Affairs-represent the SEC abroad
- The Inspector General
- The SEC Office of the Whistleblower-this office rewards individuals who voluntarily share information that leads to successful law enforcement actions.

Chapter 10: Successful Trade

Trading can only be productive when traders take the exercise seriously and conduct thorough market research.

A successful trade is one that effectively puts a trading plan into action, among other factors. The trading plan helps to ensure that a trader has a more focused trading strategy and that he or she does not take trades outside of the trading plan. Other factors include trading discipline, technology, and developing a trading style.

Consequently, successful traders take their time to understand how the investment market works and thereby improve their strategy.

Making A Successful Trade Step-By-Step

Executing trades successfully is a process that requires a trader to follow the steps below to have an effective plan.

Making a Watchlist

A watchlist is a record of stocks or securities that a trader looks at to see whether the shares or securities suit his or her trading plan. There are many stocks in the marketplace to keep an eye on, without a watchlist.

Watchlists give the trader an idea of what investments he or she may want to add to his or her collection. A watchlist should be simple and based on current information of the biggest gainers, for example. The best stocks are those whose prices keep moving in a favorable direction.

Therefore, in every single day's watchlist, a trader should try to find the winning stocks from the previous day, especially if the shares have positive news and the right chart breakout. That is because the stocks will continue trading in the market the following day.

Besides, a trader should begin with a wide range of stock selections, and then narrow down stocks according to what he or she is looking for, as he or she observes the trend. When the trader knows what he or she is looking for, he or she will eliminate stocks that do not suit his or her trading strategy.

In addition, it is wise for a trader to list the most popular stocks and to check why the stocks are popular picks for other traders. The factors that make the stock popular will most likely be issues that other traders hold in a high volume. Such considerations should then be the trading standards for the trader.

Moreover, a trader should understand how the fluctuation in stock prices directly affects the way that driving forces react to different commodities in the market. In that way, the trader will develop his or her trading style and have an easy time assessing the patterns of the stocks on his or her watchlist.

There are certain things that a trader should avoid having in his or her watchlist. First, a trader should not have too many stocks on the list. A good number would be anywhere from five to ten stocks. That will help the trader to have a better chance to understand how the trade works.

Secondly, a trader should not focus on big trades. When a trader aims small, he or she misses little, thereby cutting losses quickly. Big trades run the risk of having huge losses. The idea is to win more and get better profit on the wins than the amount one loses because losing is part of the trade.

Choosing and Purchasing Stocks

When buying a company's stock, a trader becomes a stakeholder or a part-owner of that company. The value of the trader's investment, therefore, depends on the general well-being of the business.

Therefore, when buying a stock, a trader should start with a company that he or she knows. In so doing, a trader gets a place to start and avoids buying stocks without understanding how the company intends to make money.

Additionally, a trader should take into account the stock price and valuation. More experienced investors tend to look for securities that are cheap or undervalued to reap benefits when the stock price goes up.

However, a trader should know the kind of stock he or she wants, and he or she should understand that cheap is not always right and expensive is not still bad. A commodity may be cheap because its business is slowing down, and a commodity may be costly because investors expect their earnings to increase rapidly in a few years.

In addition, a trader should evaluate the financial stability of the company before buying the company's stocks. The trader can assess the revenue growth, check the bottom line, check the company's balance sheet to know how much debt the company has, and then finally find a dividend.

After choosing a stock, a trader can buy the stock first by opening a brokerage account. When opening the brokerage account, the trader should find out the brokerage fee.

A broker that charges low or does not charge at all will be an ideal choice. Along with that, a trader should check whether the broker offers educational tools, guidance on trading, stock market research, and easy access to help centers.

Secondly, the trader should identify the stocks that he or she wants to buy by researching companies that he or she already knows from past trading experiences.

Thirdly, the trader should decide how many shares he or she wants to buy. It is advisable to start by purchasing a single stock, to get a feel of what the trade is like and the trader deciding whether he or she would want to continue in the business.

Afterward, the trader can select his or her stock order type. Most investors buy stocks either with market orders or with limit orders. With a market order, the trader is signifying that he or she will buy or sell the security at best available current market prices. A limit order gives the trader more control over the price at which he or she will buy or sell.

Finally, the trader can then improve his or her stock selection to begin the journey of carrying out successful trades officially.

Understanding Entry and Exit

An entry point is the price at which a trader buys or sells a stock. A good entry point marks the beginning of a successful trade. A trader can find a proper entry point by doing market research and maximize profits in each business.

To find valid entry points, a trader should research, study, and learn the relevant parallels and factors that are influencing the market. For example, a trader can study and find an attractive stock but feels that the price of the stock is very high. In that case, the trader will buy if the price reduces to a certain level. That level will be the trader's entry point.

Consequently, the process of finding an entry point requires a trader to practice patience and wait for the appropriate time to buy, to get returns on his or her investment.

After evaluating the market, a trader should then decide whether to enter a long position (buy) or a short position (short). Concerning that, the trader should avoid risking too much. That is, the trader should invest what he or she can afford to lose.

Additionally, a trader should utilize limit orders to buy or sell a currency pair at a particular price or a better price. The use of technical indicators will come in handy when creating trading signals. Technical indicators will give the trader essential information about the market and currency pairs.

Accordingly, a trader should make his or her transactions occasionally, because market conditions can change due to technical influences and financial news releases.

An exit point is the price at which a trader closes the position. A trader may, therefore, sell at an exit point, or buy to close the position if he or she anticipates selling it later at a higher price.

A trader can exit either through take-profit orders or through stop-loss orders. A take-profit order is a limit order that stipulates the exact price of a commodity or the exact profit level in which a trader wants his or her broker to close the trader's position. A stop-loss order, tells the broker to close the trader's position when the stock suffers losses.

When coming up with an entry-exit plan, the trader needs to decide how long he or she intends to be in the trade. In addition, the trader needs to know how much risk he or she is willing to take.

Knowing How to Stop Loss

A broker places a stop-loss order once the stock reaches a particular level. A stop-loss helps to limit a trader's loss on a stock position.

For example, when a trader buys a share at $10 per share, he or she can place a stop-loss order for $8. Therefore, is the security's price falls beyond $8, the broker will sell the trader's shares at the prevailing market price.

A trader can know where to place his or her stop-losses by using the percentage method, the support method, or the moving average method. Many traders use the percentage method.

The percentage method involves calculating the percentage of stock a trader is willing to risk before he or she closes his or her position on the trade.

For instance, if a trader is willing to lose 10 percent of the value of security before he or she exits and the trader owns securities that are trading at $40 per share, the trader would place his or her stop-loss order at $36. That will be 10 percent below the market price of the security.

The support method also allows the trader to tailor his or her stop-loss level to the commodity that he or she is trading. As such, the trader needs to find the most recent level of support and place his or her stop-loss slightly below that level.

For example, if the trader owns a share that is currently trading at $30 per share, and he or she finds $25 as the most recent support level. Therefore, the trader should place his or her stop-loss slightly below $25. Placing the stop-loss slightly below the support level gives the commodity's price space to come down and bounce back up before the trader closes his or her position.

The moving average method requires the trader to apply a moving average to his or her security chart. A moving average is a technical indicator that analyzes the price changes of stocks while reducing the impact of random price fluctuations.

A trader may want to use a long-term moving average as compared to a short-term moving average to avoid placing his or her stop-loss too close to the stock price and getting closed out of his or her trade too soon.

As soon as the trader puts the moving average, he or she should set his or her stop-loss immediately below the level of the moving average. For instance, if the trader's share is currently trading at $30 and the moving average is at $26, he or she should place the stop-loss below $26, to allow the stock price space for movement.

Knowing When to Sell

A trader should start selling his or her stock when he or she miscalculated the decision to buy the stock, when the stock price shoots up dramatically, and when the stock has reached an unsustainable amount.

A trader will know whether he or she made a profit or loss the minute he or she sells the stock. While the buying price may help the trader to know how much advantage he or she has gained, the selling price guarantees the profit, if any.

While selling a stock should not be a common occurrence because trading in and out of positions could be detrimental to a trader's investment, postponing the decision to sell the stock when it is the right time to do so may also yield unfavorable outcomes.

For example, a trader may buy a stock at $20 to sell it at $25. The stock price reaches $25, and the trader decides to hold out for a couple of more points. The stock hits $27, and the trader still holds out to maximize on profit should the stock price move further up. Suddenly, the price drops back to $24. The trader waits until the price hits $25 again, but this does not happen. The trader then gives in to frustration and sells the stock at a loss when the stock price hits $18.

Consequently, if a trader sells at the opportune time, he or she will experience the benefits of buying the stock. However, the trader should not try to time the market because timely selling does not necessarily require accurate market timing. The focus should be on buying at one price and selling at a higher price, even when the higher price is not the absolute top.

When a trader discovers that he or she made an analytical error in buying a stock, the trader should sell the stock even if it means that he or she will make a loss.

If a trade does not meet the trader's short-term earnings predictions and the price of the shares takes a fall, he or she should not sell the stock if the business is not losing market shares to competitors. If the company loses market shares to competitors, then that may be a good reason for the trader to sell the stock.

Alternatively, a trader can sell his or her stock when the stock price rises dramatically in a short period for particular reasons. The trader should take his or her gains and move on.

Additionally, a trader could sell when the company's valuation is becoming higher than its competitors are, or when the company's price-to-earnings ratio goes beyond its average price-to-earnings within five or ten years.

However, when a company's earnings decline when the demand is low, and the company starts cutting costs. That would be a chance to exit the position before any further decline in the value of the company's stock.

In addition, a trader could sell his or her stock for financial needs. That may not be a good reason from an analytical point, but securities are assets, and traders have the freedom to cash in their assets when the need arises.

Examples of Day Trades

Trading Breakouts

Given that traders always want to cut losses quickly, trading breakouts is ideal for scanning potential losses because a trader can see when he or she is making a wrong decision.

The trader first needs to identify a price level that represents his or her breakout trading level. Afterward, the trader enters the market once he or she sees that a security price goes beyond the defined range. The trader can then close the stock above the resistance level.

That means, when the price of a stock moves out of a defined price range, a trader can move to a new high or low. For example, a trader can buy when the market price breaks higher, or goes beyond a failed resistance level, and sell when the market breaks lower, or goes below a failed support level.

However, a trader should only buy when the price pulls back to the original breakout point to avoid the likelihood of being trapped in a false breakout.

Trading Ranges

When a trader trades ranges, he or she aims to take advantage of the fraction of the market that is not trending. For example, if the market only trends 40 percent of the time, that leaves the trader with 60 percent to explore.

Trading ranges take into account the support and resistance levels, which develop when the stock price oscillates. The trader first needs to make sure that the stock price does not break above or below any level in between the highs and lows, assuming that two similar highs and lows have already happened in that price fluctuation.

For example, a trader may notice that a particular stock was starting to form a price during a specified period. After the stock price forms the initial peaks, the trader may start placing long or short trades based on the stock's trendlines, along with the resistance and support levels. Trading ranges ends when the stock does not show a breakout from either trendline.

Flag Trading

Flag trading is about a trader identifying flag shapes on a price chart. Flag patterns are easy to spot. The direction in which the flag blows shows the path of the primary trend and indicates that a stock is going through a steady upward trend.

The shape of the flag forms when a stock makes a strong move upward, on high volume, and then consolidates at the top of the pole, on low volume. The trend continues when the stock breaks out of the consolidation pattern on high volume.

Flag patterns can trend either upwards or downwards while following the same volume and breakout patterns. For example, in an upward-trending flag pattern, the price action moves up during the first trend and then declines through the consolidation area. That is an indication that traders have entered the market in a new wave of enthusiasm.

In a downward-trending flag pattern, the price action does not always decline during the consolidation. That is because of fear and anxiety over the falling prices that make traders avoid taking action.

Triangle Trading

Triangle trading has three types of triangle chart formations: symmetrical, ascending, and descending triangles.

The symmetrical triangle forms when the slant of the price's highs and the slant of a price's lows meet at an apex to form the shape of a triangle. What this means is that the market is making lesser highs and lows that are more significant. Neither the buyers nor the sellers are moving the price far enough to create a clear trend.

The ascending triangle forms when there are a resistance level and a slant of higher lows. That is an indication that there is a certain level that the buyers cannot seem to go beyond. However, the traders put pressure on the resistance level for a breakout to happen. While the breakout may not occur quickly, the traders are at least able to push the price up by a margin.

The descending triangle is just like the ascending triangle only that it is inverted, and traders consider it a breakout pattern. The breakout happens when the stock price falls through the bottom horizontal trendline support while a downtrend begins again. The bottom trendline or the support, in this case, becomes resistance.

Chapter 11: Success Tips for Beginner Day Traders

Traders undertake Day Trading because it offers them the chance to take advantage of small movements of the price while avoiding the losses linked with overnight risks. An intraday day trader uses various trading strategies and analytical skills to make appropriate decisions that give him or her money. The more experienced a trader is, the more prepared the trader is to succeed in the market.

On the other hand, a beginner in Day Trading does not have the training and experience that will add additional protection against losses. Thus, he or she uses caution, technical and psychological strategies, and strict discipline to allow him or her to make money and manage the associated risks. Here is information concerning advice for profit achievement, and the dos and don'ts that provide tips for success in Day Trading for a beginner.

Advice and Methods for Beginners

A beginner starts Day Trading with the hope and belief of achieving success in the market. The trader feels that he or she is ready to undertake the trade with the knowledge and skills that he or she possesses. Nonetheless, there are some tips that he or she can follow that will enhance his or her trading experience and increase the chances of success. Some of the advice and methods that can assist a beginner in Day Trading are:

1. **Carry out Research Continuously** – Continually researching enriches a trader's knowledge and skills, which help him or her to create and apply better and profitable strategies and decisions.

2. **Prepare and Follow a Trading Strategy** – Always have a trading plan before undertaking trade and adhere to its guidelines. It helps a trader to know which position to take and the entry and exit strategy.

3. **Control of Emotions** – A trader is a human who experiences emotions as he or she trades. Day Trading is a fast-moving market with high risks involved. A trader may be in a profitable position at a time, but swings in the market can change quickly, and he or she starts experiencing losses. The fear of losing in the market can make a trader think and react to trade emotionally, which can lead to further losses. He or she should manage his or her feelings and use only the factual data to make decisions in the market.

4. **Reserve Time for Trading** – Day Trading needs a trader to commit time to the business, as he or she needs to track price movements, make trading strategies, and make appropriate judgments of the trade. It is a full-time job, and the trader needs to take it seriously by fully concentrating on the trading tasks.

5. **Prepare Funds for the Investment** – A trader must set aside some amount of money specifically for trading. Moreover, within that amount, he or she should decide on a trading formula that will determine the money to risk for each trade. In so doing, he or she will manage risks whereby he or she will still have money in the first account

even if a deal fails. He or she will only lose that small percentage in that particular investment.

6. **Having a Risk Management Strategy** – Day Trading requires risk management strategies that will help a trader to avoid or minimize any losses in a trade. Besides money management, a trader also needs to prepare exit strategies in case of unfavorable changes in the market, such as developing a stop loss.

7. **Properly Time the Trades** – Day Trading involves fast movements of prices and sudden changes in market conditions. A trader needs to get his or her timing right to ensure the entry and exit of trade results in success. It also helps him or her not to miss trading opportunities.

8. **Know When to Quit** – A trader should know when to exit a trade and abandon a particular trading strategy. If a plan or deal is not working, he or she should know when to stop to prevent further losses.

9. **Stop Focusing on the Money** – The trader should concentrate on the trading strategies to ensure that they will help him or her trade successfully. Focusing on the money will make the trader become anxious or impatient with the market and end up making rash decisions that are detrimental to the business.

10. **Realistic Expectations about Profits** – Being realistic about Day Trading will help a person to trade better and eventually succeed in the business. He or she

will know the realistic chances of success and will work within those realities. He or she will not make rash decisions in an attempt to make impossible profits.

11. **Use Appropriate Type of Orders** – Day Trading incorporates the use of orders to manage risks and minimize the losses in the market. A trader should utilize the right order according to his or her trading condition. He or she can choose to use limit orders or market orders to enable precise trading and making profits.

12. **Avoid the Penny Stocks** – They say cheap is expensive, and the same applies in Day Trading. A trader should avoid penny stocks because they have low chances of success and are mostly illiquid.

13. **Begin with Small Trades** – A trader should take small steps as he or she starts in Day Trading. He or she begins with few trades and uses them to enhance his or her skills and experience before slowly advancing and using more share in the trade.

14. **Take Full Advantage of the Technology** – Technological advancement provides a trader with access to various education, tools, and software that can help him or her to succeed in Day Trading. He or she should take advantage of these features to continually learn and practice, which will build his or her expertise and confidence in the trades. They will also help him or her to enhance his or her technical, analytical skills.

15. **Keep a Record of the Trades** – A trader needs to take notes about all the trades that he or she undertakes. He or she writes about the trading experience where he or she includes details about the planning, entry, and exit of the trade. These records will help him or her to keep track of historical data regarding a particular market. They will also provide him or her with a reference that he or she can use to make predictions about specific trades.

16. **Learning from Losses** – The trader should learn from the trading experiences that he or she goes through in the market. He or she needs to take the losses as lessons that guide him or her on how to avoid failure.

17. **Take Responsibility of the Trade** – A trader should bear the responsibility for all outcomes in his or her trade because he or she made the decisions concerned. He or she should not blame the market for any losses or failures that he or she experiences.

18. **Maintain discipline in the Trade** – The trader should always maintain control in all aspects of Day Trading. He or she should strictly follow the guidelines of the trading strategies to ensure successful trade.

Mistakes That Beginners Make

Day Trading requires a trader to spend a lot of time and effort to achieve success. An expert trader knows to follow specific trading rules and procedures to ensure that he or she will make profits and avoid experiencing losses. However, beginners lack the experience and end up making mistakes that make their trades unsuccessful. Below are some of the errors that lead to failed trading:

1. **Timing Poorly in Trade** – Day Trading is all about timing, and failure in getting it right can lead to considerable losses. The trader uses his or her timing wrong and loses trading opportunities since the price already moved to an unfavorable direction.

2. **Trading Without a Plan** – A trader starts trading without any plan or strategy regarding the trade. Hence, he or she does not know how to deal with a crisis or a sudden change in price action. It leads to an overall failure of the trade.

3. **Changing the Trading Strategy Frequently** – A trader should use a strategy that he or she understands and suits the trade. However, he or she may change the plan so much that none of them works successfully. A strategy that suits one deal may not suit another, and likewise, the trader cannot use too many plans on the same trade.

4. **Chasing Trades** – A trader becomes impatient and anxious about market conditions and decides to pursue the market in an attempt to make profits quickly. However, the market is a shadow, and he or she will not succeed in catching and controlling it. Rather than waiting for the trade to present an opportunity, his or her impatience leads to failure since he or she exposes himself or herself to more risks.

5. **Averaging Down** – A trader continues to hold on and add to a losing position in the market in the hope that the price trend will reverse and start giving him or her gains. He or she loses a lot more when the reversal does not take place.

6. **Taking a Position before the news is out** – A trader decides to take a particular trade in the market in an attempt to anticipate the news release. The unknown risk here can lead to considerable losses since the price may move against his or her expectations after the announcement of the report.

7. **Trading immediately after the News** – A trader can place himself or herself in a losing position when he or she starts trading soon after the release of the news. The price initially moves quickly and sharply after the announcement but may change direction once the volatility reduces. It can result in a trader experiencing loses as the price moves in the opposite direction.

8. **Trading Without a Stop Loss** – Trading without a stop loss exposes a trader to experience potentially unlimited losses. A stop-loss helps him or her to manage the risks by moderating losses since the trader can exit the trade when the price shifts against him or her.

9. **Risking Excessive Capital** – A trader who does not have proper money management risks the amount of money for investment. He or she uses all or a significant percentage of his or her capital on one trade instead of utilizing a smaller portion and breaking it down. Thus, he or she ends up losing his or her entire budget if the business fails to lead to reckless utilization of funds. The trader risks more money that causes him or her to lose sleep.

10. **Psychological Weaknesses** – The trader here lets his emotions decide the actions that he or she takes when Day Trading. The fear, greed, and impatience lead to him or her making rash judgments and exposing himself or herself to higher risks in the market. He or she also underestimates the market and makes hasty decisions that lead to failed trades.

11. **Trading Correlated Pairs** – A trader increases the risks when he or she transacts using correlated pairs in the market. He or she loses the double if they move against him or her since they link to each other. Hence, he or she doubles his or her losses when trading correlated pairs.

12. **Going All In** – The trader risks everything and takes a more significant trade than usual due to the temptations of doubling profits. However, he or she loses significantly if the business fails.

13. **Following the Crowd** – A trader follows the decisions and actions of other traders in the market. Rather than thinking and making his or her judgments, the trader follows the crowd. He or she does not stick to the guidelines of his or her trading strategy and instead makes moves that might ultimately lead to a losing position in the market.

14. **Having Unrealistic Expectations** – The trader has an impractical view of the market and has high expectations of profits. He or she makes highly risky decisions to try to obtain that gain. Nonetheless, the risks he or she faces leads to foreseen and unexpected losses from the trades of interest. Additionally, he or she does not accept losses since he or she sees profits as the only results in the market.

15. **Leaving Out the Margins** – A trader forgets about margins and ends up trading with money that he borrowed from a broker. Margin can help a trader to increase gains when he or she applies it appropriately. Hence, a trader leaving it out leads to the collapse and failure of a trade.

16. **Utilizing the Wrong Brokers** – A trader can use a broker who manages his or her trades poorly. The broker

may lack knowledge or access to specific essential trading software and may have poor communication skills. These features cause the trader to have a wrong broker who will create financial trouble that can escalate to trading failures.

17. **Lack of Knowledge and Training** – A trader rushes into Day Trading without having the necessary skills and experience for ensuring success. He or she ends up taking more on his or her plate and ends up failing miserably in the markets.

18. **Lack of Post Trade Analysis** – Trading without recording the trade and its aftermath can lead to a trader repeating mistakes that previously caused losses. The post-trade analysis provides him or her with an account of the trade's history, which can inform future trading strategies. However, the absence of such a report can make a trader lose the chance of identifying critical decisions and learning from them.

19. **Trading Using Fundamental Data** – A trader using fundamental data to undertake Day Trading fails because intraDay Trading uses technical analysis to make trades. Day Trading involves price movements in the short-term and a trader gambles when he or she ignores the trading strategies and starts utilizing economic data.

20. **Poor Discipline while Trading** – A trader fails to stick to his or her trading plan and becomes messy in

the market. Disorganization leads to him or her, making unclear decisions that can cause losses. He or she may want to undertake different positions at a sensitive time since the lack of discipline causes panic and confusion.

Why and How Most Traders Fail

Trading in the stock market requires a combination of skills and experience to ensure that a trader can make profits. An intraday trader also applies them to enable him or her to gain in a single day while simultaneously try to avoid losses in the market. However, many traders seem to experience more losses than gains while trading in the short amount of time of intraday markets. These traders fail because they have weaknesses regarding their knowledge, skills, mindset, and expectations of a trade. Here are how these factors affect a trader and lead to his or her failure in the market.

1. Inadequate Knowledge

Knowledge is an essential tool to possess in any aspect of life. It is especially vital to a trader as it provides him or her with the expertise that develops and improves his or her trading skills. Thus, when a trader does not have adequate and proper education concerning trading, he or she sets himself or herself up for a disastrous trading experience. He or she does not understand the trading tools and lacks analytical thinking that forms the essence of trade. Consequently, he or she cannot make trading strategies nor implement risk management rules, leading to losses and failure in the stock market.

2. Poor Skills

Some traders fail in the markets because they know but not the skills needed to achieve success. A trader who does not continually practice his or her trading will result in having poor skills. Day Trading is a business that requires a person to learn and train continuously for several years before he or she can identify as a proper trader. However, many traders have little training, experience in the markets, and view themselves as qualified. It leads to the traders taking on more than they can handle, which ultimately leads to failure.

3. Mindset

The psychology of a trader can determine whether he or she succeeds in the trade. Most traders may fail in trading despite having adequate skills and experience due to psychological weaknesses. They approach the trades with the wrong emotions and attitudes that lead to unsuccessful ventures.

a) **Emotions** – A trader lets his or her feelings influence his or her decisions and actions in the market. He or she allows his or her fear of losing money to control him or her. The trader ends up panicking and rushing into risky decisions that cause losses.

b) Attitude – A trader has a flawed approach where he or she lets greed and overconfidence dictate his or her judgments. The trader thinks he or she is invincible and views the market as a playground. He or she takes risky positions that eventually lead to failure.

4. Unrealistic Expectations

Most traders think that they will succeed and leave no room for losses. Such a trader believes that his or her trading strategies are perfect, and he or she takes trades with higher risks. He or she trades assuming in luck rather than the actual conditions of the market. As a result, he or she risks too much and applies poor trading strategies that backfire and lead to significant losses. Additionally, a trader's unrealistic expectation of profits leads to him or her being impatient and enters a trade with little training and planning. These factors combine to ensure the failure of a trader in the market.

Day Trading involves certain risks, especially since it takes place in a short amount of time. A person needs to know the conduct and attitude to have, and the mistakes to avoid when trading. Learning and understanding these tips for Day Trading will help a beginner to start and continue the trade successfully.

Chapter 12: Taking Profits, ROI and Passive Income

The primary objective for you to engage in Day Trading is to attain significant returns on your capital. For this aim to be attainable, you must apply productive strategies to your Day Trading involvement. In Day Trading, patterns in the stock price are bound to recur, and if you are keen, you can spot these trend repetitions. You can have a particular trend that matches a similar one that you encountered previously. The recurrence may not match the actual price values, but the overall uptrends and downtrends may be identical. The time frame between the similar trends may vary between days and weeks, but the resemblance is noticeable when you sharpen your focus.

Based on these recurrences, you can take advantage of this knowledge to make profits from Day Trading. If you know how the stock price behaved last time, you can accurately predict its future movement. This assumption is valid as long as the circumstances and price patterns match. Using a price action chart, you can put your newfound strategy into action. A majority of these approaches involve looking out for an event called a breakout. The following scenarios describe various setups in which the breakouts favor entry into a particular trading position:

1. IPC Breakout

This breakout acronym stands for Impulse, Pullback, and Consolidation. This phrase describes the behavior of the stock price on the price action chart. You need to look for a pattern characterized by these movements in the value of its stock. Usually, within the first few minutes, a cycle in Day Trading will start with a significant move in a specific direction in the form of an impulse wave. A pullback reaction typically follows this impulse wave.

A pullback is akin to applying instant brakes on the sharp initial impulse movement. From the pullback section, you will notice that the price hovers over a small range for a while. This period is the consolidation phase, where the stock price experiences a sideways movement. Note that the consolidation phase confines itself within the margins of the first impulse wave.

In the case of a fall in stock price beyond the open end, a different outcome may ensue. In this scenario, you will have both hovering and pullback happening at a value much lower than the opening stock price. At this point, your patience comes into play. You need to stand by for a potential breakout in the direction of the earlier impulse wave. Pay attention not to perform any trade in the event of a breakout in the reverse direction. The activation of a buying position is dependent on the stock price, breaking at a value that is greater than the consolidation level. For instance, in case the earlier scenario ensued, and the stock price pulled back after an initial drop, trading is valid only when the breakout occurs over the consolidation.

When buying, it is advisable to take a long position on a small bid above the highest point of the consolidation phase. Taking a long trading position allows you to make a profit from a later increase in the price of the stock. In case you become interested in taking a short trading position, you can make an equally tiny bid below the lowest point of the consolidation.

A short trading position enables you to make a profit from a later drop in price. In both trading positions, you will determine your entry point based on a potentially favorable future outcome. This particular pattern setup is typical of the beginning of a trading session. Movements that take place close to the opening time are usually significant and potentially profitable. Always remember to discern the price action trends carefully before trading since any setup that lacks the distinctive sections is probably wrong.

2. RC Breakout

A Reversal and Consolidation breakout lacks the smaller pullback section found in, the earlier setup. In this case, you will have the usual significant impulse section, followed by a much higher reversal. Note that the reversal occurs in a direction that is opposite to the impulse wave. The reversal section is immediate to the impulse without any signs of a previous pullback. Due to the slight difference between RC and IPC breakouts, you need to pay special attention to the reversal trend. You should ignore any movement that occurs before the reversal. Wait for an imminent pullback from the reversal spike that ought to be smaller than your first or preceding impulse. The reversal wave now acts as your point of reference with which comparisons of the pullback and later consolidation take place.

Once you achieve a level of price consolidation, follow the guidelines as before in the earlier setup. If the breakout occurs either above or beneath the extreme points of consolation, you can take a relevant trading position. Always bid small amounts of your capital in Day Trading since the margins are rather low, as well. An example of an RC setup involves an initial drop in the stock price of about 50 cents followed instantly by a reversal of, say 70 cents.

In this case, you need to concentrate your focus on the reversal rally of 70 cents that puts you back in the money anyway. The initial fall in price is the impulse wave, and it causes a distraction of which you should be wary. The more significant reversal should be your reference point, especially since you currently have an overall net trend of going upward. A pullback and consolidation phase should come after the reversal phase and finally accompanied by the awaited breakout.

3. Check for Reversal at Support and Resistance points

These two points signify the general pricing regions of a price action chart as opposed to real stock values. Support occurs when the falling trend of a particular stock price reaches its minimum point for that same trading cycle. The stock price cannot continue dropping beyond the support level. At support, the trend undergoes a period of consolidation before a reversal takes place. Upon reversing its direction, the price trend keeps rising to a point beyond which any further price increase becomes impossible.

This maximum level of the stock price is the resistance. Both support and resistance are typically indicative of how the various trading positions affect the movements of the stock market price. The economies of scale with the supply and demand forces are applicable here as well. In the context of Day Trading, excessive buyers lead to resistance, while support is the result of too many sellers. Once you identify the support and resistance regions, look out for the presence of consolidations at these levels.

A positive trading signal occurs in case of a breakout over the consolidation section at a support point. The same is valid for a breakout that happens beneath the consolidation at the resistance level. Beware of the market behaving unexpectedly. In rare circumstances, the stock price may breakout above the consolidation phase at the resistance level. In addition, the same might happen at the support region, and you encounter a breakout below the price consolidation. Although highly unlikely, these kinds of unusual breakouts are still possible. In such cases, you need to exit from your trading position immediately. You could use the breakout as your exit point. Therefore, your level of concentration has to be sharp to stay alert to such improbable eventualities.

4. Strong Area Breakout

This strategy enables you to participate in Day Trading above and below the resistance and support levels, respectively. These trending patterns are rare but still possible; hence, you need to develop and have a proper approach in place in case they arise. These regions located beyond the support and resistance points are the so-called Strong Areas. It is within these areas that you need to search for the relevant breakouts for you to conduct your trading.

First, you should take note of a trend that reached up to identical values at the resistance or support level multiple times. This pattern shows that the restrictive level is about to break. Based on the volume of trade in the stock market, such a trend is predictable. It is bound to break either its resistance or support. Trading on such values is often challenging because the margin beyond which the pattern exceeds the limit is usually small. You can decide to take a long position on a breakout trend that breaches the resistance.

However, beware of the lack of a sustaining rally beyond that level. Therefore, you should continue bidding only smaller amounts of capital on any breakout above the resistance level. The same reasoning applies to traders taking short positions on those breakouts that breach the support level. The amount of profit from such Strong Area breakouts is often insignificant compared to the larger margins experienced with the standard price action trading.

5. False Breakout

This type of breakout is useful as a confirmatory tool for other trading strategies. A false breakout is indicative of a price that attempts a particular movement, but fails and eventually goes in the opposite direction. For instance, consider an RC breakout setup where the reversal was higher than the initial impulse. After the reversal section, you would experience a brief pullback followed by a consolidation. Your expectation from the consolidation phase would likely be that the price takes an upward trend. This assumption is per the direction of the much higher reversal pattern.

However, due to the market forces, there is usually a small breakout downward for a brief moment straight after the consolidation phase. This breakout is false since the price would once again reverse and continue on its new upward trajectory. Knowing how to interpret and utilize false breakouts is essential in confirming the validity of your taken trading position. Using false breakouts in this manner is akin to proving a negative.

ROI

When you take part in Day Trading, you should expect a return on investment that corresponds to your input capital. Large amounts of capital outlay are typically disadvantageous due to the low rate of return. Investing in small amounts of money regularly usually results in a more productive rate of returns. Success at Day Trading is often a prerequisite for you to attain a significant return on your investment. The following factors affect your capital's margins of profits directly:

1. Risk on Each Trade

This risk refers to the amount of your capital that is in danger of losing its value whenever you trade. It also refers to the trading position that you take every time you participate in Day Trading. For you to maximize your returns, you should have this risk under control. Risk management is achievable by setting a maximum limit on the amount of capital with which you can trade. For instance, you can set a limit of one percent of your available equity for commitment to a particular trade.

Also, use stop-loss orders to enforce this resolution. You need to adhere to these conditions strictly, every time you engage in any Day Trading transaction. It often becomes more comfortable to estimate your position size once you have both the stop-loss and entry point values. You need to realize that risk is a potential loss, and therefore, your aim must be to gain more money than you lose. You should learn to risk as little as possible while maintaining a higher margin for any probable profits.

2. Reward to Risk Ratio

As mentioned earlier, you should strive to be in a position where your profit surpasses the amount of capital that you lose. This ratio shows you this relative association between the two outcomes. For you to get on the right track towards gaining profits, your reward to risk ratio has to be higher than one. Whenever you minimize your risk to one percent of your capital, you are in an excellent position to gain from any particular trade. This position is reinforce-able by the fact that your denominator in the ratio would become the one percent. For maximum returns, the preferable reward to risk ratio is 1.5 to 1. A reversal in the price trend or your premature exit from the trade is the only limitation to your returns. Beware of your stop-loss level whenever you seek a higher reward to risk ratio.

3. Win Rate

As the name implies, this rate describes the percentage of your trade deals that turned out profitable. This rate has a close relation to the reward to risk ratio and is often in use simultaneously. To maintain an excellent ratio that is acceptable for your level of returns, you need a win rate above fifty percent. For instance, with a rate of 1.5 to 1 and a win rate of fifty percent, you will gain an overall return of twenty-five percent on the trade. Your profits are calculated as follows: (50% of 1.5) minus (50% of 1). As you can see, win rates below the recommended fifty percent would result in a loss of your capital.

4. Number of Trades

Since your specific aims concern the win rate, and the reward to risk ratio, the number of trades in which you can trade is limitless. You can take part in trading as many times as it takes you to maintain your statistics at the recommended values. The more trades you take part in, the more your overall margin of returns. However, the trick is to keep to the fifty percent profitability rate. As a result, if you want to engage in more trades, make sure not to lose a significant number of them. With all these factors in place, you can now control your returns on investment.

Conclusion

Thank you for making it through to the end of *Day Trading for Beginners: How to Day Trade for a Living, Proven Strategies, Tactics, and Psychology to Create a Passive Income from Home with Trading Investing in Stocks, Options and Forex*. Let us hope it was informative and able to provide you with all of the tools you need to achieve your goals, whatever they may be.

Now you are aware that Day Trading is the process of purchasing and selling assets within the same day, often using borrowed funds to take advantage of small price shifts in highly liquid indexes or stocks.

Day traders use short-term trading strategies and a high level of leverage to take advantage of small price movements in highly liquid currencies or stocks. Experienced day traders have their finger on events that lead to short-term price movements, such as the news, corporate earnings, economic statistics, and interest rates, which are subject to market psychology and market expectations.

Day traders can use technical indicators to provide trading signals and assess the current trade. Keltner Channels, a popular technical indicator, use average prices and volatility to plot lower, middle, and upper lines. These three lines move with the price to create the appearance of a channel. Chester Keltner introduced these channels in the 1960s, but Linda Bradford Raschke updated them in the 1980s. Today, traders use the later version of the indicator, which is a combination of two different indicators, which are the average true range and the exponential moving average.

Created by J. Welles Wilder Jr. and introduced in 1978, the average true range is a measure of volatility. The moving average, on the other hand, is the average price for specific periods, with the exponential variation giving more weight to recent prices and less weight to less recent prices. A trader using trading charts in his or her trades receives significant additional information that helps him or her to make appropriate decisions in Day Trading.

Managing your account and the risks associated with Day Trading involves the responsible handling of the available equity in your brokerage account. You can perform account management through further investment in profitable stocks, ingenious trade maneuverability, or exiting from trade deals that stagnate. On the other hand, your risk management strategies involve responding appropriately to alleviate prospective losses in an uncertain future and limiting the degree of your exposure to financial risks.

Technical analysis is the study of the price changes and trends of a stock or security. The study involves traders inspecting a stock's trading history through technical indicators and charts in order to determine the future direction of the stock price.

Statistical trends, such as price movement and volume identified from the past, determine future trading opportunities. Technical analysts, therefore, focus on price fluctuations, trading signals, and analytical charting tools to examine the strength or weakness of a specific security.

Day Trading, like any other form of investment, is subject to influence from human emotion and psychological impact. Whenever money or capital is in play, people tend to take matters rather personally because of the inevitable consequence of the hope that comes along with the promise of significant returns.

After reading this book, your next step should be to practice what you have learned by signing up and becoming a Day trader. When you apply these tips, you will become an expert day trader much faster.

Finally, if you found this book useful in any way, a review on is always appreciated!

Forex Trading for Beginners

Simple Strategies to Make Money with Forex Trading: The Best Guide with Basics, Secrets Tactics, and Psychology to Big Profit and Income from the Financial Market

Table of Contents

Introduction

Congratulations on purchasing *Forex Trading for Beginners* and thank you for doing so. The following chapters will discuss the important steps and information a beginner should take and heed to if he or she wants to succeed in Forex Trading.

The first chapter is an introduction to Forex Trading, and it goes into the definition of Forex, and lists down the principles of forex trading. Furthermore, the chapter goes into detail to explain the different types of forex traders, the advantages an individual would enjoy by becoming a forex trader, and reasons an individual should choose forex trading over other forms of trading.

The second chapter dives into the basics of forex trading, and it begins with the definition of important terminologies and trades. The chapter provides an in-depth explanation of forex markets, currency pair basics, and concludes with quote currency. The third chapter is a guide for beginners on the things they need to do to become forex traders. The chapter begins with an explanation of the role of a foreign exchange broker, the importance of a considerable account balance, and the various tools and platforms a forex trader should make use of.

The fourth chapter is an in-depth study of Forex Trading technical analysis and fundamental analysis, and in addition to the value, they offer a forex trader. The fifth chapter is about the mindset a forex trader needs to develop, since such an individual must develop a form of discipline and way of thinking that the direction of the markets will not influence easily. The chapter discusses the attitude approach and the personality types traders have.

The sixth chapter is a study of the different strategies forex traders can implement in their business to become successful. The chapter begins with an explanation of the most popular and effective strategies traders use and then concludes with the most appropriate strategies for beginners.

The seventh chapter is about the various Forex Trading signals, and it begins with an explanation of the signals. The chapter continues to explain the most popular signals traders use out there and how they work, both the manual and automated forex trading signals. The chapter concludes with a guide to choosing the best signals and evaluating the free forex signals option.

The eighth chapter is a valuable resource on the tips an individual would need to follow to start winning in Forex Trading. The chapter explains the different tips and best kept secrets, and it concludes with the strategies a trader can implement to manage risks. The ninth chapter is about cryptocurrencies and the value they can have on a forex trader's business strategies.

The tenth chapter offers three forex trading examples that a beginner would look at to have even more insights into this business. The eleventh chapter is an explanation into the mistakes Forex Traders make, and the preventive measures, as well as solutions a new trader should look into to have better chances of success.

The final chapter is about making money as a forex trader. The chapter explains how forex signals, forex robots, and social trading can help a beginner to make the most out of every trade.

There are plenty of books on this subject on the market, thanks again for choosing this one! Every effort was made to ensure it is full of as much useful information as possible, please enjoy!

Chapter 1: An Introduction to Forex Trading

If you have been to a foreign country, you know that you cannot buy your favorite food and drinks in the country you are visiting with your home country's currency. To avoid such a predicament, individuals have the option to convert their money into the currency of the country they are visiting at the airport.

In addition, you may have received some payment for services in a foreign currency, and you needed to exchange the money into your country's currency for you to use it. Regardless of the situations you had interacting with foreign currency. It is likely highly you have participated in forex in one way or another. A person can participate in Forex Trading whether he or she is traveling to a foreign country, or doing business in his or her country.

What Is Forex Trading

The word 'forex' is short for 'foreign exchange.' It involves the process of converting one currency into another currency for reasons including tourism, trading, and business.

Although a person can participate in foreign exchange by traveling to a different country and exchanging his or her currency for the foreign country's currency, the foreign exchange market is more significant than that. The foreign exchange market is a global forum for exchanging substantial national currencies against each other.

Due to the international spread of finance and trade, the forex markets experience high demands for foreign currencies, which makes the market the most significant money market in the world.

When multinational companies intend to buy goods from other countries, companies need to find the local currency first. That exchange will involve vast amounts of currency exchange. As a result, the local currency value will move up as the demand for that currency increases. With that exchanging going on around the world, the exchange rate always changes.

When global traders exchange currencies, currencies have a specific exchange rate, the price of currency changes according to the law of supply and demand; the higher the demand, the higher the supply and the higher the exchange rate.

The foreign trading market has no centralized marketplace for foreign exchange. Foreign exchange bureaus operate electronically through computer networks between traders all over the world.

Therefore, foreign trading goes on for 24 hours a day, six days a week in leading financial centers of major capital cities around the world. Investment and commercial banks carry out most of the Forex Trading in the international marketplaces in place of clients and investors.

Principles of Forex Trading

1. Learn the Market's Trends

It is essential for one to be able to predict the changing nature of the foreign exchange market in order to be successful in Forex Trading.

Accordingly, a person should understand the general direction of the marketplace. Trends can be uptrend, downtrend, or sideways trend. Identifying a pattern can profit a person in that he or she will be able to trade with the trend.

Uptrends are trends that move upwards, indicating an appreciation in currency value. Downtrends move downwards as an indication of depreciation in currency value. Sideways trends show that the currencies are neither appreciating nor depreciating.

2. Stay Focused and Control Your Emotions

Forex Trading is a challenging marketplace that can cause a person to lose confidence and to give up in the toughest of times. That is understandable given that traders put in their hard-earned money.

As a result, when a person experiences loss, he or she can lose focus when negative emotions become overwhelming. Some of the negative emotions a person may experience include panic, frustration, depression, and desperation.

It is, therefore, essential for one to become aware of the negative emotions that result from Forex Trading so that he or she may minimize the emotional effects of loss and remain focused.

3. Learn Risk Mitigation Tactics

In order to achieve the profits that a person anticipates, the person needs to minimize the likelihood of financial loss.

Since the forex market keeps on changing, the risks, therefore, keep on changing. The most crucial risk management rule is that a person should not risk more than he or she can afford to lose. Traders who are willing to invest more than they make, become very susceptible to Forex Trading risks.

Consequently, a person can mitigate potential losses by placing stop-loss orders, exchanging more than one currency pair, using software programs for help, and limiting the use of financial leverage.

4. Establish Personal Forex Trading Limits

A person should know when to stop Forex Trading. One can stop Forex Trading when he or she has an unproductive trading plan, or when he or she is continually experiencing losses.

An ineffective Forex Trading plan may not bring trade to an end, but it will not function as well as a trader may expect. In that case, the trader can consider stopping the trade, constantly changing markets, and the decreasing volatility within a particular foreign trading tool may also cause a trader to take a break from Forex Trading.

In addition, when a person is not in a good physical or emotional state, he or she may want to think about taking a break to deal with personal issues.

5. Use Technology to Your Benefit

Being up-to-date with existing technological developments can be gratifying in Forex Trading.

Given that forex markets utilize the online forum, high-speed internet connections can increase Forex Trading performance significantly. In order to make the most of Forex Trading, a person must take it as a full-time occupation, and he or she must embrace new technologies. Similarly, receiving forex market current information with smartphones makes it possible for forex traders to track trades anywhere.

Forex Trading is an aggressive enterprise that needs a trader to have an equally competitive edge. Therefore, a forex trader needs to maximize his or her business's potential by taking full advantage of the available technology.

6. Make Use of a Forex Trading Plan

A Forex Trading plan comprises of rules and guidelines that stipulate a forex trader's entry, exit, and money management principles.

A trading plan provides the opportunity for a forex trader to try out a Forex Trading idea before the trader risks real money. In so doing, a trader can access historical information that helps to know whether a Forex Trading plan is feasible and what outcomes he or she can expect.

When a forex trader comes up with a Forex Trading plan that shows potentially favorable outcomes, he or she can use the trading plan in real Forex Trading situations. The idea is for the forex trader to adhere to the trading plan.

Buying or selling currencies outside of the Forex Trading plans, even if a trader makes a profit, is poor trading, which can end any expectation the plan may have had.

Different Types of Forex Traders

Because foreign markets become flooded with the constant demand for currency exchange, four types of currency traders facilitate the smooth operation of forex markets.

1. Scalpers

Forex scalpers are dealers who buy or sell currencies, hold on to the exchanged currencies, and then wait for them to have higher and favorable exchange rates before the dealers can change their new currencies back to their original versions.

The scalpers hold deals for seconds to minutes and open and close several positions within a single day. In other words, scalpers go in and out of positions several times each day.

Scalpers trade currencies based on real-time analysis. Scalpers aim to make a profit by selling or buying currencies and holding on to them for a short time before buying or selling the currencies back to the forex market for small gains.

Therefore, that means that scalpers should love sitting in front of their laptops or computers for the entire forex session without taking their eyes off the screen.

Scalping is widespread moments after essential data releases and interest rate announcements. That is because high-impact reports generate significant price moves within a short period.

However, while profits can accrue rapidly with profitable trades, huge losses can also accumulate if the scalper is using a faulty system or if the trader does not understand what he or she is doing.

2. Day Traders

Forex day traders control trading positions during each trading day. Day traders close the trading positions at the end of the trading day and ensure that there are no positions that remain open during the night.

Forex day traders use currency day trading systems that regulate whether to buy or sell a currency pair in the foreign exchange market. A currency pair is the quotation of two different currencies where the trader quotes the value of one currency in comparison to the other.

Day traders target day currencies that are very liquid to leverage their capital as soon as investment prices change in favorable directions. The traders pick a price position at the start of the day, act on their assessments, and finish the trading day with either a profit or a loss.

Forex day traders avoid holding positions overnight because that may result in stock price gaps, a consequence, which can be very costly.

3. Swing Traders

Swing traders take hold of a position over a few days to several weeks. They hold places for more than one trading session, although not longer than several weeks or a couple of months.

Swing traders aim to capture huge potential price moves. Some swing traders may look for volatile stocks with constant movements, whereas others prefer stock prices that are more predictable.

Swing traders have exposure to overnight and weekend risks, where prices could rift and open the following forex session with markedly different rates. However, swing traders can generate profit by using established risk or reward strategies that will help them to determine where they will enter assets, where they will place stop-loss orders, and to know where they can make profits. Stop-loss orders help to limit the loss when stock prices fall.

Swing traders come up with plans and strategies that will give them an advantage over may trades. The traders do that by looking for trade arrangements that facilitate predictable price movements in the price of the asset. However, no trade arrangement works every time.

4. Position Traders

Position traders hold on to investment positions for long periods, anticipating the investments to appreciate. The periods can extend from weeks to months. In that regard, position traders are less concerned with short-term changes in price movements.

Position traders follow trends, believing that once a pattern starts, it is likely to continue. As such, position traders incline toward obtaining the bulk of a trend's move, which would generate profit in their investment capital.

Position traders use both fundamental and technical analysis to help in making trading decisions. They also depend on macroeconomic influences, old trends, and overall market movements to get to their anticipated end.

For a trader to have success in position trading, the trader has to know the entry or exit points and have a strategy to mitigate risk mainly by placing stop-loss orders.

Advantage of Forex Trading

1. Easy to Modify

Forex Trading markets put no restrictions on how much money a forex trader can use. Forex traders can trade a variety of goods and services.

In addition, the forex market does not have many rules and regulations for the forex trader to follow. The regulations that exist guide forex traders on when to enter and when to exit a trade.

2. Individual Control

Nobody controls the foreign market. Therefore, a forex trader has complete autonomy concerning making a trade. The forex market regulates itself and levels the playing field.

There are no intermediaries involved – a forex trader trades directly in the open forex market, and a retail forex broker eases that process.

3. Lucidity of Information

The Forex Trading market gives information straightforwardly to the public about the rates and price movement forecasts. The forex market traders have free and equal access to the market's information, and that makes it easy for the traders to make calculated and risk-free trading decisions.

Forex traders also have access to past information that helps in analyzing the market tendencies and forecasting the direction, which the market will take.

4. Widespread Options

The forex market provides a variety of options to forex investors. As a result, forex investors can take advantage of the available options to trade in different currencies in pairs.

An investor has the option of getting into foreign exchange spot trade or trading in currency futures to make the most of his or her investment.

5. High Liquidity and Volume

The forex market trades in large amounts of currencies at any given time because of how active the foreign exchange is. Therefore, there are high chances for forex traders to trade currency pairs on demand.

Under normal market conditions, a forex trader can buy and sell quickly with the anticipation that there will be another forex trader on the other end who is willing to trade back.

6. Money-Making Gains

The forex market provides Forex Trading measures that guard against financial loss. To ensure that a forex trader maximizes of gaining profits, the forex market has provisions for minimizing loss through making stop-loss orders.

Stop-loss orders enable forex traders to determine the closing price of their trade and thereby avoiding unforeseen losses.

7. 24-Hour Market

Foreign exchange markets remain open for 24-hours a day and 6 days a week. That means that the market stays open most of the time, and it is not subject to external factors that may affect it.

Consequently, forex traders are flexible to work during the hours that suit them best.

8. Low Operation Costs

Operation costs in the forex currency markets are competent in trading in the forex market. The cost of operation in the currency market is in the form of spreads measured in pips. A pip is the fourth place after the decimal point of a percent.

For example, is the selling price was 2.5887, and the buying price was 2.5889, then the transaction cost is 2pips. Brokers may charge commissions on a fraction of the amount of the trade.

9. Chief Financial Market

The forex market is the biggest financial market in the world. That is because global corporations and big financial institutions participate dynamically in the foreign exchange market.

The foreign exchange market empowers major financial institutions to retail stockholders to seek out profits from currency variations connected to the global economy.

10. One Can Use the Leverage

The forex markets allow forex traders to capitalize on the advantage. Leveraging enables forex traders to be able to open positions for thousands of dollars while investing small amounts of money.

For example, when a forex trader trades at 40:1 leverage, he or she can trade $40 for every $1 that was in his or her account. That means that the forex trader can manage a trade of $40,000 for every $1,000 of investment.

Why Forex

The foreign exchange market is open to all types of traders, and it is more accessible than any other online trading platform in the world. Similarly, one can start trading with as little as $100. Therefore, foreign exchange markets have lower exchange capital prerequisites compared to other financial markets. A person can quickly sign up to open their trading account online, where most forex retail brokers operate.

Forex Trading is easy to learn, although it may be challenging to master. However, once an investor understands how the forex market works, he or she will be open to a world of vast opportunities that include becoming a foreign exchange account manager. A foreign exchange account manager can accumulate profits from trading as well as earning commissions for managing the Forex Trading accounts.

Foreign exchange markets make provisions for forex brokers to develop considerable trading volumes because of the leverage that the forex markets offer. That explains why forex traded get rewards like deposit bonuses when creating a Forex Trading account. Likewise, forex brokers give several incentives and promotions to financial institutions that enter Forex Trading. As a result, the forex market becomes a stimulating marketplace for Forex Trading.

Forex traders form international social communities as more people sign up every day. The social networks help forex investors to encounter an entire community of foreign exchange traders, thus making the forex market an interactive market to trade. In addition, forex traders can find many international forex experts, contributors, critics, and educators, among other members, in every conceivable language.

Moreover, forex traders can buy and sell risk-free, using a demonstration trading account. The account prevents traders from putting their investment at risk, and the traders can, therefore, move to the live forex markets whenever they please. The trading accounts enable forex traders to have access to real-time market information and the latest trading wisdom from foreign experts.

The forex market infrastructure is sophisticated, causing the performance of traders to be even more level. The forex market also has low spreads and commissions, thus making the transaction costs relatively small as a result. Besides, the foreign exchange market educates forex traders on global events, as the traders continue to trade online. Favorable trading conditions are crucial for foreign exchange traders.

Heavy security measures guard the foreign exchange markets, and several authorities control every forex broker. The bodies exist to make sure that forex traders have a safe space to carry out

Forex Trading activities. However, forex traders are only with regulated brokers. Therefore, one must conduct a background check on available brokers in order to ensure that he or she works with the regulated brokers.

Online Forex Trading makes use of advanced trading software that generates regular updates that help forex investors to make real-time Forex Trading decisions. Consequently, Forex Trading becomes a rewarding way to buy and sell online, also due to third-party software developers who provide add-ons and plugins for popular trading platforms.

Finally, the forex markets allow traders to buy low and sell high. What's more, forex traders can trade assets without owning them, a practice that is called short selling. Furthermore, the use of leverage enables Forex traders to buy or sell more substantial amounts than what they have in their deposits.

Chapter 2: Basics of Forex Trading

The term Forex Trading stands for foreign exchange trading, which is the purchasing or selling of one type of currency in exchange for another one. Also known as FX, it is a global over-the-counter market where investors, traders, banks, and institutions speculate on, purchase, and sell world currencies.

Forex Trading happens over the interbank market, which is a channel through which currency trading happens 5 days a week, 24 hours a day. It is one of the biggest trading markets in the world, with a worldwide daily turnover estimated to be more than $5 trillion. This is because countries, businesses, and individuals all participate in Forex Trading.

Actually, when people visit another country and convert their currency to the local currency, they are participating in the FX market. The demand for a particular currency at any given time will either push its value up or down in relation to other currencies. Therefore, people who want to venture into Forex

Trading should understand a few important things before making their first trade, including:

1. Learning about currency pairs and what they mean
2. Market pricing

Forex transactions involve the simultaneous buying and selling of two different currencies known as currency pairs, which include a quote currency and a base currency. One of the most popular currency pairs on the forex market is the Euro/US Dollar. Also called the counter currency, the quote currency is the second currency in a forex pair.

Forex prices often have four decimal places due to their very small spread differences. However, they can also have any number of decimal places. Trades on the forex market are often worth millions of dollars; therefore, even tiny price differences can add up to a significant profit.

However, such massive trading volumes mean that a small spread can also lead to significant losses. Therefore, forex traders should consider the risks involved and trade carefully.

Important Terminology and Trades

A position, in terms of Forex Trading, describes a trade in progress. A long position, for instance, means that a forex trader purchased currency expecting its value to go up. Once he/she sells it back to the market at a higher price, the trade is complete, and his/her long position closes.

A short position, on the other hand, refers to a situation where a trader sells a certain currency with the expectation that its value will decrease, with the aim of buying it back at a lower price. The short position will close once the trader buys back the currency, ideally at a lower price.

If the currency pair of EUR/USD, which refers to Euro/US Dollar, was trading at 1.0914/1.0916, for example, investors planning to open a long position on the Euro would purchase one Euro for 1.0916 US dollars. They will then hold on to the currency and hope that its value will increase, and then sell it back to the market once it appreciates.

On the other hand, investors looking to open a short position on the Euro will sell one Euro for 1.0914 US dollars, with the expectation that its value will depreciate. If their expectations come true, they will buy it back at the lower rate and make a profit.

Forex Markets

With central banks, retail forex brokers, commercial corporations, commercial banks, hedge funds, individual investors, and investment management firms participating in the forex market, it is easy to see why this market is larger than equity and futures markets combined.

Placing a trade in the forex market is quite simple. The basics of Forex Trading are very similar to the mechanics of other financial markets, such as the stock market. Therefore, traders with prior experience in any type of financial market should be able to understand Forex Trading quite quickly.

1. Basics of the Forex Market

The FX market is a global network of brokers and computers from around the world; therefore, no single market exchange dominates this market. These brokers are also market makers and often post bid and ask prices for currency pairs, which are often different from the most competitive bid in the FX market.

On a more basic level, the foreign exchange market consists of two levels, i.e., the over-the-counter market and the interbank market. The OTC market is where individual traders execute trades through brokers and online platforms. The interbank market, on the other hand, is where large banking institutions trade currencies on behalf of clients or for purposes of balance sheet adjustments and hedging.

2. Hours of Operation

The FX market is a 24-hour market, from Monday morning to Friday afternoon in Asia and New York, respectively. Essentially, unlike markets such as commodities, bonds, and equities that close for a while, the forex market does not close even at night. However, there are exceptions. Some currencies for emerging markets, for example, close for a short while during the trading day.

3. The Currency Giants

By far, the US dollar is the biggest player in Forex Trading, making up approximately 85% of all forex trades. The second most traded currency is the euro, which makes up close to 39% of all currency trades, while the Japanese yen comes in at third place with 19% of all currency trades.

The reason that these figures do not total 100% is that every forex transaction involves two currencies. Citigroup and JPMorgan Chase and Co. were the biggest participants in the FX market in 2018, according to a study conducted by Greenwich Associates. Actually, these two banks commanded more than 30% of the global forex market share.

Goldman Sachs, Deutsche Bank, and UBS made up the remaining top five places. According to a settlement and processing group known as CLS, the daily trading volume in January last year was more than $1.8 trillion. This is a testament to just how popular, and massive Forex Trading is around the world.

4. Origins of the Forex Market

Up until the First World War, countries based their currencies on precious metals like silver and gold. This system, however, collapsed, and the Bretton Woods agreement became the basis of currencies after the Second World War. This agreement led to the creation of three international organizations to oversee economic activities across the world.

These organizations were the General Agreement on Tariffs and Trade, the International Monetary Fund, and the International Bank for Reconstruction and Development. In addition to creating these international organizations, the agreement adopted the US dollar as the peg for international currencies, instead of gold.

In return, the US government had to back up dollar supplies with an equivalent amount or value of gold reserves. This system, however, ended in 1971 when Richard Nixon, the US president at the time, suspended the US dollar's convertibility into gold.

Nowadays, currencies can pick their own peg, and the forces of demand and supply determine their value.

Currency Pairs and Their Prices

These are quotations of two different currencies, such as EUR/USD. They quote the value of the first currency, which is the base currency, against the second one, which is the quote currency. Essentially, a currency pair compares the value of the first currency against the second one, showing how much of the first/quote currency can but one unit of the second/base currency.

An ISO currency code identifies currencies. This is the 3-letter alphabetic code, such as EUR for the euro, associated with a particular currency on the international market. When traders place an order for a currency pair, it means that they are purchasing the base currency and selling the quote currency. According to FX trading statistics, the most liquid currency pair in the world is the EUR/USD, followed by the USD/JPY.

1. Currency Pair Basics

Forex Trading happens in the foreign exchange market, which is the most liquid and largest market in the financial arena. Although it involves the simultaneous sale of one currency and purchase of another, forex traders should think of a currency pair as a single unit to purchase or sell.

Essentially, when a forex trader purchases a currency pair, he/she buys the base currency and, in effect, sells the second/quoted currency. The buy/bid price represents how much of the quote currency he/she will need to purchase one unit of the base currency.

On the other hand, when the trader sells a currency pair, he/she is selling the base currency and implicitly getting the quote currency. In this case, the sell/ask price for the currency pair will represent how much he/she will receive in terms of the quote currency for selling a single unit of the base currency.

2. Major Currency Pairs

There are numerous currencies in the world, which means that there are just as many currency pairs. Currencies come and go; therefore, the total number of currency pairs tends to change. However, investors categorize currency pairs based on their daily trading volume. Those that trade the most against the USD are the major currencies, and these include:

1. EUR/USD
2. USD/CHF
3. USD/JPY
4. USD/CAD
5. GBP/USD
6. AUD/USD

These major currency pairs account for almost 80% of the global Forex trading volume. They usually have high liquidity and low volatility and are indicative of well-managed and stable economies. In addition, they have narrower spreads than other currency pairs and are less susceptible to currency manipulation strategies.

3. Cross Currency Pairs

Also called crosses, these currency pairs do not include the US dollar. A few years ago, investors looking to trade crosses first had to convert them into the US dollar and then into the currency they desired. However, nowadays, investors can make direct cross currency pairs exchanges.

The most popular crosses feature minor currency pairs, such as GBP/JPY, EUR/JPY, and EUR/GBP. Cross-currency pairs are usually more volatile and less liquid than major currency pairs.

4. Exotic Pairs

These consist of currencies from smaller or emerging economies, paired with a major currency. Compared to two types of currency pairs discussed above, trading in exotics involves higher risk because they are significantly volatile and less liquid, which means they are more susceptible to currency manipulation.

Exotics also have wider spreads and are extremely sensitive to certain financial developments and unexpected changes in the political climate.

Quote Currency

Commonly referred to as the counter currency, the quote currency is the second one in both an indirect and direct currency pair. The quote currency determines the value of the base currency. In an indirect quote, the domestic currency is the quote currency, while the foreign currency is the quote currency in a direct quote.

The value of the quote currency falls as the rate in the currency pair goes up. This is the case irrespective of whether the pair is indirect or direct. It is important for forex traders to understand the pricing structure and quotation of currencies in the FX market. Forex brokers tend to trade certain currency pairs in specific ways.

Therefore, understanding the fundamentals of the quote currency is an important step towards finding success in Forex Trading. The exchange rate of a currency pair shows how much of the quote currency traders need to buy or sell to sell or buy one unit of the base currency. The value of the quote currency will be decreasing as the currency pair's rate increases, whether it is indirect or direct.

USD/CAD, for example, is a direct quote that denotes the cross-rate between the US dollar and the Canadian dollar, which is the quote currency in this case, while the US dollar is the base currency. Therefore, investors will use the Canadian dollar as a reference to determine the US dollar's value. From a US perspective, the Canadian dollar is a foreign currency.

The EUR/USD currency pair, on the other hand, describes the cross-rate between the euro and the US dollar; however, it is an indirect quote. In other words, the US dollar is the quote currency, and the euro is the base currency. In this case, the US dollar is the domestic currency that determines the value of a single unit of the euro.

The investment market can easily relieve investors of their money if they fail to prepare themselves well or adhere to the fundamental principles of trading. In any investment market, trading can be exceedingly tricky and difficult. However, success comes with adequate practice and education, and anyone with the right mindset can succeed at Forex Trading.

Learning about foreign exchange trading is the first thing that prospective forex traders should focus on. There are tons of learning materials and tools available to both experienced and new forex traders. It is also important to work with a regulated broker with several years of experience.

Chapter 3: How to Get Started in Forex Trading

Who Is A Foreign Exchange Broker?

Brokers are the intermediaries who link investors with their capital. Some traders may choose to invest in the forex trade, and therefore they will invariably become in need of a foreign exchange broker. Forex is a shortened version of the term Foreign Exchange. This phrase represents the financial market site within which various trading processes, deals, and transactions in foreign currency take place. Based on this description, a foreign exchange broker is, therefore, a registered and more qualified expert in currency trading.

Such forex brokers offer their services to prospective investors in foreign exchange and other currency traders who may require specific complex services. They identify opportunities, execute complicated trading strategies, and manage financial risk exposure on your behalf. Hence, a foreign exchange broker will assist you in achieving your aims of making a significant profit and mitigate potential losses. He or she is responsible for guiding you on how to manage your investment capital in the currency market.

Those brokers who deal in foreign exchange services typically know when and how to react or respond to volatility within the financial market. They provide the support mechanism that enables you to navigate through the uncertainty associated with currency trading successfully. In addition, such forex brokers often have extensive experience as previous traders in the forex markets. Therefore, you should always heed their advice and pay attention to their guidance or occasional recommendations.

Most forex brokers, upon hiring, will come with various trading platforms and accompanying tools to assist you in proper forex investment. Management of your available capital and exposure to risk may be your responsibility, but the advice of a forex broker is equally essential. The currency trading tools and relevant software platforms vary in their specific applications and features. Forex brokers will also make sure to teach you about the extensive range of traders and expertise required to master each of the separate platforms.

For you to understand the data and information contained in Forex Trading tools, you need to learn particular skills in technical analysis. This analytical expertise is transferable from the forex brokers to prospective traders and new investors through learning. You can grasp some knowledge of how to perform and correctly interpret the various forms of foreign exchange technical analyses. The associated foreign exchange terminology is relevant to know, as well. The foreign exchange broker can bring your attention to any other currency investment opportunities that may be available in the financial market.

Besides, the forex broker can distinguish the productive and probably profitable currency deals from the doomed ones. Due to the lax regulations in the currency market, you should beware of fraudulent brokers. You need to be highly suspicious of those brokers who claim to specialize in foreign exchange per se. whenever you encounter such seemingly dedicated brokers, you should sever ties with them instantly. You should engage a general stockbroker who has an additional registration in Forex Trading. Besides, it is rare to find phony stockbrokers due to the stringent regulation of the stock markets and stock exchanges. Select a well-known brokerage firm to have a chance of success in trading currencies.

The foreign exchange is the largest financial market in the world currently, and it is the most liquid kind of all the available markets too. Daily, it can experience currency exchanges to the tune of trillions. You will need the guidance of a foreign exchange broker to participate in this market, especially if you are new to the concept of currency trading. With the advent of the World

Wide Web, this market has had an exclusive electronic presence online.

The internet connects the various stakeholders involved in Forex Trading, such as financial institutions, private investors, retail traders, and foreign exchange brokers. Since it is an online entity, the forex market is always active throughout the day. Whenever you want to participate in the currency trade, you need to interact with the other currency queries in the market. This interaction is possible by posting relevant orders online for you to engage in either buying or selling currencies or even conduct both.

When you are new to foreign exchange, you can begin investing in retail trading. Here, profits and losses are simply the difference between your buying and selling prices of the relevant currencies. When buying currency, you will hope for a rise in its value over the allocated trading time frame. The opposite is exact of a situation involving selling money, and therefore, these two scenarios are the distinct routes to making a profit in cases of simple retail trading. You may experience motivation for a change in the currency price. Hence, you are more likely to roll over your positions on most days. Rollover positions attract a commission or fees depending on the kind of forex broker that you use. However, this charge and other brokerage costs get an automatic credit or debit to your forex account.

Spot transactions describe the types of trade deals that ensure immediate resolution without the need for a rollover. Such trades are especially useful for people who are sensitive to nagging costs, charges, and fees. Only the presence of holidays can render spot trade deals impossible and hence the need for its postponement. Another way to interact in foreign exchange involves speculating on the future value of a particular currency relative to a different one.

This activity needs your correct predictive skills in the future exchange rate between a pair of specific currencies. Speculation is a tactic that is relevant to futures and forwards in the forex market. These two types of Forex Trading differ in their customizability after the expiry of a specified trading period. It is possible to customize the forwards with the currency under trade. The possibility maintains even after the lapse of the trading time interval. The futures, however, are not as customizable as forwards, and in fact, they do not permit it. Therefore, a foreign exchange broker would advise you on how to proceed with these situations.

As earlier mentioned, spot transactions are usual in retail trading, while currency forwards and futures involve trading with some degree of speculation. You will need to deal in futures contracts when making predictions in the currency market. Its principle is similar to options trading whereby you begin by purchasing a currency futures contract.

Next, you should take a particular position on the future behavior of a specific currency relative to another different type of currency. Your contract becomes due for settlement upon the expiry of your allocated trading period. However, currency futures do not allow for any further negotiations past the expiry period. This strictness is unlike the situation with bespoke forward contracts that would enable settlement at any time. Besides, you should close your futures contract trading position before the expiration date to avoid additional settlement costs. Just like options trading, taking multiple trading positions on the future values of various currencies is possible, as well.

What Is the Account Balance, and Why Does a Broker Need It?

The account balance is the amount of equity or capital available in your brokerage account due to investment in the currency market. It is essential to have such an account to enable the foreign exchange broker to carry out the buying and selling executions on your behalf. Since your investment is in the currency market, this brokerage account is your forex account, as well. Opening a forex account for a new investor is a simple exercise that is akin to opening a personal bank account. After setting up a forex account, you should seek the services of an accomplished and registered forex broker. All foreign exchange trade deals and transactions should go through your forex broker. Therefore, he or she needs to gain access to this forex account and have permission to transact in the currency market on your behalf.

An investor's limited involvement in the daily running of the account necessitates that the forex broker takes over these duties. In addition, other financial liabilities charged to this account include the commissions and brokerage fees. You should check on the forex account regularly to keep track of the progress of your investments.

It also allows you to carry out responsible financial management based on the difference between your finances and risk liabilities. Productive risk management strategies become possible based on the available capital balance in the account at a particular moment. Since the currency market tends to turn volatile without warning, your forex account must maintain its liquidity status. The available balance provides your forex broker with the necessary leeway to take immediate corrective measures when a specific currency trade deal begins to go wrong. The best way to ensure that the brokerage account retains activity is to make regular deposits into it.

A standing order is a useful way of guaranteeing the liquidity status of the forex account. Your order will execute the transfer of a certain sum of money from your private account at regular intervals of your choosing. This automatic process eliminates the downsides associated with forgetfulness on your part. In the case of currency trading that involves derivatives, the forex broker can easily buy and sell futures contracts based on their speculation at a particular time.

Currency fluctuations require your forex broker to take a specific position promptly to take advantage of the time factor in currency trading. Financial delays from an inactive or overdrawn brokerage account are often responsible for some of your indirect losses. As a result, your forex broker will miss out on potentially profitable opportunities in the currency market.

Another importance attributed to the forex account is the possibility of a quick integration with the trading platform and technical analysis tools. Your forex broker will have access to both the forex account and the trading platform in a single place. Hence, making informed decisions becomes an instantaneous activity. The forex broker reacts to data and information from technical analyses with the appropriate monetary input.

This activity may involve either more investment in a promising opportunity or a straightforward exit from a non-productive trade deal. You can easily relate the comparison between any technical analyses performed and the balance available in your forex account. Your forex broker has the freedom to make long-term decisions and speculation only if he or she is sure of the availability of capital. Because of taking such high risks, your forex broker is more likely to make higher profits for you.

In the case of taking long positions on forwards and futures contracts, the forex broker should feel confident in his or her level of liquidity. Confidence breeds more self-belief, and eventually, the forex broker ends up conducting sensible transactions. Emotional reactions to trading positions are typical of forex brokers who are always wary of taking risks due to the fear of losing the scanty balance available. Insufficient capital and account mismanagement typically result in forex brokers who continuously engage in illogical trade deals to cover recent losses. You will find such forex brokers participating in the short-term local currency trading more frequently with your capital.

Further investigation of your forex broker may reveal the underlying cause as the fear of losing your money and, in turn, his or her commission. Always make sure that you are abreast of the condition of your forex account. You can offer appropriate instructions and proper orders on the level of risks that you may tolerate. Such instructions are only possible if you keep track of the activities in the account. In addition, you and your forex broker can plan risk management strategies together to limit your exposure to unnecessary financial risks. The forex broker will grow accustomed to your mannerisms gradually, and soon he or she will understand your objectives. At this point, the forex broker becomes comfortable enough to exert the full range of his or her trading expertise towards the attainment of your financial goals.

What Are Platforms and Tools?

A trading platform is the graphical user interface provided by computer application software, and it enables the trader or investor to interact with the aspects of his or her trading transactions. A Forex Trading platform is a standard provision from most forex brokers to their clients, investors, or other retail traders. It also acts as a source of commission for the forex brokers by charging an access fee to use it. After seeking a foreign exchange broker, most traders will get a couple of trading platform recommendations from these same brokers.

Forex brokers are often adept at their jobs, and hence these recommendations are typically advisable. When you decide to participate in foreign currency trading, you will need to familiarize yourself with the skills of taking profitable market positions. Therefore, you will have to purchase, download, and install the software on your computer and learn to navigate around the online platform.

In case you are new to online Forex Trading, it may become somewhat challenging to make your way around the platform. For you to understand and succeed in this particular endeavor, you will need the assistance of an online foreign exchange broker.

Due to the competition among different foreign exchange brokers, some of the online trading platforms may be available at a discount or even free of charge. It is essential that you know which one will work best for you based on their simplicity of use, precision, and online forex broker support. Most of your investment and capital management decisions depend on your understanding of the forex market. A robust and versatile platform should make it easier for you to come up with informed choices. In addition, an excellent online platform should have an online forex broker standing by for technical analysis and support.

Another aspect concerning Forex Trading platforms is the range of the available versions. They vary from the low end of the trading spectrum to the high end of trading end users. You can have the primary platforms consisting of rudimentary trading user interfaces for the beginners and new investors. Besides, there are sophisticated platforms that contain multiple analytical tools with enhanced graphics and live streaming capability for seasoned traders.

When choosing a relevant platform, you should keep in mind the amount of capital you intend to invest and the level of risk exposure that you can tolerate. The initial cost and the presence of subscription fees are other vital deliberations to make during the selection process as well. All the essential features needed for Forex Trading are common to most platforms; hence, the availability of multiple and excessive aspects is not such a significant consideration when buying one. You can narrow down your choice to the platforms that have the features that you will require only. As an investor, you should make decisions concerning the kind of platforms based on your forex broker's reputation.

Meta Trader is the most famous Forex Trading platform in the market currently. Its development resulted from the use of a versatile programming language that employs scripting as an execution method, i.e., the MQL program. Meta Trader can support multiple types of order executions, allows for simultaneous editing while trading, and can conduct hedging operations. In addition, the platform has an embedded email system, technical indicators, analytical, graphical objects, and the ability to chat online with fellow traders.

Currently, the Meta Trader platform is in its fifth version. Other platforms' primary purposes differ from foreign currency exchanges. However, they often have some level of forex capacity inbuilt within their structure. Examples of these different platforms include the IG group, CMC Markets, X-Trade Brokers, Pepper Stone, Forex.Com, Robin Hood, Trade Station, TDA merit trade, and Interactive Brokers.

On the other hand, foreign exchange trading tools are the indicators that show you how the market and your capital are performing. They are mainly the outcomes of technical analysis conducted on the various trading positions taken in your Forex Trading deals. The presentation of the results of such studies occurs via a graphical user interface that provides relatable information that is easily understandable. Most trading platforms have embedded tools within their structure to provide all the necessary data at one point. This platform flexibility eliminates the need to acquire separate stand-alone tools for each analytical process. The kinds of information derived from currency trading tools are in the form of graphical objects such as tables and charts for reports and analysis, respectively.

Line graphs are specifically standard in trend and pattern analysis. Monitoring currency fluctuations is better using such a graphical representation. Hence, most, if not all, trading tools are akin to the technical, analytical tools that are exclusive to foreign exchange trades. The only slight difference is that they are currently presentable online via computers as opposed to the previous use of paperwork.

The tools that are within the Meta Trader platform provide information on daily market analysis as well as Forex Trading signals on market trends and fluctuations. Consistent capital and risk management strategies are essential deliverables credited to the use of Forex Trading tools. You can adjust your trading position based on the data from these tools. The adjustments may involve reinforcing your stance on a forex position due to the use of a more valuable currency in a favorable market. In addition, you can consider exiting a trade deal altogether when the currency values become too volatile to sustain investor confidence.

Currency converters, economic calendars, financial news streams, and various types of calculators are additional tools available on most Forex Trading platforms. Computation of potential profits and losses within the Meta Trader platform is possible using tools such as profit, pip, margin, and invest-profit calculators. Your financial risk increases with the rise in the volatility of the currency market.

In such a situation, the margin calculator is also responsible for conducting your probable risk assessment. Forex Trading applications that are customizable to your smartphones are another form of tools available to you during trading. These so-called apps are beneficial in that they are portable and enable you to keep track of your financial progress at any time, as well as in real-time. Examples of such mobile forex tools include Coin Trader, FX Trader, Trade Interceptor, Forex Hours, and XE Currency.

Chapter 4: Technical and Fundamental Analysis in Forex Trading

Forex Trading involves a market of an electronic network of brokers, individual traders, institutions, and banks, which trade a variety of national currencies. Excluding a holiday, a forex market opens throughout for five days a week, and it is the liquid and most prominent financial market worldwide. Forex Trading is essential to traders and financial institutions as it offers them profits from the movements of the currency. Technical and fundamental analyses are the two primary methods that a trader can use to study and assess the forex market.

A trader needs to learn and understand how the two forms of analysis work. He or she also should be able to tell the difference that takes place in the application of each analysis type. This knowledge will help him or her to read the market better and even make fitting speculations regarding the direction of specific currency movements. As a result, the trader can take up appropriate positions in the market that will enable him or her to receive gains from the trades.

Below is information that provides a breakdown of how technical and fundamental analysis functions in Forex Trading.

Technical Analysis

Technical analysis is a methodology that a trader uses to study and make predictions concerning currency or price movements in the forex market. He or she observes the patterns of the price like flags, double bottoms, and triangles on a chart and interprets the actions of the cost to find out the market conditions. As a result, he or she should have excellent analytical skills to evaluate the technical charts correctly. A trader that utilizes technical analysis has a short, medium, or long-term view of the trade he or she undertakes.

Technical analysis bases its operation on historical information about price movements since traders believe that history will repeat itself. They think that the price on the market will move in the same way as in the past if they find any similar historical patterns. A trader would be keen on a particular price level and build his or her trades on it if it provided a necessary price action in the past. Thus, he or she studies past movements of price and use that information to find out the current market conditions and possible price movements.

Technical analysis provides the visual representation of past movements of the price that inform a trader of the situation in the market. The price patterns and statistical trends in the analysis assist him or her to know the best time to enter or exit the market. Additionally, the technical signals also show him or her significant trading opportunities. Hence, technical analysis understanding can help a trader to make decisions that bring him or her gains. Simultaneously, it will also assist him or her to avoid trades or making unnecessary moves in the market that may result in considerable losses.

A trader uses various technical indicators to analyze the Forex Trading market, technically. Understanding how the indicators function can help him or her to comprehend the market conditions. Subsequently, he or she can then choose and apply the most appropriate trading strategy that will place him or her in the most profitable position in the market. The essential indicators that technical analysts employ in the forex market include:

1. Relative Strength Index Indicator (RSI)

The Relative Strength Index is an oscillator that provides a trader with signals to help him, or her sell high and buy low. It indicates to a trader the status of a currency, whereby it shows the overbought or oversold levels. The readings of an RSI indicator range from zero to 100, and they signal the speed and shift in price movements. The currency has overbought status when the value is above 70. Similarly, when the number on the oscillator is below 30, it indicates the oversold levels of that the currency.

Moreover, the RSI places the bullish and bearish price momentums against the price's graph and compares them. Bullish dynamics of the cost can cause overbought levels, while the bearish ones can produce oversold levels. As the forex market trends, a trader enters the trade in the trend's direction as the indicator recovers from the extremes. He or she finds the RSI going through a reversal from oversold levels or readings below 30 if there is an uptrend in the market. He or she then enters in the direction of that trend.

2. Slow Stochastic Indicator

The slow stochastic is an oscillator that helps a trader to identify profitable trade points in the forex market. It also assists him or her in determining the oversold and overbought levels in the trade. Its readings interpret the same as those of the RSI. It also uses the percentageK and the percentageD lines to indicate to the trader an entry point of a deal. The movements of these two lines on the oscillator will signal to the trader about a strong buying position that is in the direction of the price trend. A trader can take up such a place if the percentageK line crosses over the percentageD line through reading at the 20-level.

3. Moving Average Indicator

The moving average indicator helps a trader to determine trends, identify trade areas, and evaluate the forex markets. It assists him or her to establish the resistance and support levels as well as the patterns that indicate great buying or selling positions in the trade. A moving average indicator is also a lagging one because it also determines the current price direction, albeit with a lag. This delay stems from the signal utilizing historical data to establish the moving averages.

A trader can use the simple moving average (SMA) or the exponential moving average (EMA) to carry out the analysis. The SMA gives the simple mean of an asset in a given amount of time by adding all the closing prices and dividing the sum by the given number of days. If a trader uses a 20-day SMA, then he or she finds the total amount of the closing prices of the last 20 days and divides the total by 20.

An EMA provides the averages of the latest prices, unlike the SMA, which focuses on a long sequence of data points. A trader uses a particular formula to calculate the EMA, that is, Current EMA = [(Current closing price - (previous day EMA) × multiplier) + previous day EMA]. The formula for the multiplier or smoothing constant in the above equation is 2/ (1+N), where N= the number of days.

A forex trader uses the momentum to determine the entry and exit points in the market. He or she enters the trade when the currency pair moves in the moving average's direction and exits when it runs in the opposite direction.

4. Moving Average Convergence Divergence Indicator (MACD)

This MACD indicator uses crossovers, divergences, and rapid rise and falls to show the link between moving averages of prices. In turn, it indicates the variations in momentum through a visual display, which helps a trader in recognizing a ranging or trending forex market. The calculation of the MACD involves the trader subtracting the 26-EMA period from the 12-EMA period, which provides him or her with the MACD line. A 9-day EMA of the MACD gives a trader the signal line in this indicator.

The trader can trade according to the movements of the MACD line concerning the signal line. He or she can buy when this line crosses beyond the signal line or sell when this line crosses beneath the signal line in the forex market. Moreover, the trader can determine a downward or upward bias of the currency pair by identifying the lines with regard to the zero lines.

He or she also can combine the MACD with a ranging or trending market to increase efficiency and minimize loss. The trader can place stops below the latest price extreme that is before the crossover. In doing so, he or she establishes a limit on the trade at the double the amount of his or her investment. The MACD provides the trader with suitable conditions when he or she uses crossovers of the MACD line in the trend's direction.

Fundamental Analysis

This methodology is the second type of analysis that a trader can use in the forex market. Unlike the technical analysis, this type concerns itself with the intrinsic value of an asset or currency. It evaluates the political, social, and economic factors that create a target price or establish value in the market. It uses information from features like interest rates, Gross Domestic Product (GDP), inflation, and others to analyze the trading conditions. A trader using fundamental analysis needs to have excellent analytical skills regarding statistical and economic data.

A fundamental trader in the forex market will assess a country's economic health by evaluating the trends of various data points and generally determine the strength and movements of the currency. He or she looks at various economic indicators and interprets them to find out the value of money. The essential economic signals that a trader can analyze the situation of the economy include:

1. Inflation
Inflation is the increase in the quantity of money in circulation due to the growth of a country's economy. The more the money

there is available, the more expensive the goods and services are in a country. When the economy of a state experiences too much inflation for an extended period, the associated currency becomes less valuable. The deprecation comes about because of there being too much supply of the money.

Conversely, the currency increases in value if an economy goes through deflation. Deflation takes place when there is little money in circulation. It leads to the country providing services and goods at lower prices. However, the value of the currency also drops when deflation carries on for a long time because there will be little money to support the economy. A country should balance the supply and demand aspects of its economy to ensure neither extreme devalues its currency.

2. Interest Rates

Interest rates are important indicators for fundamental analysis as they level the economy and can help a trader to discover trading opportunities. A common type of interest rate traders analyze is the nominal kind. The central banks create this nominal interest rate by referring to the principle that private banks pay to borrow currencies from them.

The central banks stimulate the individuals and private banks to borrow currency by lowering the interest rate as needed by the economy. It results in more valuable currency and improved performances in productivity, economics, and consumption.

However, low-interest rates for extended periods can lead to there being too much money and form economic bubbles. Thus, the central bank balances the scale by cutting the prices of borrowing and providing less money for use by businesses, individuals, and banks.

3. Gross Domestic Product (GDP)

The gross domestic product provides the best indicator of a country's economic health by measuring all the services and goods that the state produces and supplies in a given period. Typically, a trader looks at the products and services in an economy in terms of supply and demand. However, the GDP focuses on the supply side of the analysis. The indicator assumes that the state made dependable and exact approximations based on a significant understanding of both supply and demand.

Hence, the increase in GDP should have a corresponding increase in gross domestic product demand. If the supply does not grow along with a rising GDP, it indicates that the economy is unhealthy. This indicator comes about because the economy in such a state shows that the goods and services provided are unaffordable.

Technical and fundamental analyses are critical in the evaluation and understanding of the forex market. The indicators provide visual information that helps a trader to comprehend and react quickly to the trade. The factors that influence a country's currency, such as economic indicators enable fundamental analysts to determine the cause for an increase of decrease in currency value. Therefore, learning elements that make up technical and fundamental analysis can assist a trader in achieving considerable success in Forex Trading.

Chapter 5: Psychology and Mindset of a Forex Trader

Human beings can be complicated and fascinating creatures. Many factors may influence how they think and behave in a given situation. However, at the base of every decision and reaction lie two essential features that ultimately determine a person's conduct. They are the attitude and personality of an individual. How a person sees things and the personality that he or she possesses will define his or her reaction to an event.

Similarly, the attitude and personality type of a forex trader will determine if he or she will succeed or fail in trading. These elements define his or her mindset as he or she enters and participates in the market. Thus, appropriately applying them can ensure a forex trader transacts successfully while simultaneously maintaining his or her psychological wellbeing. Here, we look at the mental mindset of a forex trader from two perspectives. The first angle is the attitude approach, and the second one is personality types.

Attitude Approach

The attitude of a forex trader determines how he or she views and interprets the market and its conditions. Having the right outlook is vital as it helps a trader to control his or her emotions and handle the vicissitudes of Forex Trading. Managing feelings and maintaining objectivity while trading will ensure success for a forex trader. The following are some of the attitudes that can help a trader to improve his or her mindset and achieve success in Forex Trading:

1. Organization

An organized trader makes relevant preparations before and during a trade that enhances his or her chances of success. A person should have an organization in all the steps involved in the trading, including decisions before entering a forex trade:

- **Create a Trading Plan** – A trading plan provides a trader with a sequence of what is taking place in the market and some expectations. It helps him or her to keep track of the market conditions in a systematic way that facilitates effective decision-making.

- **Think Before Entering a Trade** – A trader should carry out extensive research regarding the trade and weigh all possible options before starting. He or she should be as objective and logical as possible when deciding to enter the market.

234

- **Maintain a Record of the Trades** – A trading journal is essential in Forex Trading as it provides the trader with relevant feedback concerning his or her situation on the market.

2. Confidence

Having confidence in the market is booster as it helps a trader to avoid making rash decisions or switching back and forth.

- **Have Full Confidence in the Decisions** – Having belief and full confidence in the decision a trader makes is vital as it signifies that he or she does not fear the trade. He or she analyzed everything in detail and logically came to that particular decision. Hence, he or she does not worry, even if he or she does lose in the end.
- **Following the Map of Price Action** – A trader should trust the information that price action provides. It indicates the market conditions and offers a useful guideline that can help a trader to make decisions without the influence of emotions.
- **Avoid Gambling** – A confident attitude helps a trader to avoid gambling in the market because he or she does not panic. Instead, he or she takes time to evaluate the situation before making a move.

3. Patience

Patience is a virtue that also applies to a forex trader. Keeping calm despite the profits and losses in the markets can help a trader to avoid the dangers of reacting emotionally in the markets.

- **Value Quality Over Quantity** – Being patient enables a trader to make profits consistently for an extended period. He or she will receive small benefits but will last for a much longer time, rather than rushing for huge gains and losing trade quickly.

- **Use the Daily Charts to Learn** – Learning using the daily charts enable a trader to develop an outlook of looking at the bigger picture of the market. It will also allow him or her to practice some trading strategies and make appropriate corrections before entering the forex market.

4. Realistic Expectation

Understanding the trade and having realistic expectations will go a long way into helping a trader to succeed in Forex Trading. It helps him or her to make the right plans, use appropriate strategies and decisions in the market. It also helps to keep his or her emotions in check.

- **Understand the Independence of Each Trade** – Regardless of previous experiences, a trader must understand and identify each trade as a different

236

transaction. It helps the trader know that the next trade's success or failure is absolute.

- **Trade Using Disposable Capital** – A trader should trade using only disposable capital. He or she should risk the money that he or she does not need; otherwise, he or she should not enter the trade.

- **Avoid Sleepless Nights** – A trader should not continue with a trade that he or she doubts. He or she should drop it if he or she loses sleep due to worrying about the risks involving his or her investment.

- **Do Not Take Trades Personally** – A trader should not have an emotional attachment to the trade. Doing so assists him or her to avoid taking the trades personally and view the forex market as a fluctuating trading environment.

5. Learning from Each Experience

Lastly, a person needs to take every experience from the market as a learning lesson. He or she needs to take into account the aspects and decisions that led to the success of failure of a particular transaction. This lesson is even more important in Forex Trading because recognizing the errors made can enable a trader to convert a loss into a profit. He or she looks at the mistakes involved, analyzes every decision, and the subsequent reactions in the market.

The failed trades will provide a trader with relevant information such as clues for what the mistake is and the reasons for the loss. Failures tend to offer a trader relevant information that can enable a forex trader to succeed in the future by avoiding repeating mistakes.

Personality Types of Traders

A person can also look at the psychological mindset of a forex trader from the perspective of the personality. Each individual has his or her personality trait that defines who he or she is. Every personality type consists of different strengths and weaknesses. Forex Trading, as is with other similar transactions, can produce a considerable profit at the moment but cause significant losses at another.

A trader experiences various emotion when it comes to dealing with money matters. He or she invests and trades his or her money to receive profits. He or she also wants to minimize risks and avoid losses as much as possible. Hence, whenever the trader experiences significant gains or losses, he or she goes through strong emotions that bring out his or her personality. The type of character that a trader has is essential because it determines how he or she will behave in the trading market. The trader's personality will define how he or she thinks, the decisions he or she makes, and the subsequent actions.

Therefore, a person needs to understand the various types of personality that a trader can possess. This knowledge will help him or her to comprehend why some traders make individual decisions in particular periods. Additionally, it will enable the individual to study his or her behavior and identify the personality kind that describes him or her. As a result, the person can recognize his or her strengths and weaknesses. It will enable him or her to know the area to improve.

Learning and understanding these types of personalities can help a person to determine the ones that suit Forex Trading the best. He or she will be able to identify and adopt the personality kind that brings about consistent gains in the trading processes. A beginner in Forex Trading can have a chance to prepare himself or herself better before entering the trade. An experienced trader can get more knowledge that will assist him or her to make appropriate enhancements that eventually lead to improved profits and overall success. The following are some of the essential types of personalities and the characteristics that describe them.

1. The Detailed Type

As the name suggests, a detailed trader pays attention to the details of the trade. He or she takes his or her time to look carefully before leaping into a transaction. The trader uses rationality to evaluate the entire situation and everything relating to the market before trading. He or she logically and systematically carry out relevant researches, take detailed notes, and combine all the information received to inform his or her decision.

Furthermore, the trader with this personality also writes trading notes regarding his or her situation in the market. He or she inputs the reasons for writing the points that he or she has and utilizes them to determine the next moves in the market. The attention to detail helps a trader to make decisions that have minimal risks. Conversely, he or she can waste time analyzing before entering a market and end up losing on potentially profitable trades.

2. The Innovative Type

A trader with an innovative personality is instinctive and thinks on his or her feet. He or she uses his or her intuitive skills to read people and events, think and make judgments when trading. Trading involves making the right moves at the correct time to ensure one does not incur losses and, instead, receive profits. An innovative trader carefully analyzes the information available and makes appropriate decisions to form or improve a trade. He or she uses creativity to assess and interpret the information at hand.

Additionally, the creative thinking that a trader with this personality possesses enables him or her to reach relevant conclusions quickly. He or she observes and interprets the significant meanings from large amounts of feedback and information. The trader then swiftly takes immediate action that helps to take advantage or solve issues arising from the market conditions. The innovative traders are keen, quick thinkers, and decisive. This personality provides them with features that can make good leaders.

3. The Playful Type

A trader possessing a playful personality kind has a fun-loving nature. He or she enters and carries out a trade with a playful attitude. This trader is optimistic, in that, he or she sees the bright side of things. He or she views the business as one that will succeed, even if a current transaction is causing losses. He or she also has a lot of positivity that makes him or her have a playful approach to the trade.

Moreover, a trader with this personality involves a certain level of social interaction as he or she trades. He or she communicates and includes other people in his or her thoughts regarding a trade. He or she may even take some advice from other traders about a particular problem. Nevertheless, the weakness of a playful trader type is that he or she is emotional due to his or her positive and optimistic characteristics. Sometimes he or she lets his or her sentiments cloud his or her rationality in the thought and decision-making processes.

4. The Spontaneous Type

A trader with a spontaneous personality does not spend time evaluating and making detailed trading strategies in a trade. He or she has a hard time concentrating on such details. Instead, he or she thinks about a situation as it occurs in the market and makes a decision quickly. The lack of concrete strategies and analysis may expose him or her to avoidable risks that he or she may not expect.

5. The Values-Driven Type

A trader with a values-driven personality is independent in his or her approach to the market. He or she does not follow the crowd and, instead, weighs up the situation, thinks carefully, and makes the relevant trading decisions. Additionally, a value-driven trader concerns himself or herself with certain aspects regarding the trade. He or she emphasizes factors such as relationships, ideas, and the substantial returns of a transaction. Independence enables this trader to look at the bigger picture of the market and make reliable decisions.

However, his or her weakness lies in the emotions that he or she experiences while trading. The trader puts significance that is more considerable on his or her values, which can lead to missed opportunities. Emotions can also make him or her less logical when analyzing the markets.

6. The Administrative Type

An administrative trader adapts to changes and makes effective decisions accordingly. He or she is realistic and practical about the trades and makes sensible moves in the market. He or she can lead other traders or delegate when necessary.

7. The Accurate Type

An accurate trader is attentive to details. He or she applies a detailed evaluation of the situation and notes down every detail concerning the trade. He or she uses a Forex Trading journal to record every assessment and market condition. He or she refers to these details to help him or her to analyze or solve a particular problem.

8. The Independent Type

A trader with an independent personality type does not follow other people's decisions. The trading market is always moving, and it can easily lead to traders making judgments according to the crowd. Emotions can cause someone to allow the decisions and actions of others to determine his or her moves in the market. However, the independent trader thinks for himself or herself.

This trader observes the situation, studies it, and even tries to look at it from different points of view. Once he or she assesses the state of the market, he or she makes the most suitable decision for his or her trades. An independent trader uses creativity and innovatively to come up with strategies and solutions to any issues that arise in his or her transactions. Consequently, the trader's independence causes him or her to be a weak team player because he or she does not have strong social skills.

9. The Facilitative Type

A trader with a facilitative personality trades in a precise and systematic manner. He or she regards trading as a serious business and uses a sober attitude when dealing in the market. He or she meaningfully think about the appropriate moves to make in the transaction and makes the final choices in an organized manner. He or she looks at not only his or her trades but also the entire market. It forms a bigger picture that informs his or her judgments.

Besides, a facilitative trader likes to engage with other traders in the market. Unlike the independent type, this trader enjoys trading in a social setting where he or she gets to work while sharing ideas with others. As a result, the facilitative trader can succeed when cooperating with others, such as in trading partnerships or teams.

10. The Socially Responsible Type

A trader with a socially responsible personality places great importance on the values he or she holds dear. Accordingly, he or she makes strategies and decisions that are in line with these values. He or she also only takes up new chances or makes moves in the market that are in consonance with his or her social ideologies. Aside from respecting and upholding the values of interest, the trader also takes delight in social life. Thus, he or she enjoys a social life while being responsible for maintaining significant social ideology.

11. The Artistic Type

A trader with an artistic personality type uses creativity and intuition while trading. He or she employs his or her artistry and uses creative and original thinking processes to make relevant moves in the market. An artistic trader is more creative and intuitive when compared to other traders in the business.

Likewise, he or she possesses flexibility in the personality that allows him or her to change and adapt to different conditions in trading. Despite this, he or she must take care not to let his or her emotions cloud his or her judgment. He or she should be wary of too much emotional connection with the trades.

12. The Supportive Type

A supportive trader owns portions of the qualities that make up complete and successful traders. The characteristics that he or she possesses enable him or her to provide support to others in the trading world. A trader with this type of personality is conscious, with a lot of insight into the factors associated with the market. He or she also approaches transactions with a somber attitude that helps him or her to make sound decisions in the trade. These qualities attract other traders; in that, they make the supportive trader dependable.

13. The Adventurous Type

A trader with an adventurous personality experiences great success while trading. The success comes from the fact that he or she utilizes factual data to make any judgments regarding the market. He or she uses data to evaluate the situation of the trade rationally before making appropriate decisions. As a result, he or she applies a systematic thought process and makes the most sensible choices that lead to success. Furthermore, an adventurous trader tends to take more risks in the market.

The more the risk there is in a trade, the higher the returns a trader will receive. Thus, he or she utilizes his or her flexible mind to assess a market critically and decide whether he is open to a particular trade. Consequently, the adventurous trader is decisive in trading as he or she uses facts, logic, and analysis to make productive and profitable decisions. Nonetheless, he or she must take care not to push his or her sense of adventure too far. The trader should be mindful of taking too many risks as the strategy may backfire and lead to considerable losses.

Ultimately, the main factors that significantly determine and influence the psychological mindset of a forex trader are emotions and the types of personality. The hope of receiving profits and the fear of losing money can drive a person to make decisions that can make trading success or complete failure. An individual need to understand the characteristics, personality, and attitude that an individual has. Understanding these elements of a person can enable a trader to know how to improve his or her approach to Forex Trading. He or she can also learn the dos and don'ts when dealing with the pressures of Forex Trading. In all, the knowledge from such comprehension will help a trader to enhance his or her mindset to ensure Forex Trading success.

Chapter 6: Forex Strategies and Strategies for Beginners

Forex Trading strategy is what forex traders do to buy or sell financial instruments at a given time to generate profits. Forex Trading strategies are nowadays done, either manually or automatically. A trader is using manual strategies when he or she interprets the trading signals and as a result, decides to buy or sell. The automated method is where a trader comes up with an algorithm that studies the trading signals and executes trades on its own.

Before choosing a Forex Trading strategy, it is important to identify which of these four trading styles fits your personality:

1. Day Trading

Day trading is a short-term trading style designed to buy and sell financial securities within the same trading day. That is closing all positions by the end of the trading day. In Day Trading, you can hold your trades for minutes or even hours. Day traders deal with financial instruments like options, stock, currencies, and contracts for difference. Many day traders are investment firms and banks. Day traders use technical analysis to make trading decisions.

Pros

- Day traders are not affected by unmanageable risks and negative price gaps because all positions are closed by the end of the trading day.
- There are a substantial number of trading opportunities
- Traders can be extremely profitable due to the rapid returns

Cons

- Traders can be extremely unprofitable due to the rapid returns
- You don't have to be concerned with the economy or long-term trends
- Huge opportunity cost
- Day traders have to exit a losing position very quickly, to prevent a greater loss.

2. Swing Trading

Swing trading is where a trader holds an asset between one and several days in an attempt to capture gains in the financial market. This type of traders doesn't monitor the screens all day, and they do it a few hours a day. Swing traders usually rely on technical analysis to look for trading opportunities. Swing trading position is held longer than day trading position but shorter than buy and hold investments. They have larger profit targets than day traders.

Pros

- Swing traders can rely solely on technical analysis, which simplifies the process
- Requires less time to trade compared to day-trading

Cons

- Swing traders are exposed to overnight and weekend risks
- Generally, swing trading risks are as a result of market speculation
- It is difficult to know when to enter and exit a trade when swing trading

3. Scalping Trading

Scalping is the fastest trading style where traders hold positions for a very short time frame. Traders here gain profits due to small price changes. The scalpers hold a position for a short period to gain profits. Traders with large amounts of capital or bid-offers spread narrowly prefer scalping. Scalping follows four principles:

- Small moves are more frequent - even when the market is quiet, scalpers can make hundreds or thousands of trades
- Small moves are easier to obtain - small moves happen all the time compared to large ones
- Less risky than larger moves - scalpers only hold positions for short periods therefore because they have less exposure the risk is also lower
- Spreads can be both bonuses and costs. Spread is the numerical difference between the bid and ask prices. Various parties and different strategies view spread as either trading bonuses or costs.

Pros

- Positions can be liquidated quickly, usually within minutes or seconds
- Very profitable when used as a primary strategy
- It's a low-risk strategy
- Scalpers are not exposed to overnight risks

Cons

- Requires an exit strategy especially during large losses
- Not the best strategy for beginners; it involves quick decision-making abilities.

4. Position Trading

Position trading involves holding a position open for a long period expecting it to appreciate. Traders here can hold positions for weeks, months, or even years. Position traders are not concerned with short-term fluctuations; they are keener on long-term views that affect their positions. Position trading is not done actively. Most traders place an average of 10 trades a year.

This strategy seeks to capture full gains of long-term trading, which would result in an appreciation of their investment capital. Position traders use fundamental analysis, technical analysis, or a combination of both to make trading decisions. To succeed position, traders need plans in place to control risk as well as identify the entry and exit levels.

Pros

- Traders have a longer period to reap fruits.
- Trader's time is not on demand. Once the trade has been initiated, all they can do is wait for the desired outcome

Cons

- Traders may fall victim to opportunity costs because capital is usually tied up for longer periods.

- Position traders tend to ignore minor fluctuations, which can turn to trend reversals, a change in the price direction of a position.

Forex Trading Strategies

There are several types of forex strategies; however, it is important to choose the right one based preferred trading style to trade successfully. Some strategies work on short-term trades as well as long-term trades. The type of Forex strategies you choose depends on a few factors like:

- Entry points - traders need to determine the appropriate time to enter the market
- Exit point-trader need to develop rules on when to exit the market as well as how to get out of a losing position
- Time availability

If you have a full-time job, then you cannot use day trading or scalping styles

- Personal choices

People who prefer lower winning rates but larger gains should go for position trading while those who prefer higher winning rate but smaller gains can choose the swing trading

Common Forex Trading strategies include:

1. Range trading strategy

Range trading is one of the many viable trading strategies. This strategy is where a trader identifies the support and resistance levels and buys at the support level and sells at the resistance level. This strategy works when there is a lack of market direction or the absence of a trend. Range trading strategies can be broken down into three steps:

- **Finding the Range**

Finding the range uses the support and resistance zones. The support zone is the buying price of the security while the resistance zone price is the selling price of a security. A breakout happens in the event that the price goes beyond the trading range, whereas a breakdown occurs in the event that the price goes below the trading range.

- **Time Your Entry**

Traders use a variety of indicators like price action and volume to enter and exit the trading range. They can also use oscillators like CCI, RSI, and stochastics to time their entry. The oscillators track prices using mathematical calculations. Then the traders wait for the prices to reach the support or resistance zones. They often strike when the momentum turns price in the opposing direction.

- **Managing Risk**

The last step is risk management. When the level of support or resistance breaks, traders will want to exit any range-based positions. They can either use a stop loss above the previous high or invert the process with a stop below the current low.

Pros

- There are ranges that can last even for years producing multiple winning trades.

Cons

- Long-lasting ranges are not easy to come by, and when they do, every range trader wants to use it.
- Not all ranges are worth trading

2. Trend Trading Strategy

Another popular and common Forex Trading strategy is the trend trading strategy. This strategy attempts to make profits by analyzing trends. The process involves identifying an upward or downward trend in a currency price movement and choosing trade entry and exit points based on the currency price within the trend.

Trend traders use these four common indicators to evaluate trends; moving averages, relative strength index (RSI), On-Balance-Volume (OBV), and Moving Average Convergence Divergence (MACD). These indicators provide trend trade signals, warn of reversals, and simplify price information. A trader can combine several indicators to trade.

Pros

- Offers a better risk to reward
- Can be used across any markets

Cons

- Learning to trade on indicators can be challenging.

3. Pairs Trade

This is a neutral trading strategy, which allows pair traders to gain profits in any market conditions. This strategy uses two key strategies:

- Convergence trading - this strategy focuses on two historically correlated securities, where the trader buys one asset forward and sells a similar asset forward for a higher price anticipating that prices will become equal. Profits are made when the underperforming position gains value, and the outperforming position's price deflates
- Statistical trading - this is a short-term strategy that uses the mean reversion models involving broadly diversified Security Portfolios. This strategy uses data mining and statistical methods.

Pros

- If pair trades go as expected investors can make profits

Cons

- This strategy relies on a high statistical correlation between two securities, which can be a challenge.
- Pairs trade relies a lot on historical trends, which do not depict future trends accurately.

4. Price Action Trading

This Forex Trading strategy involves analyzing the historical prices of securities to come up with a trading strategy. Price action trading can be used in short, medium, and long periods. The most commonly used price action indicator is the price bar, which shows detailed information like high and low-price levels during a specific period. However, most traders use more than one strategy to recognize trading patterns, stop-losses, and entry, and exit levels. Technical analysis tools also help price action traders make decisions.

Pros

- No two traders will interpret certain price action the same way

Cons

- Past price history cannot predict future prices accurately

5. Carry Trade Strategy

Carry trade strategy involves borrowing a low-interest currency to buy a currency that has a high rate; the goal is to make a profit with the interest rate difference. For example, one can buy currency pairs like the Japanese yen (low interest) and the Australian dollar (high interest) because the interest rate spreads are very high. Initially, carry trade was used as a one-way trade that moved upwards without reversals, but carry traders soon discovered that everything went downhill once the trade collapsed.

With the carry trade strategy:

1. You need to first identify which currencies offer high rates and which ones have low rates.
2. Then match two currencies with a high-interest differential
3. Check whether the pair has been in an upward tendency favoring the higher-interest rate currency

Pros

- The strategy works in a low volatility environment.
- Suitable for a long-term strategy
- **Cons**
- Currency rates can change anytime
- Ricky because they are highly leveraged

- Used by many traders therefore overcrowded

6. Momentum Trading

This strategy involves buying and selling assets according to the strength of recent price trends. The basis for this strategy is that an asset price that is moving strongly in a given direction will continue to move in the same direction until the trend loses strength. When assets reach a higher price, they tend to attract many investors and traders who push the market price even higher. This continues until large pools of sellers enter the market and force the asset price down.Momentum traders identify how strong trends are in a given direction. They open positions to take advantage of the expected price change and close positions when the prices go down.

There are two kinds of momentum:

- Relative momentum - different securities within the same class are compared against each other, and then traders and investors buy strong performing ones and sell the weak ones.
- Absolute momentum - an asset's price is compared against its previous performance.

Pros

- Traders can capitalize on volatile market trends

- Traders can gain high profit over a short period
- This strategy can take advantage of changes in stock prices caused by emotional investors.

Cons

- A momentum investor is always at a risk of timing a buy incorrectly.
- This strategy works best in a bull market; therefore, it is market sensitive
- This strategy is time-intensive; investors need to keep monitoring the market daily.
- Prices can shift in a different direction anytime

7. Pivot Points

This strategy determines resistance and support levels using the average of the previous trading sessions, which predict the next prices. They take the average of the high, low, and closing prices. A pivot point is a price level used to indicate market movements. Bullish sentiment occurs when one trades above the pivot point while bearish sentiment occurs when one trades below the pivot point.

Pros

- Traders can use the levels to plan out their trading in advance because prices remain the same throughout the day
- Works well with other strategies

Cons

- Some traders do not find pivot points useful
- There is no guarantee that price will stop or reverse at the levels created on the chart

8. Fundamental Analysis

This strategy involves analyzing the economic, social, and political forces that may affect the supply and demand of an asset. Usually, people use supply and demand to gauge which direction the price is headed to. The Fundamental analysis strategy then analyzes any factors that may affect supply and demand. By assessing these factors, traders can determine markets with a good economy and those with a bad one.

Forex Strategies for Beginners

When starting on Forex Trading, it important to keep things simple. As a beginner, avoid thinking about money too much and focus on one or two strategies at a time. The following three strategies are easy to understand and perfect for beginners.

1. Inside Bar Trading Strategy

This highly effective strategy is a two-bar price action strategy with an inside bar and a prior/mother bar. The inside bar is usually smaller and within the high and low range of the prior bar. There are many variations of the inside bar, but what remains constant is that the prior bar always fully engulfs the inside bar. Although very profitable, the inside bar setup does not occur often.

There are two main ways you can trade using inside bars:

- As a continuation move - This is the easiest way to trade inside bars. The inside bars are traded in trending markets following the direction of the trend.
- As a reversal pattern - the inside bars are traded counter-trend

When using this strategy, it is important to look for these characteristics when evaluating the pattern:

- Time frame matters - avoid any time frame less than the daily.
- Focus on the breakout - best inside bar trades happen after a break of consolidation where the preceding trend is set to resume.
- The trend Is your friend - trading with the trend is the only way to trade an inside bar
- A favorable risk to reward ratio is needed when trading an inside bar
- The size of the inside bar in comparison to the prior bar is extremely important

2. Pin Bar Trading Strategy

This strategy is highly recommended for beginners because it is easy to learn due to a better visual representation of price action on a chart. It is one of the easiest strategies to trade. Pin bars show a reversal in the market and, therefore, can be useful in predicting the direction of the price. Pin bars consist of one price bar, known as a candlestick price bar, which represents a sharp reversal and rejection of price. Candlestick charts are the clearest at showing price action.

There are various ways traders trading with pin bars can enter the market:

- At the current market price

- Using an on-stop entry
- At limit entry, which is at the 50% retrace of the pin bar

To improve your odds when using the pin bar strategy:

- Trade with the trend
- Wait for a break of structure
- Trade from an area of value

Some of the mistakes pin bar traders should avoid include the following:

- Assuming the market will reverse because of a pin bar
- Focus too much on the pin bars and miss out on other trading opportunities
- All pin bars are not the same and should not be treated as such

3. Forex Breakout Strategy

A breakout strategy is where investors find stocks that have built strong support or resistance level, wait for a breakout, and enter the market when momentum is in their favor. This strategy is important because it can offer expansions in volatility, major price moves, and limited risk. A breakout occurs when the price moves beyond the support or resistance level. The breakout strategy is good for beginners because they can catch every trend in the market. Breakouts occur in all types of market environments.

Traders establish a bullish position when prices are set to close above a resistance level and a bearish position when prices close below a support level. Sometimes traders can be caught on a false breakout, and the only way to determine if it is a false breakout is to wait for confirmation. False breakout prices usually go beyond the support and resistance level; however, they return to a prior trading range by the end of the day.

Good investors plan how they will exit the markets before establishing a position. With breakouts, there are two exit plans:

- Where to exit with profit-traders can assess the stock recent behaviors to determine reasonable objectives. When traders meet their goals, they can exit the position. They can either raise a stop-loss to lock in profits or exit a portion of the position to let the rest run

- Where to exit with a loss - breakout trading show traders clearly when a trade has failed, and therefore they can determine where to set stop-loss order. Traders can use the old support or resistance level to close a losing trade

Pros

- You can catch every trend in the market
- ·Prices can quickly move in your favor

Cons

- Traders can get caught in a false breakout
- It can be difficult to enter a trade

Tips for trading breakouts:

- Never sell on breakdown or buy on breakout both carry extreme risks
- Trade with the trend
- Wait for higher volume to confirm a breakout
- Take advantage of volatility cycles
- Enter on the retest of support or resistance
- Have a predetermined exit plan

Note

Beginners are more likely to be successful in trade than their experienced counterparts are because they have not yet cultivated any bad habits. Experienced traders have to break bad habits and put aside any emotions built over the years.

Chapter 7: Forex Trading Signals

How can a forex trader find out which Forex pair and time frame is best to buy or sell? For starters, the forex trader can move from one chart to another to identify the forex market trend. However, in view of the fact that markets change from time to time, switching through charts can be a tedious exercise. Additionally, some patterns may be erratic and unpredictable, and therefore fail to make a profit.

Nevertheless, if a forex trader could find a way to examine all the currency pairs swiftly and time frames to find the best trend, he or she can expect a dramatic increase in profitability in any method he or she trades. Forex Trading signals can help forex traders make such critical decisions about profiting from their investments.

What Are Forex Trading Signals?

Put simply, Forex Trading signals are guidelines and recommendations that help inexperienced forex traders to open

Forex Trading positions. The signals are a type of system that forex traders use to make crucial decisions about their trade. In that regard, Forex Trading signals provide details about how to open a new Forex Trade.

Examples of such details include details about which currency pair to trade, when to open the trade (open date), whether to buy or sell (position), and information on the opening price. In addition, they provide details on the stop-loss level to set if the forex market starts to experience loses, and the target profit level, that is, the point at which the trade should close so that forex traders can secure their profits.

Accurate and timely signals help forex traders to have success in their trade, whereas wrong signals reduce the opportunity for forex traders to earn and to make profits from their investments.

Forex Trading signals send email alerts that show trading arrangements for the next 24-hours. Various Forex Trading signals providers give free trial services that allow currency traders to become familiar with signal illustrations to calculate the values of the currencies. In that way, currency traders are able to evaluate the quality and the reliability of the Forex Trading signals before traders can pay subscription money.

When looking through Forex signals services, the forex trader must ensure that the Forex Trading signal provider offers the type of signals the forex trader needs.

Types of Forex Trading Signals and How They Work

Each signal is different from the other, and every forex trader needs to have a basic idea of the operation of the two types of Forex Trading signals. A forex trader can choose the type of signal to use, depending on his or her needs and depending on the signal's function.

Manual Forex Trading Signals

Manual forex signals require human traders to analyze the market before Forex signal providers distribute the signals. The human traders comprise of a team of financial analysts and experienced forex traders who carry out Forex market analysis and open the trading signals.

When the traders receive signals, they log into their Forex account and key in the trades. That means that the trader will need to be available at all times to key in the trades.

What are the benefits of Manual Forex Trading Signals?

Higher Profit Targets: The profit targets in manual trading signals are typically more significant than in the automated trading signals unless the signal provider uses a scalping tactic. Profit targets help forex traders to reduce risk by establishing a target price when the forex trader wants to take profits on a trade.

Consequently, manual signals that large financial institutions offer their clients target hundreds of pips when the high-frequency signals target fractions of a pip. A pip is short for 'point in percentage,' and it is a significantly small measure of variation in a currency pair in the Forex market.

For example, if a currency sells at 3.6997, and buys at 3.6999, then the pip is 2.

Useful Trading Tools: Manual trading signals are indicators that highlight excellent trading prospects. A forex trader can conduct his or her own forex market analysis, come up with his or her own plan and strategy, and use the manual signals to crosscheck his or her evaluation.

The use of manual signals also enables the forex trader to sort out risk levels depending on the conditions of the forex market. A forex trader is in charge of all the trading functions. Therefore, when the forex market is volatile, the forex trader can reduce the number of currency units that he or she will buy, and increase the size once the market stabilizes.

Profitable Risk-Reward Ratios: Risk – reward ratios measure how much a forex trader's potential reward is, for every amount of money that he or she risks. For example, if a forex trader has a risk-reward ratio of 1:5, it means that the forex trader is risking $1 to make $5 theoretically. It is, however, not definite that the trader will earn $5.

Consequently, manual signals often provide risk-reward ratios of 1:1 or better, compared to the automated signals, which give a minimum of 1:2 risk-reward ratio. Even with a risk-reward ratio of 1:0.5, a forex trader stands to gain $0.5 for every dollar he or she trades over the long term.

Trading News Releases: Trading news is an approach to buy or sell equities, currencies, and other financial instruments in the forex markets. Manual forex traders issue out outcomes of the news releases in ways that offer significant winning potential.

Manual forex traders or financial analysts examine news reports and identify the causes that will cause the forex market to move in a specific direction. Therefore, the forex signal providers issue out manual signals from the financial analysts, which predict what numbers, will be released.

With such expectation, forex investors start trading before the release of the actual numbers. That is unlike using trading robots, which are not always able to trade the outcomes of the news releases.

Flexibility: Manual Forex Trading signals have the capacity to adjust to market changes and fluctuations. Forex investors make profits by buying or selling as many currencies as they can.

Consequently, when a forex investor receives a manual trading signal for a trade, which appears to be heading in a profitable direction, the forex signal provider may extend that take profit level and increase the profit productively. Thus, manual Forex Trading signals provide forex investors with suck kind of flexibility in the forex market.

Human Experience: One of the most positive aspects of manual Forex Trading signals is human intelligence and expertise, which cannot compare to that of computers. Many skilled forex traders have a good feel of the forex market and can, therefore, tell the best time for buying or selling to gain profitable trades. Robots do not often perceive such upward or downward trends.

Because crowd psychology drives the forex market, human reasoning ingrains manual trading signals. As a result, the manual signals can manipulate the market trends for maximum profitability.

What are the shortcomings of Manual Forex Trading Signals?

Manual trading signals are suitable for extending profit targets, but the process of issuing out signals can be time-consuming. Even though manual signal providers may not need to conduct all the forex market analysis, they still have to open the Forex Trading platform and carry on with the trading business.

Additionally, manual signal providers are not able to follow the manual signals distributed during nighttime or work hours. In addition, manual trading signal providers do not have extensive coverage of a variety of other currency pairs. That is because many signal providers focus their attention on significant currency pairs, thus leaving out other financial instruments that include cryptocurrencies, stock indices, and commodities.

Automated Forex Trading Signals

Automated Forex signals have robotic programs, which analyze the market before the forex signal providers issue out the signals.

Due to the impracticality of trading forex on a part-time basis, many forex investors, brokers, and independent financial institutions have created trading systems that distribute forex signals that tell the user when to trade.

With automated Forex Trading, buying or selling can be as simple as pushing a button or making a telephone call to the signal provider.

What are the benefits of Automated Forex Trading Signals?

It Does Not Involve Any Paperwork: Signal providers do not go through any complex processes involving paperwork, in order for them to get started on distribution signals.

It Saves Time: A person does not have to remain transfixed on their computer monitors or screens all day long to buy or sell. The automated trading robot takes care of all the tasks 24-hours a day.

Similarly, one does not have to spend time coming up with his or her own trading plan. Instead, a person can choose to follow a forex trader who has a similar Forex Trading strategy and risk profile as his or her own. In that way, the person will have more time to set trades and to keep an eye on different forex markets.

In addition, forex traders and signal providers do not have to worry about missing trades because automated trading performs trades much faster than any human being.

Passive Trading: Automated Forex Trading signals are not subject to any human emotions, and therefore, are a clear-cut set of rules to follow.

Easily Accessible to Beginners: Precise automated forex signals help beginner forex traders to learn how experienced traders buy or sell. Beginners can achieve this by replicating the trades of the more experienced traders who have shared their successful strategies.

Similarly, beginners do not need to have minimum balances in their Forex Trading accounts to begin trading. Furthermore, automated signals can boost the confidence of beginner traders concerning the forex market. Beginner traders can relate their analysis to that of their signal's provider and thereby learn more about Forex Trading while accumulating profits.

Independent Control of Trading Account: Only the forex traders and signal providers can access their accounts. What's more, traders sign in the account in their name, and they do not have to give a power of attorney to any other person.

Back-Testing Trading Strategies: Trading robots have the ability to use historical data to evaluate the viability of a trading strategy and thus finding out how the plan will play out in the forex market.

Forex traders can fine-tune such strategies to yield outcomes that are more positive. When the trading robot performs the back-testing, signal providers can confidently open their trade because the providers will have a better idea of how the trading robots will perform in the future.

What are the disadvantages of Automated Forex Trading Signals?

Automated Forex Trading signals are not flexible. There are times when a forex investor may need to manipulate a trade or to forego a deal when the market goes in the opposite direction.

For example, when news breaks out about a hurricane hitting the investor's country, the investor will know that the trading platform will not remain stable. As a result, the investor may end up making losses following the effects the hurricane will have on assets sold on the trading platform.

Additionally, an automated Forex Trading account can breakdown potentially creating significant issues. A computerized trading account can stop endorsing trades, thus leaving trades to linger or cause the system to crash entirely. Alternatively, the automated account can have a technical error or a virus in the software where forex traders can lose all the money in their accounts at once.

How to Choose the Best Trading Signals

How can one know how to choose the best trading signals? Below are the factors a person should consider in making that decision.

The Regularity of Trading Signals: In the search for the best trading signals in the forex market, a trader should look for signal providers who issue favorable trading signals and alerts recurrently. That is because signals will not take too long to appear even if a person misses one or two signals. In that way, a trader can become consistent with his or her trading.

Variety of Financial Instruments: Signal providers who offer signals on diverse financial tools make it possible for a forex trader to choose investments from a wide range of options. Outstanding trading signals on commodities, currency pairs, stock indices, and cryptocurrencies give forex traders access to various financial instruments across different asset classifications.

Negligible Drawdowns: Choose signal providers who have minimal and negligible consecutive losing trades, but have solid equity growth curves. That will help in producing excellent performance in terms of investment profitability.

Constant Profits: It is essential to identify trading signals with excellent and consistent trading outcomes. A forex trader can accomplish this by choosing signal providers who are experts at analyzing the forex market and are therefore able to adapt to the continually changing market conditions.

Experienced signal providers demonstrate a focused effort in providing regular forex signals of the highest quality.

Therefore, how can a person know how to choose the best Forex Trading signal providers?

Credible Profitability History: Is there evidence of unrealistic profits? A forex trader should smell a rat when a signal provider issues out signals with five or more pips profit from a trade. That level of profit would be unrealistic and not trustworthy.

Consequently, a forex trader should search for signal providers who have authenticated track records. The best option would be to verify the track records through third-party online verification facilities.

The Timing of the Signal: It is wise for a forex trader to outline the schedule of the signals. That is because the trader may not have a lot of time to spend in front of his or her computer waiting for the signal provider to issue out a signal.

In order not to miss out on signals, a forex trader should check the signal provider's time zone and master the times during which the signal provider sends out signals. That is an important consideration to think about before signing up for a Forex Trading signal service.

Trial periods can help a forex trader to know the times the signal providers distribute signals.

Free Trial Period: It would be wise for a person to choose a signal provider who gives a free trial period. That will prevent the person from getting into the market without knowing how the signals work and possibly risking all of his or her investment.

Knowing whether a signal provider is right or not helps a person to develop trust with the provider. Trial periods provide opportunities for a person to test the signals and to confirm whether the set-up of the signals conforms to his or her trading style.

Random Signals: Some Forex Trading signal providers distribute random signals that seem to have no apparent strategy. Robots could generate such signals, which may lack thorough analysis.

Consequently, a forex trader should evaluate the trading positions of the signals – are they long-term or short-term? In addition, the trader should check to see whether the signals are founded on technical analysis, or fundamental analysis, or a mix of both. Therefore, a person should evaluate signals to know whether they will be suitable for his or her trading style.

Details About the Signal Performance: Are the details short and simple? Aspects such as entry point, stop loss, and take profits should be easily understandable so that a forex trader can visualize all the factors to decide whether a signal is lucrative and appropriate.

The best Forex Trading signals, therefore, take into account definitions and forex market assessments that associate with the Forex Trading signals. Forex traders may not feel confident to use signals that do not explain why a forex trader should open a particular trade.

Are the Signals Easy to Follow? Forex Trading signals that are easy to follow are those that are in a well-organized format. The structure will, therefore, have definite entry and exit prices and stop loss figures. These will help in financial management and the steady growth of a forex trader's trading account.

Additionally, the signal provider should post Forex Trading videos, webinars, and watch lists for additional customer support. Similarly, Forex Trading signal providers should be willing to answer all questions that pertain to trade formats and signals.

Should Forex Traders Use Free Forex Signals or Paid Forex Signals

Free forex signals and paid forex signals differ in terms of quality. Individuals who sell other products tend to issue out free forex signals. Therefore, although the individuals' free forex signals may work in getting a person interested in investing in Forex Trading training, the individuals have absolutely no interest in the quality of the signals themselves.

Additionally, free forex signal providers offer free trials that give beginners limited information that leaves the beginners wanting to learn more. Learning Forex Trading requires a lot of effort, which can yield positive outcomes. Consequently, even the best free Forex Trading signals do not teach beginners how to trade, because they cause the beginners to depend on other forex traders.

With paid forex signals, a person gets the experience he or she paid for. Paid forex signals give beginner traders access to support. For instance, when paid forex signals act unreliably, signal providers will provide the beginners with direction unlike using free forex signals where beginner traders will have no forthcoming support.

Therefore, a forex trader should not trust providers that guarantee results without proof. Genuine signal providers should be willing to share their performance history. Paid services provide helpful information for beginners to help them to become knowledgeable in forex money matters and the management of risks. Such data can be valuable to beginner traders who would like to control their investment directly in the future.

Forex Trading signals are instrumental in helping forex traders conduct market analysis within a short period. Similarly, forex signals mean that a trader will not have to sit down for extended hours waiting to get his or her outcomes. Moreover, forex traders can build their career within the first few months of their trading experience.

Chapter 8: Tips to Winning in Forex Trading

To the uninitiated, navigating the forex market successfully can seem like a difficult task. However, success is possible if one takes the right steps and trains properly. Just like training for a marathon, training is essential to winning in Forex Trading. Success requires targeted effort, practice, patience, and time.

Forex traders need to have specific goals in mind. With the right direction, training, and guidance, mastering the foreign exchange market is within anyone's reach. Winning at Forex Trading has little to do with hot picks, which are often fallacies created by people masquerading as experts in this field.

On the contrary, success stems from the ability to learn from both right and wrong trading choices to determine the patterns and strategies that work best for one's personality and goals. People are different; therefore, no single trading strategy will work for everyone.

Fortunately, there are several tips for winning in Forex Trading that can help beginners master the complexities of the largest market in the world. Actually, in terms of the value of average daily trading volume, the FX market dwarfs the bond and stock markets. Forex traders, therefore, have several inherent advantages over traders who engage in other forms of financial trading.

Small investors with modest capital can find success and trade their way to a fortune. The forex market is one of the few markets that can make this a reality. Trading the forex market is relatively easy. Doing it well and generating a consistent income, however, is not so easy. Therefore, it is important to learn the secrets and tips for success.

Tips and Secrets for Success in Forex Trading

1. Pay Attention to Daily Pivot Points

Forex traders should watch daily pivot points closely. This is especially important for day traders. However, it is also important for swing traders, position traders, and even traders who focus on long-term positions. It is important to do so because tons of other forex traders do the same.

In a certain way, pivot trading is like a self-fulfilling prophecy. Essentially, markets often find resistance or support at pivot points since thousands of pivot traders place orders at those points. Consequently, when a large volume of trading moves happens at these points or levels, there is no other reason for the move except that many traders placed orders expecting such a move.

However, pivot points should not be the only basis of a Forex Trading strategy. Rather, regardless of one's strategy, one should watch these points for signs of either potential market or continuation of a trend. Forex traders should look at pivot levels and the trading activities that take place around them as a confirming indicator to use in conjunction with their chosen strategy.

2. Define Trading Style and Goals

Before setting out on any journey, travelers need to have a clear idea of where they are going and how to get to their destination. In the same way, forex traders need to have clear goals, in addition to ensuring that their trading strategies will help them achieve those goals.

Each Forex Trading style or strategy comes with a different risk profile. Therefore, traders who want to win in Forex Trading need to find and adopt the right approach and attitude to trade profitably. Those who cannot imagine going to sleep with an open market position, for example, should consider focusing on day trading.

Forex traders with funds they believe will benefit from a trade appreciation over several months; on the other hand, they should think about position trading. Essentially, it is important for a forex trader to determine whether his/her personality will fit any particular trading strategy. Any mismatch will probably lead to certain losses and stress.

3. Trade with an Edge

Successful forex traders only risk their hard-earned money when a market opportunity provides them with an edge. In other words, they do so when the opportunity presents them with something that will boost the chances of their trades being successful. This edge can be various things, even a simple thing, such as selling at a price level that one identifies as strong resistance.

Forex traders can also increase their probability of success and their edge by having several technical factors in their favor. If the 100-period, 50-period, and 10-period moving averages all meet at the same price level, for example, it will likely offer significant resistance or support for a market because many traders will be acting together by trading off any of those averages.

Converging technical indicators also provide a similar edge. This happens when different indicators on many periods converge to provide resistance or support. Having the price hit an identified resistance or support level, in addition to having price movement at that level, is an indication of a potential market reversal.

4. The Trading Platform and Broker

Forex traders should spend adequate time researching a suitable trading platform and a reputable broker. It is important to identify and understand the difference between brokers and determine how each of them goes about making a market, as well as their policies. Trading the exchange-driven market, for example, is different from trading in the spot market or OTC market.

Traders should also choose the trading platform that fits the analysis they want to do. Traders who want to use Fibonacci numbers to trade, for example, should ensure the trading platform they choose has the ability to draw Fibonacci lives. A good platform with a bad broker is just as bad as a poor trading platform with a good broker. Therefore, forex traders need to find the best of both.

5. Preserve Capital

It is more important for traders to avoid huge losses than to make huge profits. For people who are new to Forex Trading, this concept may not sound quite right. However, it is important to understand that winning in Forex Trading means knowing how to preserve or protect one's capital.

According to the founder of Tudor Corporation, Paul Tudor Jones, playing great defense is the most important rule of trading. Actually, he is a great trader to learn from and study. In addition to building a hugely successful hedge fund, Tudor Jones has an excellent record of profitable trading.

He also played an important role in creating the ethics-training program needed to gain membership in all futures exchanges in the United States. Protecting the trading capital, or playing great defense, is very important in Forex Trading because many people who venture into Forex Trading are unable to continue trading as a result of running out of money.

Many forex traders drain their accounts soon after they make a few trades. Having strict risk management practices is important for people who want to win in Forex Trading. Traders who manage to preserve their trading capital are able to continue trading for as long as they want to, and might eventually become huge winners.

One great trade can fall into a trader's lap and significantly increase his/her profits and account size. One does not need to be the smartest trader in the world to make money in the forex market. If nothing else, the luck of the draw can have traders who manage to protect their capital stumble into trades that generate enough profits to make their trading careers a huge success.

6. Small Losses and Focus

After forex traders fund their trading accounts, they need to understand that their capital is at risk. Therefore, they should not depend on that money for their daily living expenses. Actually, it is better to think of those funds as vacation funds. Once their vacation is over, their money is gone.

Having this trading attitude will help prepare them to accept and learn from small losses, which will also help them manage their risk better. Forex traders should focus on their trades and accept small losses, which are normal in any type of business, rather than constantly and obsessively focusing on their equity.

7. Simple Technical Analysis

Consider this example of two forex traders in extremely different situations. The first trader has a specially designed trading computer with several monitors, a large office, swanky furnishings, trading charts, and market news feeds. He also has several moving averages, technical indicators, momentum indicators, and much more.

The other trader, on the other hand, works from a relatively simple office space and uses a regular desktop or laptop computer. His charts reveal just one or two technical indicators on the price action of the market.

Most people would consider the first trader to be more professional and extremely successful, and they would probably be wrong in their assumption. Actually, the second trader is closer to the image of a forex trader who wins consistently. Traders can apply numerous forms of technical analysis to a chart. Having more, however, does not necessarily mean having better.

Using a huge number of indicators might actually make things more complicated and confusing for a forex trader. They amplify indecision and doubt, causing him/her to miss many potentially profitable trades. Therefore, it is better to have a simple trading strategy with just a few rules, as well as a minimum of indicators to consider.

A few very successful forex traders make money from the forex market almost every day without using any technical indicators overlaid on their charts. They achieve this impressive feat without taking advantage of a relative strength indicator, trend lines, trading robots, moving averages, or expert advisors. Their market analysis involves a simple candlestick chart.

8. Weekend Analysis

The forex market ceases operation on the weekend. Therefore, forex traders should use this time to study their weekly charts to identify news or patterns that could affect their trades in either a positive or a negative way. This will give the objectivity, which will help them make smarter trading plans.

9. Placing Stop-Loss Orders at the Right Price Levels

In addition to protecting one's capital in case of a losing trade, this strategy is also an important aspect of smart Forex Trading. Many newcomers to the forex market assume that risk management simply means placing stop-loss orders close to the entry point of their trades. This is partly accurate; however, habitually placing stop-loss orders too close to their trade entry points is something that might contribute to their lack of success.

Sometimes, stop-loss orders can stop a trade, only to see the market make a reversal in favor of the trade. It is common for novice traders to endure watching this happen. Sometimes, this reversal proceeds to a level that would have seen them gain a sizable profit if the stop-loss order had not terminated the trade.

Obviously, traders should enter trades that allow them to place stop-loss orders close enough to their trade entry points to avoid making huge losses. However, they should place them at a reasonable price level, based on their analysis of the market. When it comes to reasonable placement of stop-loss orders, the general rule of thumb is to place them a bit further than the price the market should not trade at, based on market analysis.

10. Use a Consistent Methodology

Before a prospective trader enters the forex market, he/she needs to have a good idea of how he/she will make trading decisions. Essentially, forex traders should know the information they will need to make smart decisions on entering a trade or exiting one. Some traders choose to analyze a chart and the fundamental of the economy to decide the best time to trade.

Others, however, prefer to perform technical analysis to determine the ideal time to execute a trade. Whichever methodology or strategy a trader chooses to employ, he/she needs to be consistent and ensure the chosen methodology is adequately adaptive. In other words, it should be flexible enough to handle the forex market's changing dynamics.

11. Choosing the Right Entry and Exit Points

Most inexperienced forex traders do not know how to judge conflicting information that often presents when analyzing charts in various timeframes. Certain information, for example, might indicate a sell signal on a weekly chart, but show up as a purchasing opportunity in an intraday chart.

Therefore, if a trader is using a weekly chart to determine his/her basic trading direction and a daily chart to tie his/her entry, then he/she should try to synchronize the two charts. If the weekly chart is providing a buy signal, for example, he/she should wait for the daily chart to confirm this signal. In other words, keeping signal timing in sync is a good tip for winning in Forex Trading.

12. Calculating Expectancy

The formula to use to determine the reliability of a trading system is expectancy. Forex traders should analyze and compare past winning trades against losing trades, which will help them determine the profitability of their winning trades versus how much money they lost in their losing trades.

A simple way to do this is by looking at their last 10 trades. New forex traders who have not yet made any trades should study their chart to identify points where their trading system suggests an entry and/or exit point. In other words, new forex traders need to determine whether their system is profitable.

Having done this, they should write down their observations, total their winning trades, and divide the amount by the number of successful trades they made. For example, if a trader made 10 trades, four of which flopped, and six of which were successful, his/her win ratio would be 60% or 6/10. If the six winning trades made $4,800, then his/her average win would be $4,800/6 = $800.

If the trader's losses amounted to $2,400, then his/her average loss would be $2,400/4 = $600. By applying these results to the formula for calculating the reliability of a system, the trader will get E = [1 + (800/600) x 0.6 – 1 = 0.4, which is equivalent to 40%. A positive expectancy of 40% means that the trader's trading system will likely generate 40 cents to the dollar over the long term.

13. Positive Feedback Loops

Forex traders create a positive feedback loop following a well-planned and executed trade. When they plan a trade and execute it as expected, traders tend to create a pattern of positive feedback. In other words, success tends to breed success, which, in turn, builds confidence. This is especially true if the trade generates significant profits.

Even if a trader suffers a small loss following a well-planned trade, he/she will still build a positive feedback loop.

14. Keeping Printed Records

Printed records serve as a good learning tool for forex traders. Therefore, traders, especially new ones, should print their charts create a list of reasons for any particular trade, including the things that sway their trading decisions. They should mark the entry and exit points on the chart and make any relevant comments, such as emotional reasons for taking specific actions.

Forex traders need to objectify their trades to develop the discipline and mental control needed to execute trades according to their systems, instead of their emotions, greed, or habits.

15. Stress Less

This is an obvious Forex Trading tip. Trading the forex market under stress tends to lead to irrational decisions, which can end up costing a trader a lot of money. Therefore, forex traders should identify the source of their stress and try to get rid of it, or at least limit its influence on their actions.

When stress threatens to take control, a trader should take deep breaths and try to focus on other things for a few minutes. People have different ways of overcoming stress. Some exercise, while others listen to classical music. Traders should learn what works best for them.

Risk Management in Forex Trading

One of the most debated topics in financial trading is forex risk management. On one hand, forex traders want to get the most out of every trade, but on the other hand, they want to limit the size of a potential loss. Sometimes, traders need to take greater risks to gain the best returns. This is where the issue of risk management in Forex Trading arises.

Forex traders are in the business of making money. To do this, however, they need to learn how to limit potential losses. Unfortunately, many novice traders are just anxious to start trading without giving much thought to their total account size. They do not think of ways to minimize their potential losses before hitting the 'trade' button.

This type of investing is more akin to gambling. When forex traders make trades without following the rules of risk management, they are, in fact, gambling. They are hoping to land that jackpot, instead of focusing on the long-term returns on their investment. Risk management rules do not offer 100% protection; however, they can make traders very profitable in the end.

Consider this; people go to Las Vegas every day to gamble in hopes of winning a jackpot. Some do win; however, casinos still make tons of money. If people are winning big jackpots, how are casinos making so much money in the end? The answer is that they are still profitable because they earn more money from losing gamblers.

Casinos are excellent statisticians. They know that numerous gamblers will lose, and their money will be more than enough to pay for the jackpots won by the few successful gamblers. This is a good example of how casinos know how to control their losses. In the same way, forex traders need to know how to control their losses to improve their chances of being profitable.

Forex Trading, in the end, is a numbers game, which means that traders have to tilt every factor in their favor. Essentially, they need to be the statistician and not the gambler. Everyone knows that it takes money to make money. The money one needs to start trading largely depends on one's approach to a new trading business.

Losses are a reality of business, and traders will suffer some losses at some point in their career. This is the reason why it is important to have some risk management rules. Forex traders should only risk a small percentage of their accounts on each trade so that they can survive losses and avoid large drawdowns in their accounts.

New forex traders tend to assume that making money through Forex Trading is easy and fast. To find success in this business, however, traders need patience, commitment, dedication, and time. Traders should not just open trading positions without considering the currency risk, trading conditions, and risks that can affect their invested capital.

They need to use techniques and tools to manage their investments and risks. Those who fail to do this will be gambling instead of trading. Some of the best ways to manage risks in Forex Trading include:

1. Only Investing Money, one Does not Need

The first rule in any form of trading, including Forex Trading, is to invest the money one can afford to lose. Most beginners tend to skip or ignore this rule since they assume that it will not happen to them. Even gamblers do not take all their money to the casino to bet on black. Forex traders should not take unnecessary risks by investing the money they need.

Trading with money they need for their daily living expenses will only add emotional stress and extra pressure on their trading, which will affect their decision-making abilities and increase the likelihood of making costly mistakes. In addition, there is a chance they could lose all their trading capital.

The FX market is an unpredictable and volatile market; therefore, it is safer to trade conservative amounts from one's disposable income.

2. Think About Risk Tolerance

Before traders start trading, they need to identify and understand their risk tolerance, which will depend on the following:

1. Investment goals
2. Their age
3. How much they are willing to lose
4. Their experience
5. Their knowledge of the foreign exchange market

By determining their risk tolerance, forex traders will know they are in control of any situation because they are risking the right amount of money in terms of their financial objectives in relation to their personal financial situation.

3. Set Risk to Reward Ratio (RRR) to a Minimum of 1:3

Having a good understanding of the RR ratio will improve a trader's chances of being profitable, in addition to setting limit orders to protect his/her trading capital. The RR ratio compares and measures the distance between a trader's entry point and his/her take-profit and stop-loss orders.

For example, suppose that a trader is investing in the EUR/USD currency pair. If 50 pips is the distance between his/her entry point and stop-loss point, and 150 pips between the entry point and take-profit point, then he/she would be using a risk/reward ratio of 50:150, which is 1:3 because he/she is risking 50 pips to gain 150 pips.

The risk to reward ratio is an important tool to help traders set their take-profit and stop-loss orders, depending on their risk tolerance. Smart forex traders should control their downside risk. Although the RRR depends on a trader's risk tolerance, most traders use a ratio of 1:3, which means that they hope to earn 3 times what they are willing to lose.

4. Control the Risk per Trade

When thinking about their trading risks, forex traders should consider their trading capital. A smart risk management strategy would be to invest a small percentage of their trading capital in each trade. For example, 1% to 2% of their available capital per trade is a good starting point.

If a forex trader has $10,000 in his/her trading account, for example, the maximum loss allowable would be 2% of the available capital, which will amount to $200 per trade. Controlling the risk per trade is very helpful, especially if a trader goes through a losing streak. It helps forex traders to avoid huge drawdowns in their trading accounts and protect their trading capital.

5. Keep the Risk Consistent

As soon as they make their first profits, some forex traders, especially beginners, increase the size of their positions, which is a good way to wipe out their trading accounts. Forex traders should understand the importance of keeping their trading risk consistent. Just because a trader is on a winning streak does not mean that the next trade will make a profit.

Traders should avoid becoming risk-averse and over-confident since it can lead to them to change their risk and money management rules without good reasons. When they were working on their trading strategies, they probably set up rules to guide their trading positions. This is a necessary step towards setting up a winning trading strategy; however, they also need to stick to their rules to achieve long-term success.

6. Understand and Control Leverage

Due to its high volatility, the FX market is a leveraged market. In this case, leverage refers to the ability to invest more than the initial deposit through margin trading. Forex brokers will only ash traders to set aside a small amount of the total value of their positions as collateral.

By using leverage, traders can increase their profits quickly; however, they need to understand that this also applies to their losses. Therefore, they need to understand how margin trading and leverage work, in addition to how they affect their overall trading and performance.

However, using high leverage to generate huge profits, as some inexperienced traders do, is not a good idea. This is because a small change in the market can easily wipe out their trading accounts. In fact, the European Securities and Market Authority set limitations on the leverage brokers offer in August 2018.

7. Consider Currency Correlations

Since forex traders trade currency pairs, such as EUR/USD, it is important to understand the correlation between currencies linked to each other. Having a good understanding of currency correlations will help them control their trading portfolios more effectively by reducing the overall risk.

Correlation describes how one currency behaves in relation to another currency. When two currencies have a positive correlation, it means that they usually move in the same direction. Those with a negative correlation, on the other hand, will move in opposite directions.

To use currency correlations to their advantage, traders need to understand a few important things:

a) They should avoid opening several trading positions that conflict or cancel out each other
b) They should have a good understanding of commodity currencies

c) They should avoid opening trading positions with the same quote currency or base currency

No matter how unrealistic it may sound, many people going into Forex Trading expect to get rich overnight. The world of FX trading can be complicated and overwhelming, especially for beginners who do not know the rules. Before people go any deeper, they need to dip their toes into the forex pool.

Chapter 9: Cryptocurrency in Forex Trading

A cryptocurrency is a digital currency that acts as a medium of exchange. Currencies have gone through a series of changes since the barter system in the Stone Age period, to the paper currency in later years.

The term 'crypto' in cryptocurrency comes from the word 'cryptography.' Cryptography is a technique of using encryption and decryption as a means to safeguard communication in the company of third parties with ill motives. In order to work, cryptography requires a computational algorithm, a public key that the trader shares with everybody, and a private key, which acts like the trader's digital signature, which the trader keeps secret.

In Forex Trading, forex traders use cryptocurrencies as modes of payments and as trading instruments, forming currency pairs with other cryptocurrencies and currencies.

At this point, the future of currency could be cryptocurrencies. There are two major cryptocurrencies in the market: the bitcoin and ether. The bitcoin is a type of digital currency that is independent of a central authority. That is, the central bank does not regulate the distribution of bitcoins in the market. Instead, bitcoin uses a blockchain to carry out transactions on a peer-to-peer network.

Bitcoins started circulating in 2009, and its success has generated several competing cryptocurrencies called 'altcoins' or alternative coins. Altcoins include Litecoin (LTC), Namecoin, Peercoin (PPCoin), Ripple, EOS, and Cardano, among thousands of other cryptocurrencies currently in existence.

Ether is a type of currency that the Ethereum network acknowledges. Ethereum runs on blockchain technology to establish an open-source platform to create and redistribute applications that are decentralized, or independent of central authority.

Bitcoin and ether are the most significant and most valuable cryptocurrencies in the international market. While bitcoins transactions are manual, ether transactions can be both manual and automatic. A trader can use bitcoins for transactions involving goods and services, whereas ether uses blockchain to create ledgers that activate operations once a trader meets the required conditions.

Litecoin is similar to bitcoin in that Litecoin relies on an open-source global payment network that is not under any central authority's regulation. However, Litecoin has a more rapid block generation rate compared to bitcoin, since Litecoin uses a different algorithm.

Namecoin is more of an experimental open-source technology that boosts security, independence from a central regulating authority, censorship resistance, speed of internet infrastructure such as the Domain Name System (DNS), and privacy. Traders can use Namecoin to record and transfer random keys or names in a safeguarded manner. It also has the ability to attach data to the random names. In that regard, Namecoin offers advanced privacy competences.

Peercoin (PPCoin) is one of the leading forms of cryptocurrencies with regard to market capitalization. It is the first digital currency that employs a combination of proof-of-work and proof-of-stake. The proof-of-stake algorithm formulates from the coins that individual traders hold. A trader holding 2% of the currency should receive a reward of 2% of all proof-of-stake coin blocks.

The proof-of-work blocks are less rewarding because the portion of the proof-of-work algorithm requires intensive energy for generating blocks compared to the minimal energy the proof-of-stake algorithm uses to create blocks. Consequently, the Peercoin network will become more energy-efficient as proof-of-stake rewards do not need a lot of processing power.

Ripple is both a cryptocurrency and a payment system. With regard to Ripple's cryptocurrency aspect, it follows an algorithm like every other cryptocurrency. Ripple's payment system makes it possible for users to transfer money in any currency to another user on the Ripple network in a matter of seconds. That means that Ripple transactions are much faster than other crypto coins, including bitcoin.

EOS is a robust infrastructure for decentralized applications that is blockchain-based and facilitates the development hosting and performance of economic-scale decentralized applications (dApps) on its platform. EOS uses the proof-of-stake idea to make instant high-level decisions among designated stakeholders.

Cardano is both a cryptocurrency and a decentralized platform that authorizes transactions without high-energy costs. Cardano seeks to safeguard the privacy of traders while being regulator-friendly. The platform uses the Ouroboros Pos algorithm to authenticate transactions.

Why use cryptocurrencies?

Little to No Operation Costs: When traders use traditional ways of carrying out transactions using paper currencies, they lose some amount of money when transferring currencies to or from bank accounts.

Cryptocurrencies have the lowest transaction fees, which amount to only about $2. An individual may encounter only three transaction fees. The charges include the exchange fees, the network fees, and the digital wallet fees when a person wants to store his or her crypto coins in the digital wallet.

24/7 Access to Money: Unlike using banks, individuals can access cryptocurrencies anytime, any day. Given that cryptocurrencies are not subject to any central authority, an individual can have access to the crypto coins any time of the day, even in the middle of the night.

Similarly, an individual can make unlimited purchases and withdrawals. That is contrary to using bank services where the bank places limits on the amount of money an individual can spend within 24-hours.

Available for Anyone: Billions of people around the world do not have access to bank accounts. However, many people have access to mobile phones and can use cryptocurrencies and blockchain technology to execute financial transactions through biometric, thus promoting prosperity.

Additionally, the process of signing up to use cryptocurrencies is brief and requires no paperwork.

Fast International Transactions: Unlike in banks, where transferring money from one place to another can take hours, transferring cryptocurrencies is a matter of seconds. That is because when moving cryptocurrency from one place to another, transactions do not need to go through all of the same checks and balances processes that banks follow before depositing funds.

Cryptocurrency transfers, whether within a country or outside the country, are quick and instant and do not require any transaction costs. Additionally, individuals can track their transactions in the blockchain.

High Privacy Levels: With cryptocurrencies, an individual does not have to provide personal information. That is contrary to banks, where individuals have to provide extensive personal data.

Moreover, individuals can carry out safe transactions because of the encryptions that go into the code of cryptocurrencies. Therefore, traders can have confidence in the cryptocurrencies security guarantee as more people use the specific blockchain.

People Have Control Over Their Own Money: Cryptocurrencies are not subject to the rules and regulations that the banks and other financial institutions enforce. If an individual remembers the password or the passphrase of his or her digital wallet, the cryptocurrencies are entirely under the control of the individual, and no one else can have access to the crypto coins.

Cryptocurrencies allow individuals to carry out trade with other people independently, without the presence of a third party or bank interference. That is because transactions with cryptocurrencies are peer-to-peer, meaning from people to people.

Reliable Alternative to Unstable Currencies: Cryptocurrencies does not bring about inflation and economic instability that individuals often experience from using traditional paper currencies. While not all individuals are subject to the incredible rates of inflation, other individuals can benefit greatly from shifting to use cryptocurrencies.

Many countries around the world allow the use of cryptocurrency, which is not affected by forex rates and interest rates. In fact, cryptocurrency offers more solidity and assurance to people living in economically unstable countries.

Accountability of Individuals and Companies: Regrettably, there are several business entities and big industries out in the business world, which allow corrupt and illegal business tendencies. Individuals want to ensure that they carry out their trades with honesty and integrity, upholding the trading rights and following the rules of conduct. However, trusting that a company or an individual has integrity based on the information they provide about themselves is not a reliable way to know the morals of their real practices.

Luckily, cryptocurrency introduces the blockchain technology that will change the way individuals and companies practice a trade — blockchain technology, which is not subject to change, unlike the traditional paper currency. Cryptocurrencies and blockchain technologies make companies and individuals answerable to clients. Moreover, traders get the opportunity to know more about the companies they trade with.

Strengthen E-Commerce: Given that many people like to carry out most of their transactions online nowadays, cryptocurrencies provide a safe option for shoppers to buy as many things as they would want, without concerns for fraud.

Cryptocurrencies not only reduce the risk of fraud for online shoppers, but they also protect the business vendors and merchandisers. Cryptocurrency transactions are permanent. That is because the cryptocurrency's electronic network ledger records the transactions. As a result, the transactions become irreversible and unchangeable, thus mitigating risk.

Additionally, using cryptocurrency creates endless opportunities for global commerce.

Secure Handling of Smart Contracts: Blockchain technology enables individuals to computerize practically every physical object or service in the blockchain. For example, when selling property, an individual can enter the value of the property into the blockchain and sell the property through automatic or smart contracts.

Consequently, banks, notaries, and financial advisors will no longer be necessary because individuals are able to carry out trades in faster and inexpensive ways. Additionally, an individual can securely manage his or her personal information in the blockchain and use it for taking loans, insurances, or even purchasing travel tickets.

Governments can also use automatic or smart contracts when giving out permits, when holding elections, and when collecting taxes, among other government tasks. Blockchain technology will also ensure transparency in government operations.

What are the disadvantages of using cryptocurrencies?

To begin with, cryptocurrency is a concept that is difficult to understand. People who are not tech-savvy may not understand how the blockchains work, or how blockchains store cryptocurrencies. In that regard, individuals are cautious of taking advantage of the benefits that cryptocurrency can offer.

As such, most people do not know the benefits of using cryptocurrency. However, it appears that, that more and more people are acquiring information about the digital currency. The response, therefore, is slow because people are not yet ready to make the switch from using banks to using cryptocurrency.

As more individuals enter into the cryptocurrency domain by acquiring their crypto every day, there is still a long way to go and a lot of work to do with regard to the teaching people how cryptocurrencies work. Consequently, a cryptocurrency needs to circulate the money market more, so that people can have exposure to it and they can begin to accept to use it

The other significant drawback that cryptocurrencies have is the challenge of constant fluctuations in their market prices. As a result, traders find it challenging to use the crypto because traders can never be entirely sure what the value of the crypto will be in the upcoming days.

Additionally, most traders do not accept digital money. That is because the concept of digital money is still new, and many traders do not trust digital money yet. What's more, many companies have not embraced the use of digital funds, even though cryptocurrency is a growing trend. The reason for that could be that companies are not willing to take a risk with the constantly changing prices. In addition, companies may not be aware of how cryptocurrency can generate profits.

Lastly, most people may not know where to get cryptocurrencies, how to store, and how to use the cryptos. Although people can search for information on cryptos online, the idea is that no person, young and old, should have any challenges when it comes to dealing with cryptocurrencies. Instead, the trade should become an organic or natural part of people's lives, the same way that paper currency is.

In conclusion, the rate at which the world is becoming technologically interconnected calls for a complete transformation in the process of buying and selling products and services. Cryptocurrencies are one of the ground-breaking innovations in the context of technological interconnectedness that will revolutionize global forex trade.

Consequently, more traders will accept cryptocurrencies, and more people will switch to using cryptos. In that way, cryptocurrencies have a huge potential to become the most widely used medium of exchange in the future.

Chapter 10: Examples of Trade

Forex trade involves a trader going long for the first currency and short for the second one. He or she purchases the first currency using money and then waits before selling it to make a profit. The trade takes place utilizing the current rates of exchange at the time of the transaction. Thus, the fluctuations in the exchange rates determine if the value of a particular currency is high or low. It helps a trader decide when to enter or exit a trade, or when to buy or sell a currency.

For example, a trader followed the prevailing GBP/USD exchange rates and paid USD 24,200 to purchase GBP 20,000 in mid-January 2017. The value of the British pound increased over the following months against the dollar. The trader then decided to sell the £20,000 that he has for approximately $27,000. He or she closed out his or her position and received USD 27,000. Thus, he or she made a profit of USD 2,800 because initially, he or she started with USD 24,200 and closed out with USD 27,000.

A trader can utilize various strategies and means to ensure that he or she achieves success in Forex Trading. He or she can use trading instruments such as disposable risks, leveraged features, spread bets, and CDF contracts. A CDF contract is a deal between two sides to trade the difference between the closing price and opening price of a contract. It stands for 'Contract for difference' and is a complicated, advanced, and high-risk instrument as a trader can experience a rapid loss due to leveraged features.

The following are some examples of forex trade and the outcomes that indicate a winning or losing trade:

Example 1

A trader can calculate his or her profits and losses when he or she closes out a forex trade. He or she finds the difference between the price of buying and selling the currency and multiplies it by the transaction size. The difference will determine whether he or she experiences a winning or a losing trade. For instance, a trader purchases Euros (EUR/USD) at 1.2166 and later sells them at 1.2156. The transaction size of that trade is 100,000 Euros. He or she will calculate the profit using the formula: ($1.2166 - $1.2156) × 100,000. This will lead to $0.001 × 100,000 = $100. Hence, his or her profit from that forex trade will be $100.

Likewise, the forex trader will calculate a loss if he or she sold the Euros (EUR/USD) at 1.2060 and buy them at 1.2070. He or she will use the formula ($1.2060 - $1.2070) × 100,000. This will give

-$0.001 × 100,000 = -$100. Thus, he or she will have a loss of $100 from that trade.

Moreover, the trader can use the current bid to find out his or her unrealized losses and profits on open positions. He or she substitutes that bid accordingly in the formula to calculate the unrealized profit or loss. For example, if he or she purchased Euros at 1.2166, and the current rate of a bid is 1.2116, then his or her unrealized loss is $50. The calculation is ($1.2161 - $1.2166) × 100,000= -$0.0005 × 100,000 = $50. If he or she sold the Euros at 1.2060 and the current bid rate is 1.2055, the unrealized profit here is $50: ($1.2060 - $1.2055) × 100,000= $0.0005 × 100,000= $50.

The trader subtracts any extra charges in the transactions like commissions, to find out his or her exact profits and losses.

Example 2

A trader can transact in the forex market in terms of the amount of money he or she is willing to risk. He or she takes a certain amount from his or her investments fund account and uses it to trade. He or she can win and double the initial risked amount or not succeed and end up losing the money. For instance, a trader has $10,000 in his or her account as the money available as a disposable risk. During an investment, he or she decides to use $2,000 and ventures that amount in the forex trade.

The trader researches and finds out that the chances of achieving a profit goal of interest are 70%. He or she can then choose to invest that amount in the trade in two ways. First, he or she can risk the entire $2,000 and form a profit goal of $2,000 while going long at the opening. Additionally, he or she can also set a stop loss of $2,000 in the trade. If the deal succeeds, he or she wins an additional $2,000 in profits. Nonetheless, he or she may also lose the business, and the entire invested amount since the risk of failing, in this case, is at 30%.

The second way that the trader can invest the money is to split it and risk only $200 per trade. He or she also modifies the profit goal to $200. Thus, he or she can make ten trades and significantly reduce the chances of losing the entire $2,000 since the risk associated here is less than 1%.

Example 3

A forex trader can also use a leveraged instrument to trade, which provides him or her with a trading margin. He or she makes a profit if the trade moves in his or her direction margin. Conversely, he or she loses the deal if it pushes against the trader. For instance, a trader with an investment amount of $6,000 trades on a margin of 1:50. This margin means that he or she can practically manage a capital of $300,000.

A beginning trader utilizes a smaller margin of 1:20 to minimize the risks associated with contrasting trade moves that can result in a 100% loss of capital. Thus, he or she uses a margin of 1:20 with the initial money of $6,000, which enables him or her to control $120,000. He or she decides to bet that the USD will fall against the Euro and then enters a trade on a long side to transact the EUR/USD. The current exchange rate of the EUR/USD is 1.405, while he or she will practically be trading $120,000 to Euros. He or she calculates it by the 120,000/1.405 = 71,174 Euros.

Forex Trading involves several strategies that a trader can employ in the market. He or she can study the various ways of Forex Trading and select the ones that best suit his or her profit goal and trading tactics.

Chapter 11: Mistake That Beginners Make in Forex Trading

All traders have passed through the beginners' phase, and they have made their share of newbie mistakes. Most traders continue to make mistakes as they venture deep into trading, but smart ones view these mistakes as learning opportunities rather than sulk over then. People can be very emotional where their money is concerned, but it is important for traders to detach themselves from this mindset so that they can make rational decisions.

The occasional lapse is forgivable, but at the end of it all, the trader's money is at stake, so he or she should work hard to protect it and grow it. If you are new to trading, you can learn from those who have gone ahead of you and avoid some of the common mistakes that they have made which include:

1. Trading Without Much Knowledge

The first mistake that people make when they decide to try Forex Trading is getting into the forex market without proper knowledge of how to maneuver and make money. Forex Trading is something that takes years to master. In addition to trading knowledge, experts in trading have vast experience in trading. Although newbies might have the former and not the latter, they can still succeed in trading but with proper planning and guidance.

Investing in the forex market is similar to investing in a business. People hardly invest in sectors or businesses that they have little knowledge. They usually take their time to study how to conduct business in a particular area. People interested in Forex Trading should also treat trading as a business that they are interested in investing in. They should not forget that they need to protect their capital just as they would if they were putting it in a business venture by stocking up on information.

New traders can gather information from trading books, articles, and any other material available that touches on the subject. There are also people who offer classes in the form of webinars and seminars. Beginners can also practice with demo accounts. Successful traders are well informed; they know the markets they operate in as well as indicators and strategies for investing in the stock market.

2. Trading Without a Plan

Trading plans are very crucial in investing in the financial markets. They offer a trader with a guideline of how they will invest their money in the forex market. More specifically, they detail the amount of money a trader is willing to put in a trade, the market conditions that are favorable for a person to trade, the duration of stay in the market and the exact time to get out of the market either after experiencing a loss or even after making a profit. Without such guidelines, traders conduct their business blindly with no focus.

Many new beginners in Forex Trading are guilty of this mistake. They enter the forex market without any plan and wonder why they keep failing in the trade. New beginners can formulate trading plans then test them in a demo account. They can keep adjusting their plans as they see fit until they are ready to test in the real market.

Once a trader begins to use his plan, he should ensure that he follows it. This way, he is able to remain rational when trading and keep his emotions at bay. The stop loss and stop profit serve to guide the trader on when to exit the market to avoid losing money and when a trade has been exhausted. More importantly, as traders write down their plans, they should focus on the right goals. If chasing after huge profits are all a trader wants, then he or she is bound to get disappointed. Setting realistic goals is crucial, even if it means making a little consistent profit.

3. Lack of Money Management

New traders are at free will to decide how much they are willing to invest in a trade. However, a number of beginners overleverage their capital. They put money that they cannot afford to lose in a single trade and risk a huge percentage of their portfolio or investment in the trade. Since making profits is never guaranteed, there is always the risk of losing money or the entire investment if one is not careful about how they manage their money.

New traders should calculate how much money they are willing to risk in a single trade according to their risk appetite. They should not make some decisions on a whim. The best way is to have a guideline from the beginning, in the form of a trading plan. A trader should know how many trades he or she should enter at any one single time. Without understanding, his or her risk/reward ratio, or win/loss ratio, a trader can end up investing his or her capital in the wrong way and lose the entire investment.

Therefore, it is crucial that traders and especially the new ones to learn a few money management skills before they join the market; otherwise, they may not survive in trading.

4. Overtrading

Some new traders are very fond of overtrading. This can mean that they either trade with money that they do not have or risk a big portion of their investment in a single trade. Insufficient capitalization is dangerous and is ill-advised. Traders should only trade with money that they have and not money that does not exist or money they have borrowed.

It is always devastating for a trader to lose money that they did not have. This often leads to them borrowing money elsewhere to compensate for their loss, or they have to struggle to get back above the margins. Even when a trader begins to make money, they should have a guideline of how much of their profit they should reinvest back in the market and how much of their capital they should put back.

Another mistake new beginner is fond of making is trading when the markets are not favorable as stipulated in their trading plan. When traders deviate from their plans and get into markets that they should not, then it means that they are overtrading. New traders should not assume that their strategies are faulty when the markets do not favor even if it is for a long while. Instead of getting into shaky water, new traders should always choose to save their money over spending it then losing some of it.

5. Trading Without a Stop Loss

A stop loss is very important as it acts as a warning sign to a trader and tells him or her when to stop trading because of the risk of losing further amounts with an investment. Due to possibly a lack of experience, some beginners never know when to cut their losses and move on to the next trade. When they start losing money, they always think that they can recover their money, so they continue trading despite their margins running out.

Other traders may have stop losses, but they do not have the discipline to stick to them. This group is no different from the one without a stop loss. Another set of traders may be tempted to move their stop loss in the negatives or readjust it to accommodate more losses when they trade, but this is also ill-advised. Traders should always move stop losses upwards and in the direction of a win rather than down and to an even larger loss position.

6. Ignoring News and Market Trends

New traders should also stick to their plans when they venture or approach trading markets. However, their plans should be flexible to accommodate market conditions as well as any news or events that might affect the movement of the market. For example, a trader might spot a good USD to EUR exchange. However, something might happen in Europe that might blow up the deal without the trader's knowledge. Without this information, from let us say the balance trade report from Europe, a trader cannot make an informed decision. Traders are supposed to make event calendars as they catch up with their daily news, this way, they are able to monitor and keep in mind what could affect their future trading decisions as well as any curveballs that they might encounter. Various tools can assist traders to check on prevailing ranges and trends. Understanding the history of a certain market can also help a trader know what the future market might look like.

7. Trading with Emotions

Trading with emotions or gut feelings is very common with all traders, not just new ones. Rather than use hunches, traders should study markets and read the statistics in order to make rational decisions. When the market seems to be favorable, it is very easy for a trader to put in more money or stay for a bit longer.

This is risky because trading markets can sometimes be volatile; they can change in an instant or overnight, leaving a trader in regret. It is important for beginners to stick to their trading plan. They should know when to collect their profit bags and leave. Similarly, when a new trader encounters a loss, they also take a break from the market but not a long one. Refraining from trading or sulking over previous losses is emotional trading. Even expert traders make losses and mistakes, but they always choose to pick up the pieces and move on to another trader rather than seat down and sulk.

If a trader is also too cautious, they can miss great deals that are within their trading plans. This fear can also make a trader deviate from his or her plan and try out trades that are not within the plan. This decision has the potential to lead to even further losses. In most cases, a good trading plan can recover losses. If this does not happen, then the trader can pull away from the forex market, assess their plan, or look for the problem in their plan, then adjust accordingly and get back into the game.

8. Adding to a Losing Trade

Sometimes beginners in trading are tempted to continue adding to an unprofitable trade, but eventually, even they can attest that this is a wrong move. No matter how sure a trader is about the next move in the market, multiplying losses is never a good idea. In most cases, it leaves the trader in a deeper loss position. Most traders in this situation are also incapable of making unbiased decisions that are within their trading plans. It is always better for the trader to close with a negative position than to increase their loss. It is okay to step back and regroup. The trader can also try another trade or wait for the market to be favorable again.

As earlier deduced, it is never a good idea to move the stop loss in an effort to avoid closing at a loss. New traders must learn the discipline of sticking to their plans and observing any guidelines that they had set before entering the market. Traders should also refrain from revenging on the market. Revenge trades can even make a trader double or triple the current loss that they have.

9. Choosing the Wrong Broker

The first and probably the most critical decision for a new trader is choosing a good broker. Giving money to another person is the first and biggest gamble that a trader will ever make. Whichever company the trader decides to give his or her trading capital should be legit. There have been incidents of people giving away their money to scammers.

A good broker should allow a trader to trade freely with his or her money and withdraw it whenever he or she wishes to do so. The first step in choosing the right broker is to look for one that matches your needs. If you have a small amount of capital, you should look at brokers who allow trading in micro-lots. The broker should also be regulated in the country they operate in and have a stable financial system.

It is important to carry a background check on the broker by researching on reviews about the broker. A trader should also check whether a broker allows them to deal directly with the market, or they normally redirect them to a dealing desk. He should also look at the willingness of the broker to address his concerns. Once the trader is okay with the above, he can open a demo account to test whether the broker offers what they say they offer. Smart traders do not deposit their entire trading capital with a broker; instead, they test the water first to assess the broker's availability, support, and accessibility to their money. If a broker proves worthy, a trader can go ahead and deposit the rest of his money.

Chapter 12: How to Make Money with Forex Trading to Create Passive Income

According to experts in the field of Forex Trading, it is possible to create a passive income through this form of financial trading. However, before jumping headlong into this type of financial trading, prospective traders need to ask themselves whether it is suitable for them, in addition to learning as much as possible about this line of business.

A passive income is the income stream traders or investors get at regular intervals and require little or no effort on their part to maintain it. Some of the common types of passive income include dividends from stock owned in a listed corporation, rental income, and interest income from bonds.

Other less common forms of passive income include royalties from a music record or publishing a book, or dividends from a non-listed company run by a family member or friend. Passive income may also arise from a new business model or income from a multi-level marketing network, where the income originates from other people's activities.

Some internet marketers, such as affiliate marketers, also receive passive income from internet traffic that continues to stream in from blogs they posted a long time ago. Nowadays, traders can make a passive income through the forex market.

In fact, one does not have to participate directly in the trading process or have tons of experience in this field of business. Forex traders can earn a passive income from this form of financial trading in several ways, with some requiring more work or input from the trader. Some of these include:

Forex Signals

These are short messages new traders can use to determine the best currency to trade and the right time to trade. Traders can receive important trading information through email, text messages, or any other type of communication, including social media platforms such as TX forums, Twitter, and other leading financial trading platforms.

These signals or messages are usually brief snippets of information, which instruct users to take specific actions, such as purchasing EUR/USD at a certain price. Sometimes, these signals feature various types of orders, such as a market order, pending order, or limit order. There are tons of sites that teach traders how to read and understand forex signals.

These signals can also be premium or free, with the former leading to better trades. Many providers of forex signals freely send important trading information to investors to boost their reputation in the financial trading industry. Forex signals are also great for people who want to earn a passive income trading options but do not have the time or opportunity to learn much about Forex Trading.

However, it is important to perform adequate research into providers of forex signals to avoid losing money. Forex traders, however, should approach these signals with utmost caution to make a good passive income.

Forex Robots

One of the best ways to make a passive income from the forex market is using a tool known as a forex robot, which performs automated trades on a trader's behalf. Once traders set up these forex robots, they do not have to do much else; however, they should keep an eye on the trades the forex robots are making for them.

To get started, traders need to perform adequate research into the software available for forex robots. They need to choose software that will meet their needs, in addition to being reliable when it comes to executing the right forex trades. After setting up this software, it will make forex trades based on preset signals.

In addition, it will use its acquired knowledge to purchase or sell at specific times, earning users a passive income in the process. However, it is important to understand that not all forex robots make passive income for investors as claimed. In the same way that a human can make a losing trade, a forex robot can also make the same mistake.

It is also important to understand that many so-called forex robots are frauds, which is why respected news platforms such as the Wall Street Journal and Forbes refuse to promote or advertise them. Unfortunately, this is particularly true when it comes to free forex robots. Therefore, new forex traders should analyze testimonials and reviews carefully before entrusting their investment to a forex robot.

Fortunately, several leading sites focus on reviewing different trading platforms. These sites try to give an honest opinion of different investment platforms and outline all the benefits and limitations of each platform. They also offer a detailed analysis of how these platforms work and how traders can get started on them, which is especially helpful to new traders.

Social Trading

The social trading network works in the same way as a social networking platform. Instead of sharing selfies or pictures of pets playing the piano, however, social traders share important information about forex or financial trades. This allows others to copy them and make passive income as well.

New forex traders simply need experienced traders they trust and copy their trading strategies to make money. In addition to making a passive income, they will also learn when, why, and how successful traders make their trading moves, which will give them more insight and understanding into the forex industry.

However, finding traders, they can trust and emulate is not as easy as it may sound. New traders need to set aside adequate time to perform thorough research into different social trading platforms, in addition to learning more about forex traders they want to work with and copy.

In certain situations, they might need to spend some money on the trader whose trading strategies they copy. However, this commission is negligible and not a big concern for new traders who want to make a passive income. Forex Trading is something that most people looking for ways to make some extra cash look into.

However, most of them do not know where to start. This discussion provides three great ideas for Forex Trading beginners to consider. Each of the options above requires a different investment in terms of time and effort. The most important thing to remember is that beginners should perform adequate research before picking a trading platform or strategy to use.

Nowadays, Forex Trading is one of the best ways for people to make a passive income working online. Millions of traders are earning a passive or active income every day through Forex Trading. This line of business is just like any other online money-making concept, but its profit potential is unrivaled. With modern technological advances and the availability of detailed information, anyone can make a passive income through Forex Trading.

Conclusion

Thank you for making it through to the end of *Forex Trading for Beginners: Simple Strategies to Make Money with Forex Trading: The Best Guide with Basics, Secrets Tactics, and Psychology to Big Profit and Income from the Financial Market.* Let us hope it was informative and able to provide you with all of the tools you need to achieve your goals, whatever they may be.

Now you know that the word 'forex' is short for 'foreign exchange,' and it involves converting one currency into another for reasons including tourism, trading, and business. The foreign exchange market is a global forum for exchanging substantial national currencies against each other.

The foreign exchange market is open to all types of traders, and it is more accessible than any other online trading platform in the world. An individual can start trading with as little as $100. Therefore, foreign exchange markets have lower exchange capital prerequisites compared to other financial markets.

Forex Trading happens over the interbank market, which is a channel through which currency trading happens 5 days a week, 24 hours a day. It is one of the biggest trading markets in the world, with a worldwide daily turnover estimated to be more than $5 trillion.

If the currency pair of EUR/USD, which refers to Euro/US Dollar, was trading at 1.0914/1.0916, for example, investors planning to open a long position on the Euro would purchase one Euro for 1.0916 US dollars. They will then hold on to the currency and hope that its value will increase, and then sell it back to the market once it appreciates. On the other hand, investors looking to open a short position on the Euro will sell one Euro for 1.0914 US dollars, with the expectation that its value will depreciate. If their expectations come true, they will buy it back at the lower rate and make a profit.

Brokers are the intermediaries who link investors with their capital. Some traders may choose to invest in the forex trade, and therefore they will invariably become in need of a foreign exchange broker.

The account balance is the amount of equity or capital available in your brokerage account due to investment in the currency market. It is essential to have such an account to enable the foreign exchange broker to carry out the buying and selling executions on your behalf.

A Forex Trading platform is a standard provision from most forex brokers to their clients, investors, or other retail traders. It also acts as a source of commission for the forex brokers by charging an access fee to use it. After seeking a foreign exchange broker, most traders will get a couple of trading platform recommendations from these same brokers.

Forex Trading signals are guidelines and recommendations that help inexperienced forex traders to open Forex Trading positions. The signals are a type of system that forex traders use to make crucial decisions about their trade. In that regard, Forex Trading signals provide details about how to open a new Forex Trade.

To the uninitiated, navigating the forex market successfully can seem like a difficult task. However, success is possible if one takes the right steps and trains properly. Just like training for a marathon, training is essential to winning in Forex Trading. Success requires targeted effort, practice, patience, and time.

Your next step should be to get a Forex Trading account, implement the strategies within the pages of this book, and start smiling all the way to the bank.

Finally, if you found this book useful in any way, a review is always appreciated!

Options Trading Crash Course

The Beginner's Guide to Make Money with Options Trading: Best Strategies for Make a Living from Passive Income and Quick Start to Your Financial Freedom

William Rogers and George Evans

Table of Contents

Gamma

Vega

Rho

Minor Greeks

What is Swing Trading?

Support and Resistance

Trade with the Trend

Swing Trading Options

Going Long on a Stock

Shorting Stock Using Put options

Tools to Spot Trend Reversals

Chart Patterns That Indicate Trend Reversals

Candlestick Charts

Moving Averages

Relative Strength Indicator

Bollinger Bands

Removing Direction from the Trade

Central Goal of the Iron Condor

Iron Condors are Income Strategies

The Lower Legs

The Other Legs

The Complete Iron Condor as a Single Trade

The Iron Condor Relies on Time Decay

The Iron Butterfly

Introduction

Congratulations on purchasing the *Options Trading Crash Course,* and thank you for doing so.

The concept of options trading strikes most investors as obscure and even dangerous and risky. However, as we are going to learn in these pages, investing and trading in options is actually a smart and effective way to make money and build wealth. We'll begin the book by explaining what options are and how they work. There are different types of options and multiple strategies used to trade options, and we'll learn about the most popular that are available. You'll learn how to go about trading options and how to work with your broker.

The goal of this book is to demystify options trading. When you learn what they are and why they exist, the shroud of mystery that surrounds these supposedly exotic financial instruments will vanish. You'll find out that options trading, when done with care, is actually a straightforward way to engage with the financial markets. By the end of this book, you'll be able to clearly define a call and a put, an iron condor, a spread, and even the so-called "Greeks".

We'll also learn about the psychology and mindset that are necessary for successful options trading. You'll come to understand how options trading differs from stock trading and investment, both in mindset and goals and techniques. You'll also learn about the most serious mistakes that beginners make when trading options and how to avoid them. You'll also learn how to use options in order to generate regular income.

Until recently, options trading has only been available to financial insiders. The development of technology associated with the markets has changed all that, and now anyone can trade options, and you only need a few hundred dollars to get started. With all the user-friendly trading platforms that are now available through the internet and on mobile, the only obstacle is that most investors don't understand options. This book will help to remove that obstacle so that you can join those earning profits and income from options trading.

So, thank you for choosing this book. There are a number of various titles on this topic out there. So, your choice of this book is certainly motivating. We hope that you will get the most out of this book as great care has been taken in making sure that it is both useful and informative.

Chapter 1: An Introduction to Options Trading

The first step to consider when engaging in options trading is to have a clear and accurate understanding of what an option actually is. Unfortunately, one of the things that is lacking in our society is a good financial education. Most people barely understand what the stock market is and how it operates, and options are a level above even that. In this chapter, we are going to lay a foundation for the rest of the book by helping you to understand what options are, why they exist, and what the different types and characteristics of options are. Then we will go into detail in the rest of the book so that you'll learn everything you need to learn in order to actually be able to trade options with success. Remember that all forms of investing and trading carry financial risk, and not everyone who invests or trades on the markets is going to succeed.

What Is an Option?

Options are not restricted to the stock market. The name option gives us a clue as to what these financial instruments are, however. An options contract is one which enables the buyer to have the *option* to do something. Options contracts can exist in any context where you are interested in buying something. The proverbial example that is used is the option to buy a new home.

Let's say that Jane is moving to her new job in Houston, Texas. She is interested in buying a new home in a good neighborhood that is reasonably close to her job. She has two kids, so she's also interested in buying a home in an area with a low crime rate and good schools.

She finds out that there is a new housing development near her job. She also finds out that it will take about 4 months to have a home ready for her to move in. Because of the high demand in the area, home prices are changing rapidly. She'd like to lock in a price for a home but wants to look around in the meantime. How can she do that? The answer is she can enter into an options contract with the developer.

The type of homes that Jane is interested in are currently going for $350,000. Jane tells the developer she is willing to buy a house at this price, but she needs 120 days to decide. The developer knows that prices are rapidly increasing, but to make a deal. He offers the possibility for Jane to lock in a lot and home for $360,000. She must buy the home on or before the date the contract expires 120 days from the date, she signs it. If she fails to close by that time, the contract expires, and the developer is free to sell the lot to someone else at market prices.

Jane is not taking too much risk because she is not forced to buy the home; she has the option. If prices end up dropping, she can simply let the option contract expire. If prices stay about the same or keep rising, and she doesn't find another home she is interested in, Jane can go ahead and exercise her rights under the contract and buy the house for $360,000. This is true even if the price of new homes in the area has jumped to $400,000 at the time the contract expires. So, by locking in a price, Jane may have put herself in a position where she could save a significant amount of money yet get the home (investment) that she wanted.

While laws may vary based upon the given specific contract type, though generally speaking, the contracts themselves can be bought and sold. The contract itself becomes valuable because of the *underlying* asset (in this case, the home), and the ability to buy that asset at the fixed price. In an environment of rising prices, this can provide a big advantage to buyers. In many cases, the buyers won't go through with the contract. Actually, executing the contract is called *exercising* the contract. Of course, if home prices in the area were to rise to $400,000, it would be worth it to exercise this options contract.

Jane may not want to do so. Maybe she found a different home more to her liking. However, since the contract has obvious value, she could sell it to someone else. Ever since financial instruments were invented, secondary markets were created soon afterward, where people traded them. Options are no exception.

Since an option derives its value from an underlying asset that is not directly traded or even owned by the person who buys the option, it is called a *derivative*. The media often talks about derivatives as if they are extremely exotic and complex, but it is really nothing more than that. A derivative is a financial instrument or contract that derives its value from an underlying asset.

Options on Stocks

The basic concepts of options that we described above apply to options on stocks. Since we now understand those basic concepts, let's define the specifics when it comes to options contracts on stocks. It turns out that options contracts on stocks are slightly more complicated than what we've described so far, but it's not horribly complicated if you take it step-by-step.

The first thing to note is the underlying. As far as options on stocks are concerned, its corresponding asset is 10 shares of a specific stock. That stock is a stock of a publicly-traded company on a major stock exchange. Options on stocks also include index funds. So, you can trade options on Apple, Facebook, or Boeing. You can also trade options on SPY, DIA, and QQQ, which are exchange-traded funds for the most significant stock markets such as the Dow Jones Industrial Average, the Standard & Poors 500, and NASDAQ 100, respectively.

For example, using a home purchase, we only talked about the option for someone to buy the home – we never considered having the option to sell a home. But with stocks, both concepts are equally important. The most basic concept is imagining having an option that would give you the possibility of purchasing those 10 shares of a given stock at a pre-determined sale point on or prior to the expiration date of the contract. This kind of deal is known as a *call option.*

You can see that in a market of rising prices, a call option favors the buyer. The potential buyer can lock in a price, and if they choose to do so, if the price per share actually rises by a significant amount (and by significant we mean significant enough to earn a profit if you turned around and sold the shares on the market), the buyer can buy shares at a discount.

In an environment of rising prices, since the option contract would give buyers such an advantage, that means the contract itself becomes more valuable. So, with everything else remaining equal, the price of said contact will be going up in a market of rising prices. People will be bidding up the price as more investors excitedly want to get their hands on the option.

There are going to be two types of buyers in the marketplace. Some buyers are really interested in getting a hold of the stock at a discount price. Others are simply hoping or anticipating that prices are going to continue rising, and so they anticipate that the price of the option is going to be higher in the future. In other words, they want to buy the option, and then turn around and sell it for a higher price a few days or weeks later at a higher price, so they can make a profit *from the option contract itself.*

When we are talking about anticipating making a profit from future changes in price, this is called speculating. The term speculating is associated with *trading*, which can be defined as short term purchase and sale of a financial asset with the sole intent of generating profits. It is important to keep this concept distinct from *investing*. The first difference between trading and investing in the time frame. Trading is generally done on short-term time frames of one year or less. In contrast, investing generally means five years or more. Investing is a long-term commitment to something you believe in.

Of course, investors hope that their assets are going to increase in value as well. Otherwise, they wouldn't invest. But they are in it for the long haul and are not going to be getting rid of their assets soon after they acquire them. The reasons for investing often go beyond simple profit. Investors may be passionate about the companies they invest in and the products they offer or believe that the companies they invest in represent the future of the economy. They may also take a broad view, and invest in index funds, based on the idea that the economy will grow with time.

It is crucial to have a clear understanding of the difference that lies between trading and investing, and understanding what "speculating" is, as an options trader. As we'll see later, you might have to express the fact that you understand the difference as an options trader to satisfy regulators.

Put options

Now let's turn our attention to the other major type of option on the equities market. The option we are going to be discussing is known as a "put option". This kind of contract entitles the buyer to acquire a set quantity of stock at a pre-determined sale point. That might appear to you as somewhat bizarre at first, so why would anyone want to do that? The answer is that put options are valuable to buyers in a market of declining prices. If the stock is dropping significantly below the fixed price agreed upon in the options contract, then it makes sense to either do one of the following. If you already own the shares, maybe you purchased them at a much higher price, and you want to limit your losses. In that case, a put option allows you to cut your losses at a given price point that may be significantly above the market valuation. You don't have to worry if the market price keeps dropping, you can sell your shares at a price agreed to in the contract at any time before it expires. So, in this case, a put option can be a form of insurance for a buyer that has invested in a lot of shares.

It's also possible for speculators to profit. The first case is where you really want to sell the stock. To do this, you wait until the stock price drops low enough so that making a move on the option would be profitable. So, you buy the 100 shares and then sell them to exercise your rights under the option. Of course, the way this would work is you would sell them to the originator of the options contract, who is obligated to honor the contract and buy the shares.

But just like call options, if prices are moving favorably, the value of put options themselves is going to be increasing. This means that if stock prices are dropping, the price of put options will be rising, all other things being equal. That provides many opportunities for traders to earn profits. You buy the put options when they are at a relatively high pricing point, and then you sell them when the stock price drops, for a profit. The buyer may be a speculator who is simply interested in trying to sell the option at a later date for a profit, or it may be someone who owns the shares and wants that insurance that we talked about earlier.

Selling Options and Options Strategies

Of course, there are all these options on the market to buy, but who sells them in the first place? Lots of people sell options. Options are not issued by the companies themselves, so in other words, Facebook does not issue options on its own stock. However, in some cases, big institutional traders might sell options. We say that the creator of an options contract *writes* the contract. Another way to put it is to say that they *sell to open*. As it turns out, not only can you buy options as an individual trader, you can sell to open options contracts as well.

This is a more advanced way to deal with options, so we will be talking about this later in the book after we've gotten a thorough understanding of trading options. Generally speaking, selling to open is an income strategy. So, people sell to open options and get paid when someone buys the option they are selling. They hope that this is the end of it (see below). Traders, on the other hand, will buy to open their positions, and then hope to make profits and trade away the option before it loses value. Trading is significantly riskier than selling options for income.

There are many strategies used when selling options. This can be used to reduced risk, but many experienced options traders sell what are called "naked" options. This is just straight up selling of options contracts to earn income. Of course, there is a risk with a naked option that you'll have to buy or sell the shares of stock. Since we are talking about 100 shares at a time (a single options contract covers 100 shares of stock), that can be a non-trivial amount of cash that you need to have on hand. It is also possible to sell options that are backed by either the full amount of cash or shares of stock that you already own. We will be talking more about this later.

Selling options can also be used in complex strategies in combination with buying options at the same time. This is done in multiple ways in order to minimize risk. These types of strategies also allow you to play different kinds of market situations. For example, many times, the stock doesn't go up or down very much. Instead, it stays trapped – often for very long periods – within a narrow range of prices. In that case, we say that the stock is "ranging". There are options strategies that allow you to earn profits when the price of a stock doesn't change very much. That may seem mysterious right now, but later in the book, you'll learn exactly how that works. An astute observer will note that this is a way to earn money that simply isn't possible investing in or trading stocks. This illustrates the explosive power that options provide.

Another strategy that can be used with options is you can sell options while limiting risks. These types of strategies are known as "spreads". Moreover, either selling naked options or trading in spreads, you can set up trades that make profit either when the stock price rises, or when it falls. This is another illustration of the power that options provide to traders, that is not available to stock traders. You might note that stock traders can "short" a stock to earn profits from market declines, however, to do that you have to be a major player with a large account. For most individual traders, shorting stock is going to be out of reach.

There are also strategies that can be used to earn profits if the stock goes up a large amount very quickly, or if it drops a large amount very quickly. So, you can make a profit no matter which way the stock moves, but there has to be a situation where there is going to be a large movement in stock price. A common time that this type of strategy is used is when there is an earnings call for a large company.

We are going to discuss all the details behind options trading strategies throughout the book so that you can become an expert in short order. You'll also learn all the meaning behind all the jargon behind these strategies that are probably floating around on the internet. For now, just be aware that there are many different ways that you can trade options as a buyer and a seller in order to earn money, and that you can do it under any condition that the market happens to be in. This type of flexibility is something that stock traders and investors, even "day traders", simply don't have access to.

Chapter 2: Options Basic Definitions

In the last chapter, we went over the basic concept of an options contract as a derivative that gets its value from some underlying financial asset. In this chapter and from now on, we will turn our attention strictly to options on stocks (and index funds trading as stocks). The purpose of this chapter is to define and explain all the basic properties of options and the basic terminology.

Strike Price

For a call option, there is a fixed price that is a part of the contract, which allows the buyer to purchase any amount of stock corresponding to a specific company at a pre-determined. The set price contained in the contract can be termed as the "strike price". The strike price of this kind of contract is one of its most important characteristics, and when you go to look for options to trade, you are going to see them listed in order by strike price. So, who do you purchase the shares from? You would buy the shares from the seller of the options contract. In the event they were not able to fulfill their end of the deal, the broker would step in and do it for them (with consequences to the seller). The strike price must be used independently of the stock's current market valuation. As such, if there is a strike price of $50, but the stock's current market valuation has risen to $350 per share, it's not relevant. The seller of the call option would still be required by law to sell you 100 shares at $50 a share.

The concept is the same for put options. In this case, the strike price of this kind of contract entitles the holder to trade a specific amount of a stock. As in the case of call options, you would be selling the shares to the originator of the put option. They would be legally bound to buy the shares of the stock whose valuation has been determined by the seller regardless of its perceived current market valuation.

Expiration Date

Next, we come to the other crucial piece of information, which is the date of the expiration date of the contract itself. Generally speaking, the most common way in which options can be traded are listed is first by expiration date. When you select a given expiration date, you will then see options listed by strike price. On some platforms, options are all listed on the same page but grouped according to type. So, you will see all the call options listed at the top, and then this will be followed by the put options. In other cases, you will see a tab that lets you move back and forth between call and put options for the same expiration date.

As we will see, the expiration date is very important for many reasons. As this critical deadline approaches, if the contract does not have an appropriate valuation with regard to stock's current market valuation, it's going to be rapidly losing value. Let's get some insight into this with this sample situation. Let's assume that you are looking to purchase a contract for a call option that has a current strike valuation of $10. With this trade, you are looking to make a profit when its price increases. As such, the option has the greatest value when its current market valuation exceeds $10. Consequently, you profit more, the higher the price gets. Now, let's assume that its current market valuation falls to $7 instead. Then that call option simply isn't worth anything. People can just buy shares for $7, so why would anyone enter into a contract that required them to buy shares at $10 a share? Of course, they wouldn't do that. The longer you have remaining on the deal, the greater the value it has. If there are three months left on the contract, then it might still have a little value, because there would be a chance that the stock could move significantly in that time frame. But, if there are only three days left on the contract, the chances of the stock increasing from $7 to above $10 are pretty much nil (unless an earnings call is coming up and it turns out to be unexpectedly rosy), so the option will be rapidly losing value.

The expiration date is also important because when an option expires, it may be in a position where it can be exercised. Of course, there are as many approaches to this situation as there are unique individuals. Some people are small traders and simply don't want to buy or sell stock, and they may not have the capital to do so even if they wanted to. Remember, we are talking about 100 shares for each options contract.

On the other hand, others may be looking to buy and sell the shares. So, they may want to exercise the option when it expires, or even beforehand. If you are not able to buy and sell shares, you'll probably want to get out of the option before it expires to avoid this situation. In other words, you'll want to get whatever profits you can from selling the option. So, you want to sell it prior to the expiration date.

The expiration date is closely associated with a concept called time decay (and time value), so let's go ahead and discuss that.

Time Decay

Time decay is an important factor to consider when trading options. For buyers, time decay works against them. For options sellers (that is people who sell to open options contracts), time decay works in their favor.

Earlier, we touched on the basic idea of time decay. When there is a long time until the option expires, there is a higher probability that the price of the option can move in one direction or the other. That means that the market price of the shares can move in such a way as to make the option profitable. On the other hand, as time passes, that probability that this is going to happen decreases. In fact, each day, that probability drops. This is known as time decay.

Time decay actually refers to a drop in the price of the option on the options market. Options pricing is complicated and described by mathematical formulas, and a part of that is value that comes from the time remaining until the option expires. This value is called time value, and time value translates into real dollars and cents. Again, as we will see, there are several elements that influence the valuation of an options contract, so it might so happen that an option is gaining overall value even as it loses time value. Down below, we'll discuss that a little bit more. In other cases, time value will be dropping rapidly, and the price of the option is going to be dropping with it.

Time value is also known as extrinsic value. Time value is extrinsic because it only relates to the time remaining on the options contract. We are simplifying a little bit, but this is generally the way to think of it. So, it's not derived from the underlying market valuation for this stock. Pricing of the option that comes from the underlying stock is known as intrinsic value.

Options Chain

The list in which options for stocks and even index funds that are up for sale is known as the options chain. Every option has a ticker, although many modern platforms don't bother with that anymore since options information can be displayed in a user-friendly manner using computer and mobile technology. The options ticker includes information on the option such as which underlying stock the option is for, the expiration date, type of option, and the strike price. It might look something like this:

AMZN200103C1530000

The first part of the options ticker is the stock ticker of the underlying stock or index fund for the option. This is followed by the expiration date, which is given in a 2-digit year, month, and day format. So here we see:

200103

This means January 3, 2020. So, the format is YYMMDD. Following this, we see a single letter representing the type of option. In the case of AMZN200103C1530000, since we see a C in this position, that means that we are dealing with a call option. Had it been a put option, we'd see AMZN200103P1530000.

The last part pertaining to the contract is its strike price. This valuation (strike price) will have three decimal places and leading zeros if the strike price uses up all the digits. In other words, 1530000 represents a strike price of $1,530. If the strike price had been $851, the ticker would look like this:

AMZN200103C0851000

Tickers are displayed grouped by expiration date, with calls first, followed by put options, but probably with the ability to switch between them.

yahoo! finance	Search for news, symbols or companies					Q	
Finance Home	Watchlists	My Portfolio	Screeners	Premium	Markets	Industries	Personal Finance	Videos
AMZN200103C01835000	2019-12-31 3:59PM EST	1,835.00	19.75	18.45	20.15	-2.02	-9.28%	477	0	16.53%
AMZN200103C01837500	2019-12-31 3:59PM EST	1,837.50	17.70	16.65	18.15	-2.30	-11.50%	614	0	15.97%
AMZN200103C01840000	2019-12-31 3:58PM EST	1,840.00	16.57	15.45	16.80	-2.72	-14.10%	3,457	0	16.22%
AMZN200103C01842500	2019-12-31 3:59PM EST	1,842.50	15.20	14.05	15.50	-3.10	-16.94%	1,228	0	16.42%
AMZN200103C01845000	2019-12-31 3:59PM EST	1,845.00	13.75	13.50	14.10	-2.74	-16.62%	1,840	0	16.38%
AMZN200103C01847500	2019-12-31 3:59PM EST	1,847.50	12.70	11.60	12.85	-2.47	-16.28%	967	0	16.43%
AMZN200103C01850000	2019-12-31 3:59PM EST	1,850.00	11.55	11.05	11.75	-2.89	-20.01%	4,883	0	16.58%
AMZN200103C01852500	2019-12-31 3:59PM EST	1,852.50	10.40	9.55	10.60	-2.45	-19.07%	675	0	16.56%
AMZN200103C01855000	2019-12-31 3:59PM EST	1,855.00	9.40	8.45	9.40	-2.90	-23.58%	1,197	0	16.37%
AMZN200103C01857500	2019-12-31 3:58PM EST	1,857.50	8.30	8.00	8.55	-2.90	-25.89%	918	0	16.55%
AMZN200103C01860000	2019-12-31 3:59PM EST	1,860.00	7.50	7.00	7.80	-3.07	-29.04%	2,591	0	16.77%
AMZN200103C01862500	2019-12-31 3:59PM EST	1,862.50	6.90	6.60	7.05	-2.80	-28.87%	446	0	16.90%
AMZN200103C01865000	2019-12-31 3:59PM EST	1,865.00	6.15	5.75	6.35	-2.68	-30.35%	836	0	17.01%
AMZN200103C01867500	2019-12-31 3:59PM EST	1,867.50	5.56	5.15	5.65	-2.60	-31.86%	634	0	17.04%
AMZN200103C01870000	2019-12-31 3:59PM EST	1,870.00	5.05	4.85	5.15	-2.52	-33.29%	1,813	0	17.28%
AMZN200103C01872500	2019-12-31 3:59PM EST	1,872.50	4.60	4.20	4.70	-2.27	-33.04%	271	0	17.54%
AMZN200103C01875000	2019-12-31 3:59PM EST	1,875.00	4.12	3.65	4.25	-2.23	-35.12%	1,029	0	17.72%
AMZN200103C01877500	2019-12-31 3:59PM EST	1,877.50	3.75	3.40	3.80	-2.09	-35.79%	351	0	17.83%

The options chain for Amazon.

As we said, many platforms no longer use the tickers and simply display the options by strike price in a user-friendly, readable format. Below, we see the contrast between the traditional display used by Yahoo Finance, and a newer user-friendly display used by the mobile trading platform Robin Hood:

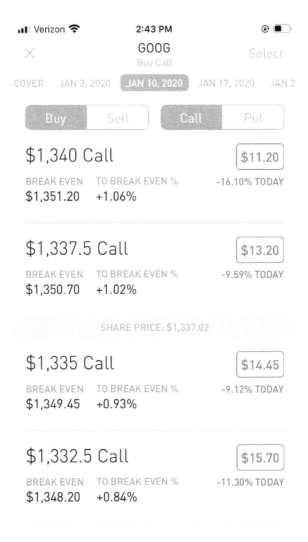

Here we see that you can simply click on a date at the top of the screen. For that date, we are able to move between call and put options with a single tap, and also between the purchase and sale. The options are listed in rows, going from highest strike price to lowest one, with the prevailing market valuation noted on the screen. The actual price of this contract is displayed on the right side of the screen, along with some other information.

How Options Are Priced

Options prices are quoted on a per-share basis. For the vast majority of options contracts, there are 100 underlying shares of stock. So, the quoted price is for one share, but to buy a single options contract, you'll be doing it for all 100 shares. Fractional purchases of options are not allowed. So, if you see the price of an option quoted as $2, that means to buy the option, you actually have to pay $200.

As you can see, some options are quite expensive, but the price varies considerably. In the example using Google above, the last option at the bottom has a price of $15.70. That means to actually buy this option. You must pay $1,570. Of course, looking at it another way, you could sell the option for $1,570, and that might clue you in as to why people are interested in selling options contracts. More on that later. Next, we are going to cover some industry jargon that refers to the relationship between the market valuation of the individual stock and its strike price.

In the Money

An option can be said to be *in the money* when it would be prudent to exercise it. In doing so, the transaction would generate a profit. As such, the term "in the money" means that the current valuation of a call options contract is greater than the current market price of the shares. The same can be said about a put options contract when its share price is below the valuation of the contract itself. But in reality, we need to take into account the price paid for the option. So, let's look at a more formal and more accurate definition.

In the case of a call option, this implies the market valuation of the shares is higher than its strike price in addition to the *breakeven* (note that in the options trading world, breakeven is two separate words). The breakeven price is simply the price paid to enter into the options contract. So, if the strike price of a call option is $100, and you buy that option for $1 (per share – so total of $100), the breakeven is $100 + $1 = $101. What this tells you is that its market valuation must increase to $101 in order for the option to be worth exercising.

For put options, remember that profit is earned from declining share prices. So, to get the breakeven price of a put option, you subtract the price per share spent on the option from the valuation of the contract. So, if we have a put contract containing a $90 valuation that costs $0.80, then the breakeven price would be $90 - $0.80 = $89.20.

Also, if the valuation of the stock drops below the strike valuation of a put contract minus the value paid, in other words, share valuation has fallen beneath the breakeven point. This is when the contract is said to be in the money.

At the Money

The term "at the money" means that the valuation of the shares is the same as the market valuation of the contract. We use the same definition for both call and put options. Keep in mind that in reality, you can basically consider an option as "at the money" when the valuation of the shares goes below its breakeven point, but at or above the market valuation for the contract in questions. For a put option, you would for practical purposes consider an option at the money in the event the valuation of the shares was over the breakeven point but below the strike valuation. An at the money option isn't really anything special, other than being close to the possibility of going in the money at some point. The more time remaining until the option expires, the more useful an at the money option is. If you have a strong reason to believe that a stock is going to move one way or the other, using the money options could be a lower-cost way to get into the trade.

Out of the Money

An out of the money option is one that is in a position relative to the market price of the stock such that it would not be worth exercising. For a call option, it will be out of the money when the strike price is above the strike price. Using the logic of the last section, in practice, you could consider it to be out of the money when it is above the stock price plus the break-even, but that is really a distinction without a difference when the option expires. An out of the money option will expire "worthless". Let's use a simple example to see why.

Remember the point of a call option. The purpose of a call option is to give someone the right to buy 100 shares of stock at a discount. So, let's say we buy a call option on some stock with a strike price that is $200 a share. Our speculation that the price of the stock was going to rise turns out wrong, and instead of going up, the price of the shares drops. As the option is nearing the expiration date, the price of the shares drops to $195 a share.

You can ask yourself if it would be worth exercising an option that gave you the right to buy 100 shares at $200 a share. Of course, it wouldn't be worth doing this. So, nobody is going to do it, and fewer people will want to buy the option from you if you wanted to get rid of it by trading it. Of course, some people will still buy it, as some naïve traders (and there are a lot of them – but we are educating our dear readers) will buy out of the money options because they are cheap, and there is always the "hope" that the stock price will reverse and gain value.

In most cases, that hope is not realistic, so it is not advisable to buy out of the money options, except in a narrow situation that we will discuss in chapter 4.

Now let's turn our attention to put options. Since put options earn profit when the stock price drops, that means a put option is going to be out of the money if the strike price of the option is lower than the share price of the stock.

Open Interest

When you are looking for options to trade, there are other factors besides the strike price and expiration date that you should be looking at. One of these is called open interest. Open interest is the number of contracts that are on the market for a given stock, strike price, and expiration date. Some options are really popular, and you will see open interest in the tens of thousands. Others are not so popular – but could still be worth trading. A good rule of thumb that is used by professional options traders is you shouldn't get into options trades if the open interest is lower than 100.

There is a simple reason for this. You might need to find a buyer very quickly for an options contract to get out of a trade. This can happen when the price is moving in a favorable direction and when it's moving in a bad direction. The reason is that the relationship of the price of an option to the underlying shares is such that price movements of the stock are magnified in price movements of the option. Remember that there are 100 underlying shares of the option. So, a $1 price movement in the share price could, in theory, have up to 100 times the impact on the price of the option. We will discuss the actual values when we discuss the Greeks, but for in the money options, the relationship will be $0.50 to $1 per share, meaning that the price of the option can rise or fall $50 to $100 for in response to a $1 shift in the price of the underlying stock.

For at the money options, the relationship is $0.50 per share, so even at the money (or close thereto) options are massively impacted by price shifts in the underlying stock. It is this magnifying effect that makes options so attractive to many traders. In fact, although its operating at a lower level, large price shifts can even have a large impact on the prices of out of the money options, even a few days before expiration.

The bottom line here is that you can gain or lose money very quickly. When you've made a large profit, you're going to want to sell your options to someone else before the price moves in the opposite direction, and you end up losing money as fast as you've made it. These cuts both ways. Sometimes an option is destined to simply lose a lot of value. If you find yourself in a losing trade, you are going to want to cut your losses before they get too dramatic.

And if the open interest is too low, it's going to take a long time to find a buyer. To sell an option, although it seems like magic on the computer screen, you still have to find a real buyer to take an option off your hands. When open interest is only 30, that means there are only 30 contracts out there, and it might take you a long time to find someone to buy it. That can mean lost profits or catastrophic losses.

Check around, and you will find that there are plenty of options that have an open interest above 100, and some have very high levels of open interest.

Volume

Volume is another measure of an options popularity. Volume tells you the number of times per day the contracts were traded. The closer you get to expiration, the higher the volume is going to be. Volume can be higher or lower than open interest, but popular options such as on the index fund SPY can have a very high level of volume. A high volume isn't the only thing you are going to look for when deciding whether or not to trade an option, of course, but if the trading volume is high, this is an indicator in the options favor. Like open interest, a high trading volume indicates that it will be relatively easy to get in and out of trades quickly.

Options Exchanges

Options trading takes place on separate exchanges. They are not traded on the stock floors of the New York Stock Exchange or NASDAQ. Most options exchanges are located in Chicago, and there are several options exchanges. For an individual trader, indeed, for many large traders these days, that is all irrelevant. This is all hidden from you by the broker and by a computer interface. All you know is that you are placing an order to buy or sell an option, and the computer reports back on the trade. How it actually gets executed on the other end isn't that important. But you might want to keep it in the back of your mind that a real person is taking the other side of the trade. That can help you to make better trading decisions since you might think about whether a given trade would be something other people are going to be interested in. Usually, however, that isn't too much of a problem. The reason is that the options market is large, and although it is not as large as the stock market, there are enough people around to get the full range of different and competing interests represented. Sometimes when a trade seems like a disaster for you, someone else might feel they can do something with it. What their reasons are you can't possibly know, and it really doesn't matter anyway.

The Market Maker

Options markets have so-called "market makers". In the old days, these were high flying individuals that made large trades. Today they are likely people with large accounts that work for major institutions like major banks. The purpose of the market maker is to keep the options market running and running as smoothly as possible. Market makers will take the other side of many trades. The point of doing this is largely to keep the market as "liquid" as possible. If you are not sure what liquid means, basically liquid means how easy it is to convert an asset into cash. Something that takes six months to sell is less liquid than something you can sell in 1-2 days. As for options themselves, liquidity means you have the opportunity to purchase and trade options quickly. Sometimes, if you are doing lower volume trades, the market maker might help you by taking the other side of the trade. Once again, we can't always guess the motivations of the market maker or anyone else taking the other side of the trade, and it's not really worth worrying about it. The only thing to think about as an individual options trader is getting in and out of trades when you need to.

In the next chapter, we will discuss the topic pertaining to the so-called "Greeks". Learning about the Greeks will explain how options prices are determined. You will learn specific values and relationships that will tell you how much the price of an option will change in response to a variation in the asset underlying in the contract. You will also learn how much the price of an option will drop in response to "time decay" and some other factors that can influence option pricing.

Chapter 3: The Greeks

In this chapter, we are going to look at five important parameters that an option has that go by the name "the Greeks". Understanding these parameters will help you estimate where an options price is going to go when different factors that impact that price change. Options pricing is based on mathematical formulas, but you don't need to understand the details. The Greeks will help you make estimations at a glance once you understand what they are all about. Your brokerage trading platform will allow you to look up the Greeks for any option so that you can make the best choices for your investments.

Delta

The first Greek parameter that we are going to look at is called delta. In many cases, this is the most important of the Greeks. It describes the relationship between the valuation of the stock in question and the options contract. More specifically, it tells us how the price of the option changes in response to variations pertaining to the variation of the equities on the stock market. Consider call options first. The value is given in percentage terms, and if you think of the stock price rising or falling by a dollar, that means the price of the option will rise and fall by the fraction listed as delta. In other words, the option price will change by:

Delta x change in stock price x 100

So, if delta is 0.6, if the underlying price of the equity increased by $1, the price of the contract will rise by 60 cents per share, for a total of $60. If the stock price had only risen by 50 cents instead, then the option price would rise by 30 cents on a per-share basis, or by $30.

These figures show how dramatic options prices can change with small changes in share price. If you are trading options on Apple, Netflix, Tesla, or Google, for example, a one-dollar change in share price is not all that significant. And by extension, a 50-cent change in share price certainly isn't very significant.

Keep in mind, of course, that these cuts both ways. If the valuation of the equity drops by one dollar, the price of the option is going to drop by 60 cents per share if delta is 0.60. One thing this tells you is that you have to keep a close eye on your options trades so that you can get out of bad trades before they become disasters. However, trades can also change direction quickly, since we are talking about relatively small price movements on the stock market. In some of my trades, I had stuck it out when the price of an option dropped by $50 and then saw it rise by $120 in a matter of hours. Panic is not a reason to get out of a trade. We will be discussing this later.

Delta is not a fixed quantity. You will see that it changes depending on changing conditions in the markets. The more in the money an option is, the higher the delta is going to be. Options that are significantly in the money will have delta values that approach 1.0, so their prices can really move with changes in the stock price. If a contract happens to be out of the money, delta will be smaller. A rule of thumb you can use is that for an equity that is at the money, delta is 0.5. Then, for an options deal that is in the money, it will have delta higher than 0.5, while options contracts that are out of the money will have delta lower than 0.5. You can see how this will work to make out of the money options less lucrative. For example, and out of the money option might have a delta of 0.25, so that a $1 increase in the valuation of the equity might only bump the price up $25.

But this also raises the issue of tradeoffs. Options contracts with are out of the money are more affordable to buy, and you can still earn significant profits. Apple is trading at $293 a share as I am writing this, and you can buy a $302 call for $247. Delta is 0.2862. A $1 rise in the stock price is only a 0.34% change, so that is not something outlandish to expect. That would earn you a $29 profit on a $247 investment, a 12% ROI which isn't too shabby. Of course, you can earn more from in the money options, but a

$290 call would require a $793 investment. So how much you can invest is obviously going to be a part of weighing what you trade.

Unfortunately, a lot of online articles, usually written by people who are financially trained but not active options traders, give a lot of bad advice. One thing you are going to see discussed on many websites is advice that you shouldn't trade out of the money options. The truth is that depends on the situation. Later we will discuss situations where trading out of the money options can be a viable strategy.

Now let's turn our attention briefly to put options. The concept is the same, but when you look at put options, you are going to see delta listed as a negative quantity. This is because of the inverse relationship between share price and a put option. Remember that with a contract for a put option, as the share valuation drops, the valuation of the contract increases. Conversely, when share prices rise, the valuation of the corresponding contract decreases. As such, the point of a put options contract is to be able to sell declining shares at a higher price, and the negative delta expresses this fact.

Otherwise, delta for a put option means the same thing. So, you can take a drop in share price and use delta to estimate how the price of the option would change, in the inverse manner described.

As the expiration date approaches, you'll see delta getting very small for out of the money options. Again, that doesn't mean you can't profit from out of the money options.

Remember that delta is dynamic. As the price shifts and time passes, delta might change as well. So, if you look up delta for an option today, it might be different three days from now. You need to keep track of these parameters on a regular basis, so you understand what is going on and what the possibilities are.

In the chart below, we show a perfect example of why these fluctuations are important for options traders. In a short time, frame after the market opened, the stock gained a dollar and twenty-four cents. So, with large, high volume stocks, one dollar or more fluctuations are easily going to happen, and this can cause big swings in options prices (and they might represent opportunities for profits). Notice that the stock also dropped back down but rose back up over $205 per share by the closing bell.

Theta

Next, we consider a parameter called theta. The purpose of this Greek is to tell you how much value the option is going to lose due to time decay. The losses that you will see from this occur every single day at the market open. So, once the decay happens at the market open, then theta won't impact the option again until the following day. The decline in options price due to theta can be significant, but it can also be overwhelmed by other factors impacting price. We just saw that delta can lead to large changes in options price, and if you have delta at 0.54, theta at -0.12, and the stock rises by $1 at market open, when all is said and done you actually have a 42-cent gain per share, or $42. Of course, if things are not moving your way with the stock, or the delta on an out of the money option is small, that means that theta is going to be working against you.

Theta is expressed as a negative value because it always means the price of the option is going to decline because of time decay when a new trading day opens. This is true for both call and put options, and so theta is always expressed as a negative number, ranging from 0.0 to -1.0. Realistic values range between -0.13 and -0.30. As time to expiration approaches, theta values tend to increase. Also, out of the money options tend to have smaller theta values. However, out of the money options get *all* of their pricing value from time value or extrinsic value, even though their price will fluctuate because of delta. To take an example, consider a stock trading at $220 per share, and suppose we have an out of the money call option with a strike price of $235. At 39 days to option expiration, the price of this option is $408. Theta is -0.105, and delta is 0.29. The extrinsic value is $408, and the intrinsic value is $0. Under the same conditions with 5 days to expiration, delta has dropped to 0.05, and theta has dropped to -0.082. The option is only priced at $160 at this point.

Let's compare values for an in the money call option. Suppose that we have the same $235 strike price, but with a share price of $240. At 39 days to expiration, the price of the option is $1,295.

386

Delta is 0.60, theta is -0.129, and the option has $795 in extrinsic value with $500 in intrinsic value. At five days to expiration, the price is $670, delta is 0.71, and theta is -0.317. The extrinsic value of this option is $170, and the intrinsic value is $500 at this point.

This example shows us a few important things. The first is that without the money options, buying and holding them over a significant period is foolish. It is this fact that misleads many people that write about options trading to make a mistake to say you shouldn't trade out of the money options. In the trading strategies chapter for calls and puts, we will discuss this in more detail.

We also notice that the intrinsic value is the difference between the share price and the strike price. So close to expiration, as extrinsic value is declining, and in the money, option can make large profits from changing share prices as delta gets closer to 1.0.

The important thing about theta is to have an awareness of it and to be ready for it to work its wicked ways each morning when you hold the options overnight. As we said earlier, whether or not theta turns out to be important for your specific trades is going to be something that depends on the situation.

Gamma

Gamma is a bit of a more obscure Greek. For math geeks out there, it's a second derivative term. Or in English, it tells you the rate of change of another parameter. In this case, gamma tells us how delta is going to change, in response to a price change. Gamma is the same value for both calls and puts. It's also usually a small value.

Going back to our example, take call and put options with a strike price of $223, and an underlying share price of $220. Gamma for both the call and the put is 0.04. This means that if the share price goes up a dollar, delta for the call will rise by about 0.04, but delta for the put option will decline by 0.04. So, a rising share price will make delta grow for a call option, but it's going to make delta shrink for a put option. In this example that we are using, before the stock price increases, delta for the call is a bit more than 0.37, while for the put, it's -0.63. After the rise in share price by one dollar, delta for the call rises to 0.42, while for the put, it declines to -0.58.

It can be handy to know gamma depending on how deeply you're getting into the analysis. However, most individual traders don't pay much attention to it. I'd say that especially for a beginner spending time worrying about gamma isn't particularly productive. You should devote your time to delta and theta, which will help you focus on what is important for coming profits or losses.

Vega

The next Greek is Vega, which is related to the implied volatility of an option. Remember that with options, it is all about probabilities that the option is going to end up in the money. The higher the probability that this is going to happen, the higher the price of the option, and therefore more profits for options traders. Assuming that some readers are new to the world of options, let's explain volatility just briefly so that everyone knows what we are talking about.

You probably have a commonsense notion of volatility, and you can visualize it on any mathematical graph, and certainly on a stock chart. Volatility is a reference to the amount of fluctuation in the price when it comes to stock. If the price is making wild price swings, that is having large changes in price up and down for a given time period, then that's high volatility. Low volatility would be more of a smooth curve. Maybe the price is steadily going upward, but there isn't much fluctuation.

Of course, generally speaking, stock price charts are not smooth. There is an inherent amount of volatility baked into the system. This occurs from the random nature of the business. People are buying and selling shares, and fluctuating supply and demand is causing the price to move around basically in random ways, in addition to the overall price trend. But not all stocks fluctuate in the same manner. Stocks that are in heavy demand often have high amounts of volatility, since heavy demand can mean lots of buying and selling activity.

You can visualize volatility just looking at a stock chart, and it's pretty intuitive to determine which stocks are more volatile and which stocks are less volatile. At the same time, this is also precisely quantified. Each stock has a measure of its volatility, which is called Beta. You can look up beta for any stock using your brokerage provided trading platform or on free sites like Yahoo Finance.

Here is how to understand the values given for beta. The larger beta is, the more volatile the stock is. The way this is measured is that the average volatility for the entire market is calculated and assigned a value of 1.0. This means that any stock that has a beta that is higher than 1.0 is more volatile than the market average. If beta is 1.25, that means the stock is 25% more volatile than the market average. If beta were 1.4, that would mean the stock was 40% more volatile than average. When beta is less than 1.0, that means the stock is more quiescent, or less volatile than the market average. Beta can also be negative. That means that the stock is actually fluctuating against the market. So, when the overall market is increasing in price, that stock is decreasing, and vice versa. As you might imagine, negative beta values are actually pretty rare.

For options, it is implied volatility that we are interested in. This is a measure of what volatility is expected to be in the future. This can have a large impact on options prices. This goes back to that fundamental principle, which is that the higher the probability that the option ends up in the money, the higher the price of the option. More volatility means that probability is going to be higher. In fact, high levels of volatility can really cause options prices to rise. Implied volatility is expressed as a percentage.

Implied volatility tends to get large when there is an expectation of something that is going to impact the price of shares. The quintessential example of this is when there is an upcoming earnings call. Earnings calls are something that is big in the options world. If you are an options seller, you might want to avoid earnings calls. So maybe for that week, you don't trade. But for options buyers, earnings calls represent a big opportunity. The key here is to get in on your trade a couple of weeks prior to the earnings call of a big stock. Stock prices change a lot when there is an earnings call, depending on whether or not the company was profitable and more importantly, whether they managed to beat expectations or not. In the weeks leading up to the earnings call, implied volatility gets larger and larger. For some stocks like Tesla or Netflix, implied volatility can get quite large, over 50%.

One strategy you can use is to buy an option a bit of time out before the earnings call and then sell it the afternoon before the earnings call.

Let's see how implied volatility impacts options pricing. We'll go with a $220 share price again and say that we are 10 days to expiration with a strike price of 223. We'll take a relatively average implied volatility of 18%. A call option is $141, and a put option is $439 under these conditions. To understand the impact of implied volatility, we'll keep everything else constant.

Now move to 5 days to expiration. If implied volatility hadn't changed, the call option would be worth $74, and the put option would be $373. That is due to the effects of time decay. However, if the implied volatility had risen to 35%, the call option would be $232, and the put option would be $531. So, you could sell either option for a profit just from the increase in implied volatility alone. And remember, the call option is out of the money, but despite 5 days of time decay, it has increased in value because of the increase in implied volatility.

Now let's go to 2 days left to expiration and suppose that implied volatility is 55%. Now the call option is $230, and the put option is $529, leaving everything else unchanged. The prices haven't changed much, but there has been a lot of time decay, and the increase in time decay is not impacting the options prices hardly at all because of the high level of implied volatility. In fact, at this point, theta is sitting at -0.85 for both the call and the put option. If implied volatility goes up to 65%, the price of the call goes up to $292 and the put to $592.

In some cases, with highly sought-after stocks, if big results are expected in an earnings call, implied volatility can go higher than 70%.

So, Vega is the parameter that tells us how the price of the option is going to change in response to a 1-point change in the implied volatility. You will find that Vega is the same for both calls and puts with the same strike price and expiration date.

Rho

Finally, we come to the last major Greek. This Greek goes by the name rho. It measures the sensitivity of options prices to interest rates. Specifically, a long-term "risk-free" interest rate is used. It changes in the interest rates that are important, and of course, in today's environment interest rates are pretty steady and only change by small amounts when they do. The best example that you can use to understand the "risk-free" interest rate is the interest rate on a ten-year U.S. Treasury. When interest rates rise, this can have a small but negative impact on options pricing. When interest rates fall, there will be a small but positive impact on options pricing. This is not really a Greek to concern yourself within today's environment, where significant changes in interest rates are unlikely and infrequent. Also, it requires a pretty large change in interest rates to produce a measurable impact on options prices.

Minor Greeks

There are even more "Greeks". They are known as the minor Greeks. The vast majority of options traders don't pay much if any attention to the minor Greeks, so we aren't going to discuss them. Most options traders don't even pay attention to all of the major Greeks, focusing only on delta, theta, and Vega. If you understand delta, theta, and Vega, you have all the information you need in order to be a successful options trader.

Chapter 4: Swing Trading with Options

The most straightforward way to trade options is to make a bet on the direction of the stock market and buy call or put options accordingly. Most beginning options traders are going to have to start with this method because more advanced strategies are closed off to beginning options traders. That isn't all bad, however, because you should get a feel for the options market before attempting more complicated trades.

What is Swing Trading?

The type of trading that we are going to be discussing in this chapter can loosely be described as swing trading. If you are not familiar with it, swing trading is a simple trading philosophy, where the idea is to trade "swings" in market prices. In a commonsense kind of way, there is nothing special about swing trading because it's a buy-low and sell-high method of trading with stocks. You can also profit from a stock when the price is declining by "shorting" the stock.

So, what distinguishes swing trading from other types of trading and investing? The main distinction that is important is that swing trading is different from day trading. A day trader will enter their stock position and exit the position on the same trading day. Day traders never hold a position overnight.

Swing traders hold a position at least for a day, which means they will hold their position at a minimum overnight. Then they will wait for an anticipated "swing" in the stock price to exit the position. This time frame can be days to weeks, or out to a few months' maximum.

A swing trader also differs from an investor, since at the most, the swing trader is going to be getting out of a position in a few months. Investors are in it for the long haul and often put their money in companies that they strongly believe in. Alternatively, they are looking to build a "nest egg" over a time period of one to three decades or even more.

Swing traders don't particularly care about the companies they buy stock in. They are simply looking to make a short-term profit. So, although swing traders may not be hoping to make an instant profit like a day trader, they are not going to be hoping for profits from the long-term prospects of a company. A swing trader is only interested in changing stock prices. Even the reasons behind the changes in the stock prices may not be important. So, whether it's

Apple or some unknown company, if it is in a big swing in stock prices, the swing trader will be interested.

The chart below shows the concept of swing trading. If you are betting on falling prices, you can earn profit following the red line in the chart. If you are betting on increasing prices, you would follow the upward trending blue line. A bet on falling prices is often referred to as being short, while a bet on rising prices means you are long on the stock. This, of course, is another difference between swing trading and investing; investors don't short stock.

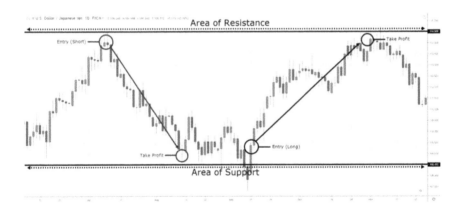

Swing trading can be used in any financial market. In the chart above, we are actually showing a chart from the Forex (currency exchange) market. The principles are the same, so the specific market we are talking about doesn't really matter, which is why it works with options.

Support and Resistance

An important concept often used by swing traders is spotting support and resistance. Support refers to a local low price of the stock. It's basically a pricing floor that, for the time being, the stock price is not dropping below. To find support, you just draw straight lines on the stock chart. The share price should touch the support level at least twice in order for it to be a valid level of support.

Resistance is a local high price. So, this is a high price level that the stock is not able to break above. Again, expect it to touch the resistance level at least twice, and drop back down, before you consider a given share price for the resistance level.

As the share price moves in between support and resistance, there are opportunities to buy-low at the support level price and then sell-high at the resistance level. And you can do the reverse in the case of shorting stock. You can enter your position at the relatively high resistance level, then exit your position at the support level.

Of course, support and resistance are not going to be valid price levels for all time, and a stock will often "break out" of support or resistance. This happens when the share price starts a declining trend and goes below the support level, or if it breaks out above the resistance level in an uptrend. These can be more opportunities to make a profit. But, when a stock price is stuck between support and resistance levels, we say it is *ranging*.

Trade with the Trend

The best thing to happen to a swing trader (or a trader of straight call and put options) is for a stock to enter into a unidirectional trend. So, it could be a trend in upward prices, giving you a chance to make large profits before it starts reversing. Alternatively, of course, trends can head downwards, opening up opportunities for those who are shorting the stock.

Trends can exist in many different time frames. It might only last part of a day, or it could last weeks and even months. Learning to spot trends and take advantage of them, with a sense as to when the trends are going to come to an end, is something that comes with experience and education. A new options trader can benefit by studying educational materials related to both swing and day trading so they know what to look for in stock charts to spot not only trends worth getting into, but also how to spot a trend reversal which would eat up your profits.

The chart below of AutoZone stock is a simple example of this concept. It's a dream trade, with prices going steadily up with time. But remember nothing lasts forever.

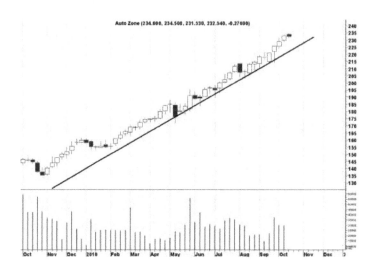

Trading with a trend is definitely something you'll want to look for as an options trader. The time scale of the trend is going to be something important, of course, because you are going to be concerned about time decay when trading options. Time decay is a concept that a swing trader does not have to worry about.

So rather than being beholden to specific rules, like saying you are going to trade options like a day trader or like a swing trader, an options trader has to be flexible. You will need to be ready to take advantage of very short term moves in stock price that only last for a day or less, and you'll also want to be in trades that can last days to weeks or even months.

Swing Trading Options

Since options are time-limited, they are a natural fit for the concept of swing trading. Although many of the advanced strategies attempt to take out the direction of share price movement from the equation, if you are buying single call or put options in order to make a profit, then you're definitely behaving at least in a qualitative sense like a swing trader.

Since put options gain in value when stock prices are declining, buying put options is like shorting stock. It's actually quite a bit more accessible, however. In order to short stock, you must have a margin account so that you can borrow shares from the broker. The basic idea of shorting stock is to borrow shares from the broker when the stock price is at a relatively high point and sell them. After this, the trader will wait for the share price to drop. Then when the share price is low enough to make a profit, the trader will buy the shares back and return them to the broker.

Of course, shorting stock using options is far easier. The reason is you never have to buy the stock to make a profit from the declining price. You simply profit from prices of put options which will increase as the stock price goes down.

Going Long on a Stock

If you believe that the price of a stock is going to rise, then you want to buy call options. So, call options represent the most straightforward or common-sense way to trade options. When you buy a call option, you are betting on that stock. Another way to say this is that you are bullish on the stock.

A good way to go about trading options is to pick a few companies and limit yourself to trading them. The reason is that you are going to have to be paying attention to the markets, company news, and general financial news for any option that you invest in. If you spread yourself too thin, you are not going to be able to stay on top of things and will find yourself getting caught up in losing trades. The best approach is to keep your trading limited in scope so that you can know what is going on. That doesn't mean you only trade a single call option; you might trade a large number of them on the same stock.

There are two ways to go about swing trading options. The first way is to look for ranging stocks that are trapped in between support and resistance. Then you can trade call and put options that move with the swings. So, the idea of this type of trading is very simple. First, you need to study a stock of interest and determine what the price levels of support and resistance are. Then, when the price drops to the support level, you buy call options. Now hold them until the price goes back up near resistance. It can be a good idea to exit your trades before the price gets all the way to resistance so that you don't end up losing some of your potential profits if the price reverses before you get rid of the options.

Trend trading call options can also be very lucrative. In this case, you are looking for significant news and developments related to the stock or even the economy at large. For example, when a company announces that it had big profits, this can be an opportunity to earn money with call options, as the price will go up by large amounts as people start snapping up the stock. When trading in this fashion, you're going to need to know how to spot trend reversals. We will talk about that later in this chapter. The idea is basically the same when you identify a trend in the making, you buy call options, and then ride the trend until you are satisfied with the level of profit and sell the options.

Again, it can't be emphasized too much. You always need to take time to decay into account when trading options. So, remember that with each passing day, your options are going to automatically lose value. Check theta to find out how much value they are going to lose. And as we discussed before, often, other factors overwhelm time decay in the short term.

A big opportunity with call options is trading on index funds. SPY, which we mentioned earlier, is one of the top choices for trading call options. In the case of SPY, you are going to be paying attention to overall economic news to look for opportunities. Any information related to the economy at large can cause large moves with this index fund. This includes changes in interest rates (or even leaving them the same when that is what the market would prefer), announcements of GDP growth rates, changes in trade policy, or release of jobs numbers. One of the best things about options on SPY is that they are extremely liquid, making it very easy to get in and out of your trades. You can also trade many other index funds, tracking virtually anything financial.

Shorting Stock Using Put options

Put options may be one of the most powerful tools available to the individual trader. To earn profits from shorting stock, you have to be a big player in the market. That means you have to get a margin account and have enough financial resources that you are able to borrow large numbers of shares from the broker. Most new traders are not going to be at that point. Keep in mind that to earn profits from shorting stock, you'll have to be shorting 100 shares or more of stock in order to make money.

With put options, you can leverage the stock through the option. By investing in Put options, you get control of the stock and earn profits from the price movements in the stock without actually having to buy shares. A single put option might cost $30, $100, or $400, but you will control 100 shares.

Some traders actually hope to profit by selling the shares when they buy put options, but most traders simply want to get into a put option early when a downward trend in stock price is expected, and then sell the put option for a profit when stock prices have actually declined. The same basic things to look for apply, except you'll be doing it in reverse. So, you can trade put options for profits when stocks are ranging. In this case, you start the trade by purchasing put options when stock prices are relatively high, at the resistance level. Then you hold your put options until prices drop down again to support and sell them for a profit.

Likewise, for an options trader, downward trends in stock prices are just as nice as upward trends. When a downward trend is developing, you invest in Put options and then sell them when the stock price has dropped enough such that you are taking an acceptable profit. As with call options, traders using put options will need to learn about signals that indicate trend reversals so that you have some quantitative tools to help you make solid trades.

Keep in mind there are no guarantees on the options market. When trading options, we are really looking for probabilities. This means that you can expect to have some losing trades, and the goal is to be profitable overall without worrying about specific trades.

Tools to Spot Trend Reversals

Swing traders use tools that help them estimate changes in the direction of stock market prices. Some of these tools are more qualitative in nature and involve spotting particular chart patterns that usually indicate a trend reversal is coming. You can think of these tools more in the sense of being rules of thumb or even "art of trading".

Many other tools used by swing traders are more mathematically based. These tools go under the umbrella of *technical analysis*. We aren't going to have space in this book to delve into all the details and tools used, but we will cover the most fundamental tools which are enough to get you started, and in fact, are often all that you need. Let's get started looking at a few chart patterns.

Chart Patterns That Indicate Trend Reversals

A trend reversal is important for an options trader because it's a point that you will use to either enter a trade or exit a trade. Over the decades, traders have come to recognize certain chart patterns that will indicate a coming trend reversal. This is a bet, in a sense. The given chart pattern is no guarantee a reversal is coming, but most of the time that will be the case. Chart images below were created by Altaf Qadir on Wikipedia.

The first chart patter we are going to look at is the "head and shoulders". This pattern occurs at the top of an upward trend before the price begins declining. It is characterized by three peaks in the chart. The middle peak will be the highest, and it will be flanked by two smaller peaks that are generally the same height. The pattern emerges because there are still traders coming into the stock, but the numbers are such that not enough of them are still entering the position in order to push prices up further. So, as they enter their positions, these late arrivals push up prices a little bit, and then it drops back down again. When the pattern is forming, prices drop down to a level called the neckline. Then they rise back up.

By the point of the right shoulder, traders are going to be looking to take profits. So, they will be exiting their positions, and as the number of people selling increases, the increased supply of the stock on the market relative to willing buyers will start pushing prices down. So, if you are trading call options and the stock underlying the call shows this pattern, it is a good time to sell.

You can simply flip the chart over to see a trend reversal developing after declining stock prices.

A double top is the same type of phenomenon, but with only two price peaks.

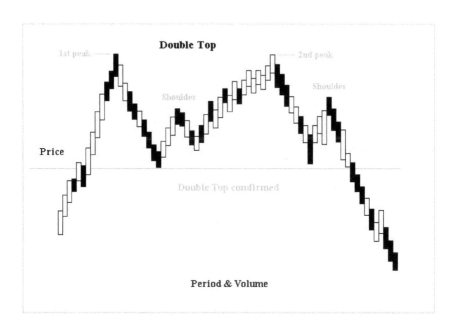

Double Top

1st peak — 2nd peak

Shoulder

Shoulder

Price

Double Top confirmed

Period & Volume

Next, we consider a cup and handle. This takes place in an uptrending stock before there is a large breakout. In this case, the stock will rise to a peak, and then gradually drop down in a relatively smooth fashion, forming a bowl shape. So, it will drop to a minimum and then gradually start rising to the previous level, which forms the "cup" part of the pattern. Then there will be a period where the stock price is ranging between two values, not really doing much. This is the handle part of the pattern. After the handle, the stock is likely to break out to the upside.

DCM SRIRAM LTD
WEEKLY

There are many chart patterns like these used by traders, but we can only cover a few because there are large numbers of them, and it would be outside the scope of this book. There are many online resources available that can be used in order to study and learn chart patterns. Consider using the site Investopedia to learn all of them if you are so inclined.

Candlestick Charts

Candlestick charts show stock prices divided up into small trading periods. This is done so that you can determine changing investor behavior before there is a major trend reversal. Each trading period is a microcosm of the trading day, week, or month, with its own opening and closing price, and high and low price. This way, you can see whether or not investors are in a buying or selling mood, and how strong that mood actually is.

411

Candlesticks are colored according to whether or not the closing price for the trading period was above or below the opening price. If the closing price is higher than the opening price, that is a bullish candlestick, and these are normally green in color (although different trading platforms sometimes use different coloring schemes). Candlesticks have "wicks" that are sometimes called shadows that extend out of the top and bottom, indicating the high and low for the stock for that trading period. A candlestick chart is illustrated below.

By examining how candlesticks are forming in a series, it can be possible to spot trend reversals in price. Candlesticks can be used on many different time frames, from 1 minute to 5 minutes, to 1 hour, 4 hours and more. The time scale to use is going to depend on what your goals are at the moment. If the price of a stock is fast-moving and you are looking to sell options to make a profit by exiting your positions, you might want to go with a 5-minute time frame, for example.

There are many different patterns on candlestick charts that can indicate future direction in price. Remember that price is really a reflection of demand for a given security, so declining price means that fewer buyers are willing to close a sale for the given price, and the price must continually drop until an equilibrium between buyers and sellers is reached. As an options trader, you are looking for changes or reversals in the trend.

When you see three candlesticks in a row of the same type, this can be an indication of a trend reversal. We actually see this in two spots in the chart above. These have been marked to draw your attention to them in a reproduction of this chart here, showing a trend reversal turning into a significant downward trend in price:

This pattern goes by the name "three black crows" when there are three bearish (or red) candlesticks in a row. Although the sighting of a black crow may be taken by some to be an indication of bad luck, the term "black crow" in this context is really historical. Options trading began in the 1920s but was suspended in the Great Depression and not revived again until 1973. Prior to the widespread adaptation of colored printing, candlestick charts used solid black candlesticks to represent bearish trading sessions, thus the name "black crows". For stock traders, declining prices are always a bad sign, so that is another reason why "bearish" denotes a bad situation, but remember that as an options trader, you can profit in either case. If you saw a chart like the one above, the three red candlesticks in a row would be a very good indication that you should buy put options. Then, you hold your put options until either a) you have made a level of profit that you find acceptable, or b) you see signs in the charts of another trend reversal, which is going to start eating into possible profits and possibly even turn them into losses.

When you see three green or bullish candlesticks in a row, this is a sign of a coming uptrend, and in the business, it is known as "three white soldiers". Again, the name is historical. It comes from the fact that in the days before color printing and computer screens, bullish candlesticks were outlined and hence "white" in color.

Another important candlestick patterns every options trader should be aware of is the engulfing pattern. This can happen at the end of a downtrend in prices or at the end of an upward trend in prices. In either case, and engulfing pattern occurs when a candle of the dominant trend type is followed by a large candle of the opposite type, such that the following candle completely covers the length of the previous candle. This concept is illustrated below.

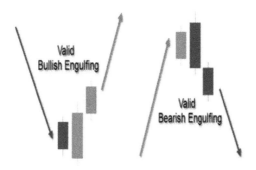

Let's focus on the bullish engulfing pattern to understand what is going on here. Notice that the closing price, which is indicated by the bearish candlestick to the left, is a bit higher than the opening price of the bullish candlestick immediately to its left. This indicates that at the start of the trading period, people were still selling off, pushing prices down lower. In fact, in the example given, you can see a wick sticking out the bottom indicating that prices continued to drop. However, by the end of the trading period, prices reversed and went much higher than the previous close, and also higher than the previous open. This indicates that the trend is reversing because buyers are now pushing prices up with increasing demand. In the given example, there is a follow up bullish candlestick, but that isn't strictly necessary although the appearance of one would increase confidence. It is the trend that starts to develop over the next few candlesticks that are important. In the example given, we see that at the next time period prices continue to be pushed higher. This kind of pattern would indicate that it's either a good time to buy call options on the underlying stock or a good time to sell put options if you've got some in your inventory.

In the bearish example, it's a similar situation but with everything reversed. In the engulfing candle, remember that the top of a red or bearish candle is the opening price for the trading session, while the bottom of the candle is the closing price. So, in this case, the trading session for the engulfing candle opened with a small continuation of the previous trend – and prices jumped higher. Then they were pushed down by a large amount, even further down than the opening price (and indeed for the low price) of the previous trading session. This indicates that the opening price of the bearish candle indicated only a slight increase in prices; in other words, demand was starting to peter out. The fact that the candle engulfs the previous one indicates that the selloff became overwhelming, as compared to the previous trading session.

Another important candlestick pattern that is often used is a "hammer". Depending on the orientation of the hammer, it can be a plain hammer or an inverted hammer. It is also called a shooting star if present at the start of an uptrend. A hammer has a wick that only comes out of one end of the candlestick and a relatively narrow body. This means first of all that opening and closing prices (regardless of whether we are talking about a bullish or bearish situation) were fairly close to each other. Second, it means that during the trading session, prices were pushed strongly in one direction, only to be pushed way back towards the opening price level for the trading session. A shooting star occurs when an inverted hammer occurs at the top of an uptrend, indicating that prices were pushed up high, only to drop down below the opening price (so for a shooting star you are looking for a bearish candlestick.

Here are two examples so that you understand what a hammer or inverted hammer actually looks like:

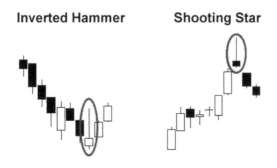

To get a hammer, you just flip it over.

While these are the main trend reversal signals with candlesticks, there are literally dozens of them. You can learn what they are and how to spot them using many resources, including free resources that are available online. A good options trader, however, is not going to rely on only using one or two techniques, so you don't need to devote your entire life to studying candlestick charts. Looking to spot the most compelling chart reversal signals is usually enough for most traders when used in conjunction with other tools.

Be calm when looking at stock charts. You don't need to enter or exit a trade in a matter of seconds when trading options in most situations. So, it isn't necessary to spend hours memorizing candlestick.

Moving Averages

One of the most powerful tools that you can use in order to spot trend reversals is using moving averages. Moving averages are used in conjunction with candlestick charts by most stock traders, but in my opinion moving averages are actually a stronger signal indicating a trend reversal, and it is even possible to rely only on moving averages in a lot of cases. But to play it safer, a typical approach would be to look at moving averages for a trend reversal and then confirm by looking at the candlestick patterns.

First, let's take a step back and make sure we understand what a moving average is. Anyone understands the concept of an average, we take a set of data points and add them up, and then divide by the number of data points. A moving average is like this, except at each point along the line, we compute the average at that point. So, the average at each point is going to be different and reflect market conditions at the point in question. Moving averages require that you specify the number of points used in the calculation. Note that stock charts extend far back in the past, so you could use 10 points, 30 points, 200 points or more.

For stocks, we can compute averages on nearly any time frame we desire. For the sake of simplicity, suppose that we are averaging daily, using the closing price. So, each point on our chart, assuming that we are using a candlestick chart is going to be one day. To compute the moving average for 9 days, we could create a 9-day moving average curve and add it to our chart. At each day along the chart, it would get the past 9 days of data and compute the average. So, you can see why it's "moving", as it goes to the next day on the chart, the first day used in the previous calculation drops off and is replaced with the current day.

If the stock prices used to calculate the average are just added up and then divided by the number of days in the calculation, then we call this a simple moving average. Many traders get by quite well using simple moving averages, and there really isn't an argument that you can frame against them. We are not looking for ultimate precision. We are looking for indicators that trader sentiment on a given stock is changing.

However, many traders argue against the use of simple moving averages. The reason that you might not want to use them is that notice the simple moving average treats all prices with equal relevance. That might be fine if you are only using a moving average over the course of a few days, but the longer the time frame you use in your moving average, the less relevant prices in the past are to the calculation. The simple moving average fails to recognize this basic fact.

To get around this, different types of moving averages were created to weight the data, so that more recent prices would get more "weight" in the calculations. The most popular type of moving average used for weighting is called an exponential moving average. Another popular method used is called a Hull moving average, after its creator. These types of moving averages are pretty accurate, and you will notice that they track the actual pricing trends quite closely.

One of the benefits of moving average curves is that they remove noise from a stock chart. Rather than seeing the typical jagged up and down zig-zag line that you are used to seeing, you will see a smooth curve that represents the real, underlying trend in stock prices.

To use moving averages to spot trend reversals, we will add two moving average curves to the stock chart. These moving averages will have different periods, or in plain English, they will use a different number of trading sessions. So, if you are using a chart of daily stock prices, the moving averages will use a different number of days for each curve. The point of doing this is to see whether or not the short-term price movements are going higher or lower than the long-term average at each point. When this type of event happens, this usually indicates a trend reversal. That apparent trend reversal can be compared to other indicators like candlestick patterns to confirm what you are seeing with the moving average curves. In most situations, you can be pretty confident that a crossover of moving average curves will mean a coming trend reversal.

Different choices are used to spot trend reversals with moving average curves. For example, a popular method is to use 50-day and 200-day moving averages. These curves work pretty well under a wide variety of circumstances, but I find the 200-day moving average too long. Let me tell you why.

When you are looking for a long-term moving average, you have to keep in mind that it's going to be impacted by many factors. For example, it might be impacted by earnings calls, and the more you extend the moving average into the past, the more impact moving averages are going to have. Earnings calls can have a pretty dramatic impact on stock prices. Over the past year, there have been earnings calls that have moved stock prices by $20, $40, and more in a single day or even in overnight after-hours trading. The impact of earnings calls can be long-lasting. For example, a boost in share prices from an earnings call might set a new support pricing floor for the stock in question. But it may not be long-lasting, and so it's an outlier data point that is distorting prices.

Also, no matter what, when it comes to tomorrow's stock price, recent events and stock prices are simply a lot more relevant. And trading options, unless you are investing in LEAPs, you're definitely interested in short-term price movements, often of 30 days or less. In fact, many options traders only trade on weekly time scales. So, what the stock was doing 200 days ago doesn't seem as relevant to what it's going to be doing in the next few days.

For this reason, I like to use a 9-day moving average in conjunction with a 20-day moving average, or you can use a 50-

day moving average. My advice is to try different values and see how it works for you. Apply these moving averages to *past* stock market data, so that you can get a feel for how it really worked with real data. Your trading time frame will also be important. Shorter time frames that you are looking at to enter or exit trades are going to demand shorter moving averages.

So, what are we looking for? We are looking for the behavior of the short-term moving average curve with respect to the long-term moving average curve. Sticking to my preferred values, we are looking for the 9-day moving average curve to either move below or above the 20-day moving average curve. When the short-term moving average moves below the long-term moving average – this is a very strong signal that stock prices are going to decline in short order. On the other hand, when the short-term moving average goes above the long-term moving average, we have the reverse condition – so this is a strong indication that there is a coming uptrend in stock prices. Always confirm by looking at other signals, such as the candlestick chart, before entering or exiting a position.

When we see the short-term moving average drop below the long-term moving average, this is called a "death cross". Once again, the terminology used is reflective of the mentality of straightforward stock traders, where they view increasing stock prices as strictly positive, and declining stock prices as strictly negative. As an options trader, you should adopt a view that a particular move in one direction or the other is neutral. So, when you see a "death cross", you should consider investing in Put options. If you are already invested in call options, a death cross is a selling signal. Here is an example, via Market Watch, of a death cross for Apple stock prices:

Here, the green line represents the short-term moving average, while the red line represents the long-term moving average. Of course, prices are going to fluctuate up and down constantly, but by looking at the relationship between the two curves, you can not only spot buy and sell points but also false signals. For example, a bit after the death cross in the figure, we notice that the stock price started climbing, which may have led novice traders to buy calls or to sell put options. But if you are looking at the moving average curves, you'll see that the short-term moving average remained below the long-term moving average even as the stock prices momentarily rose to a higher level. Whenever you see the short-term moving average staying clearly below the long-term moving average, you should take the view that bearish conditions are still in existence no matter what the stock price is doing in the moment. Since the stock market is a pretty chaotic system, we can expect that it is going to be doing a lot of up and down movement that is not going to be significant at all over any time period of interest. And you can see clearly from the figure that the indication given to us by the death cross proved quite accurate, as the curve of stock prices continued to decline to a significantly lower value.

When the short-term moving average goes above the long-term average, this is called a golden cross, because it is an indicator of a coming upward trend in stock prices. A golden cross is, therefore, an indicator that represents a buy signal for call options and a sell signal for put options. The example below shows simple moving averages, using a 50-day simple moving average for the short-term curve, and a 200-day moving average for the long-term curve. This particular example is a textbook example, showing a very strong upward trend that followed the golden cross:

Pay attention to the slopes of the moving average curves. When one of the curves has a much stronger slope than the other curve, this can indicate that the trend is either going to be weak or strong. In the example above, the short-term moving average curve has a larger slope, and so it grows faster (for a time), indicating that this is a very strong upward trend in price. You can also note that at the marked entry point in the figure, the candlesticks certainly agree with the information that you are getting from the golden cross. There is a "three white soldiers" pattern just before the golden cross; in fact, there are more than three bullish candlesticks at that point. That is a strong confirmation signal that would give you confidence in using this moving average crossover as an indicator that you should go ahead and invest in call options.

Relative Strength Indicator

The next item we are going to look at, which can be used in swing trading, is called the relative strength indicator. This is a technical tool that can be used in order to estimate "overbought" and "oversold" conditions. In my opinion, it should not be used as a primary tool, but only to give confidence to the type of information that you are getting from your other tools. So, the general procedure you should utilize is to first look for moving average crossovers. Then confirm with the candlestick chart and then look at the relative strength indicator to solidify the information that you are getting.

The relative strength indicator will put a curve below your stock chart, and it will range over the values 0-100. If the relative strength index is between 30-70, it is considered neutral. If it is above 70, this represents "overbought" conditions. This means that buyers have been too enthusiastic about entering this stock and have pushed the price of the stock up to levels that aren't justified by external conditions. When a stock is overbought, this can be an indication that the price is going to start declining, since the only way out of an overbought stock is to sell it.

However, this technical indicator can only be described as suggestive. In many cases, I have seen stocks labeled as overbought, but the price kept going up and up. At least for a time. For this reason, my advice with the relative strength indicator is to only look at it when you are unsure even after looking at the candlestick charts and the moving averages. For example, you can come to a tentative conclusion with a crossover on the moving averages that the candlestick charts seem to confirm, and if you are still not confident, you can use the relative strength indicator to back up what you think your move should be.

When there are overbought conditions, this indicates that you should sell call options, or alternatively, buy put options. An overbought indicator is a bearish indicator. But again, it's no guarantee by any means.

Overbought conditions will form at the top of an upward trend in prices that are coming to an end.

When the relative strength indicator is 30 or below, this indicates oversold conditions. That means that people have been too active getting out of the stock, and prices are likely to start rising again soon. So oversold conditions are a strong indicator that you should be looking to exit your position if you have been investing input options. If you are looking for stock prices to rise, this could suggest an entry point for buying calls.

Oversold conditions are going to occur at the bottom of a downward trend.

Again, you are probably going to want to be using the relative strength index on a secondary basis. So if you see a golden cross and it seems to be confirmed by the candlestick patterns (which would indicate a trend reversal to the upside), if you can confirm this with an RSI below 30, that is a strong indication that you should be investing in call options or getting out of positions that are invested in Put options.

Bollinger Bands

Another very popular tool used in swing trading goes by the name of Bollinger bands after its creator. Bollinger bands involves defining some boundaries for a stock, using moving averages. It relies on simple moving averages by default, but you can customize it. It forms "bands" by using a simple moving average and then also plotting one standard deviation above the simple moving average, and one standard deviation below the moving average. The basic idea here is that under normal conditions, a stock is going to stay within a standard deviation of the mean. If it goes outside of this range, then that is an indication that there is going to be a trend reversal. Of course, there are special situations (again, think earnings calls) when this might not be true because breaking news can cause unusually large movements in stock price. However, under normal circumstances, the stock can be reasonably assured to stay within a standard deviation of the mean. After all, that is the meaning of standard deviation.

Bollinger bands are overlaid on the stock chart. Most traders are going to use Bollinger bands in conjunction with candlestick charts, and so you are looking for the candlesticks to fall above or below the Bollinger bands. So, if there has been an upward trend of the stock price and then the price touches or goes outside the upper Bollinger band, that is a point where you can expect a trend reversal in the price to the downside. This means that you would either be investing in puts or selling your positions that were invested in call options.

Alternatively, if prices have been dropping and then the candlesticks touch or go outside the lower Bollinger band, then we can expect a trend reversal to the upside. This is taken to be a signal that you should buy call positions or exit put options.

In short, Bollinger bands are a way to dynamically add support and resistance to your stock charts. So, we can take the lower Bollinger band to be supported, while the upper Bollinger band is taken to be supported.

Chapter 5: The Iron Condor and Iron Butterfly

In the previous chapter, we learned about straight trading of calls or puts. In short, this represents a style of trading that is something that goes along with swing trading stocks. You either want to short the stock, that is bet the price is going to be entering a decline or go long with call options and make profits from rising prices. This is a basic strategy that involves basically making a bet on which direction the stock price is going to move. The cold reality is that while there are certain circumstances when you can make bets on trends in stock prices, that is a very difficult game to play overall. Most professional options traders do not do straight trading of calls and puts, because it is a high-risk bet on stock direction. Instead, they use one or more of several advanced trading strategies.

Advanced trading strategies seek to do one or both of two things. The first thing that advanced trading strategies seek to do is to reduce your risk. This can be done by reducing the probability of engaging in a losing trade or by capping losses. And actually, there are more ways to reduce risk. For example, you can remove the direction of the stock market from the equation, which is something that we are going to talk about here.

Removing Direction from the Trade

The iron condor is a trading strategy that does something that is quite unusual. Rather than betting on the stock moving one way or the other, it bets instead that the stock is going to stay within a certain range of prices. Over short time periods, unless there is a dramatic event, be it something unpredictable or something expected like an earnings call, stocks are basically going to flail around within a certain narrow confine of pricing. In other words, most stocks will spend most of their time range.

This is where an iron condor comes in. An iron condor is a limited risk strategy that bets that the stock price is going to be trapped within two values over the lifetime of the trade. Now, of course, if you were to trade stocks over a matter of weeks or years, stock prices would probably be hard to pin down within a range. But most traders enter into iron condor positions with time frames of a maximum of 45 days all the way down to a single week.

An iron condor has four "legs". As a new options trader, it is important to become familiar with the jargon, and my legs, all this means is that there are four options involved in the trade. We will spell it out later in the chapter.

Central Goal of the Iron Condor

The central goal of an iron condor (or an iron butterfly) is that the stock price is going to stay within a bounded range of values over the lifetime of the options contracts. What the stock price does within that time frame really isn't of concern. It might go up, go down, or hardly move at all. For the trader, that isn't important.

All that matters to the trader of the iron condor or iron butterfly is that the stock doesn't move very much. Very much is a relative term for the iron condor, you can define any range you like. The narrower the range, the more money you are going to make. However, that means higher risk. If the stock's price goes outside of the range, this could end up being a losing trade, in the event that the options go to expiration. If you have a smaller range of values, that means that there is a higher probability that the stock is going to go outside the range. You can have a wider range to reduce risk, but that will decrease potential profits as well.

Iron Condors are Income Strategies

When you buy a call or a put, note that you are buying to open your position. This is a speculation strategy; you are speculating that you can earn profits from certain moves in the stock price.

434

However, with an iron condor, we meet a new and different way to think about the stock markets and options trading. An iron condor is an income strategy.

This means that you are going to open a position in an iron condor by selling it for a credit. Since an iron condor has four legs, that means it's a trade that involves buying and selling four options simultaneously. But you will be buying options on net as we will see. But the point is not to speculate, although there is always a small amount of speculation in any stock or options trade. The point is to earn income. Many options traders sell iron condors on a revolving basis so that they can receive options premium on a regular basis. Options premium refers to the payments that are put in by people buying options.

As an income strategy, this means that you are going to be selling iron condors, rather than buying them. The idea is that you sell them for a credit, provided the stock price does not violate some conditions that you set on the trade; you get to pocket the credit as a profit.

The Lower Legs

The lower legs of an iron condor consist of two put options that form the lower boundary or support region for our trade. The boundary is formed using the strike prices of the options. So, we are hoping that the stock price never goes as low as the strike prices of our put options. There are two put options that form the lower boundary of the iron condor. We need the stock prices to be above the strike price of the higher put option at closing to make a profit.

We set this up using what is called a vertical spread. This just means that we have to options of the same type, that have different strike prices on the same stock and with the same expiration date. In this case, you are going to sell the put option that has a higher strike price. The idea with an iron condor is that you are going to be selling options that are out of the money.

Selling a put option can be lucrative, but it carries some risk. The risk is that we would be assigned, meaning that if the share price moved below the strike price of the option minus the breakeven price, a buyer out there might decide to exercise the option. In that case, we would be assigned, and we'd have to buy the shares from the buyer at the strike price on the options contract. Depending on circumstances, this could result in a substantial loss.

However, we can mitigate that loss substantially by simultaneously buying another put option. In this case, we buy another put option with a lower strike price. It's going to be cheaper, and if prices crash, while we will make profits, we will also reduce our risk since we can exercise that option in the event things don't work our way with the overall trade.

To understand how this works, let's make up a simple example. Suppose that a stock is trading at $200 a share, and there are 10 days to expiration. We could sell the $217 put option for $9.37 a share, for a total credit of $937. In the event that the share price moved low enough to make the $217 call profitable for a buyer, we might be assigned, which would mean that we'd have to come up with $217 x 100 = $21,700 in order to buy the shares of stock. That might be an unpleasant thought if the stock price was dropping substantially. For the sake of example, suppose the stock crashed to $200 a share.

However, we can cut our risk by purchasing another put option with a lower strike price. In fact, we could purchase the $210 put for $6.37. Since we are buying this while selling the other option, this means our total profit is cut substantially. In this case, our total profit would be $9.37 - $6.37 = $3. While that is a big cut in possible profits, we've also cut our risks massively. Suppose that the stock price drops below $210, also covering the breakeven price. If the option were exercised, we'd have to buy the 100 shares at $217 a share, resulting in a loss of $21,700. However, since we entered into the contract with the $210 put, we can turn around and sell the shares to someone else. Using the second options contract, we can sell the shares for $210 and make $2,100 back. Now we've reduced our loss to $21,700 - $21,000 = $700.

That may not sound good, but had we not bought the second option, we'd be stuck buying the shares at the sale price. At best, we could sell them on the open market. If they were trading at $200 a share, that means selling them for $20,000. So now our loss is $1,700. So, we've cut our losses by 41%.

The Other Legs

The upper legs of the trade are created by selling a call option and buying a call option with a higher strike price. The strike price of the lower call option forms the boundary of range for the stock to the upside. So if a stock is trading at $200, and we create an iron condor by selling a put option with a strike price of $195 and buying a put option with a strike price of $190, and then we sell a call option with a strike price of $205 and buy a call option with a strike price of $210, if the stock price stays in between $195-205, we earn profit. On the other hand, we lose if it goes above or below this range. So, with the legs involving the call options, you buy a call option with a certain strike price, and then sell one with a higher strike price.

The basic ideas are the same as compared to what we've looked at before, but in this case, we don't want the price to move very substantially. We are going to be in trouble if it breaks to the upside or the downside.

The Complete Iron Condor as a Single Trade

When you enter into an iron condor position, you are going to enter it as a single trade. So, you buy a call and a put, and you sell a call and a put, simultaneously. The important point here is that you are selling the position. You have to know that your inner strike prices set the acceptable range over which the price of the stock can move.

The following chart illustrates the iron condor:

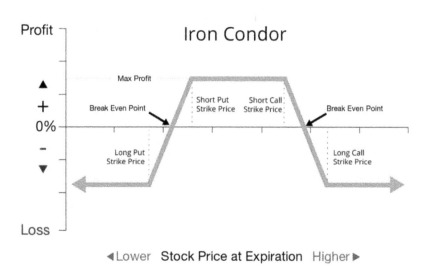

The Iron Condor Relies on Time Decay

You can buy an iron condor with respect to any expiration date of options. However, the main strength of the iron condor is time decay. Put another way. You are going to earn more from an iron condor that expires further out in the future. However, most iron condor traders will work in a time frame that ranges between 30-45 days. Some traders will opt for shorter time frames. Many will take a mere week's time frame or 7-14 days. By reducing the amount of time until expiration, you also reduce the probability that the stock is going to move outside the bounded range. So, while buyers are hoping the stock is going to break one way or the other and get outside the range set up by the iron condor, you're playing the role of the house and making the opposite bet.

So, keep the following in mind:

- Less time left, lower risk to seller, but less possible income. In this case, with a shorter time frame on the contract, the probability of the stock exceeding the range set up by the strike prices is lower.
- More time left, higher risk to seller. This is because the stock has more chances to go above or below the range set by the iron condor. However, there is more possible

income. With more time left until expiration, you will earn more money from time decay.

Since you are selling a call option with a lower strike price(relative to the call options that you buy) and selling a put option with a higher strike price(relative to a put option that you buy), you are going to get a net credit for the transaction.

The Iron Butterfly

The iron butterfly is essentially a derivative of the iron condor strategy. So, like the iron condor, the iron butterfly has four options, two puts, and two calls. It will have a put option with a relatively high strike price that you sell. It will have a put option with a relatively low strike price that you buy. Then it will have a call option with a relatively low strike price that you sell, and a call option with a relatively higher strike price that you sell. All options have the same expiration date.

In the case of the iron butterfly, however, you are going to have a call option and a put option that have the same strike prices. This means that for an iron butterfly to be profitable, the share price has to stay on the strike price, which defines the mid-value for the trade. You can see this in the graph for the iron butterfly shown below. It has a spike, rather than a range of prices over which the trade is profitable:

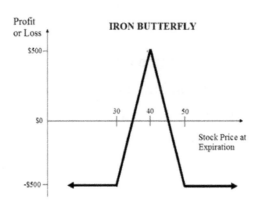

The Buyback Strategy

Now we are going to briefly mention an important advantage when selling options that can be used to mitigate risk. This is the buyback strategy. In short, if at any time it looks like an option or strategy that you have sold is not working out, or is likely to finish such that you would lose on the trade and have substantial financial obligations, you can buy the trade back. This doesn't mean you buy the trade back from the exact same person (who might not even have it anyway), you can buy it back from any trader on the market. Traders will buy positions back under two circumstances.

The first is that you have simply made a good profit, and the stock is still ranging within the values set by your inner strikes. In this case, you may buy the position back to exit the position, in order to protect yourself from the possibility that something unusual will happen on the last day of trading that could cause the stock to break out, and go below the strike prices of the put option or above the strike prices of the call option.

The second case is when your position is obviously not going to work. In this case, you could buy back your position in order to cap your losses. There is no requirement, as a seller, for you to hold onto the position if it is a losing position. The way that you get out of it is you tell your broker that you want to buy it back. This is done automatically by placing an order to buy that position.

Maximum Losses

Maximum losses are set to the upside and the downside. If the stock breaks toward the upside, the maximum loss is the difference in the strike prices of the call options plus the breakeven. On the other side, if the stock price collapses so that it ends up lower than the lower strike price of the put options, then the maximum loss is the difference between the strike prices less the breakeven price. The strategy does not require symmetry, but in most cases, traders construct symmetric iron condors or iron butterflies.

Summary

When do you get into an iron condor or iron butterfly? You do this when you don't expect the share price to move very much. In the case of an iron butterfly, you expect the stock to stay within a range of prices until the expiration date. For the iron butterfly, you expect the share price to stay at the strike price used for the inner call and put options in the trade.

Chapter 6: Strangles and Straddles

What if there was a strategy you could use to profit if the stock rose high, but you also earned profit if the stock crashed? It sounds too good to be true, but the reality is with options you can do this. The strategies used to accomplish this are called strangles and straddles. In this chapter, we will learn how to set them up, how they work, and when to use them.

Strangle Options Strategy

The strangle options strategy is designed in a way that is somewhat opposite that of an iron condor. While an iron condor is set up to earn profits if the stock price stays within a certain range, a strangle will earn profit only if the stock price breaks out of this range. It doesn't matter if the price rises or falls; a strangle makes a profit either way. So, this is an ideal strategy to use when you expect big price movements on the stock, but you are not sure which direction the price will go.

The classic situation where a strangle can be used is with an earnings call. Prior to an earnings call, it is not known for sure how the earnings of the company will be reported. The benchmark used by the markets is analyst expectations. If the earnings of the company exceed the predictions made by major analysts prior to the earnings call, this usually results in jubilation and rising stock prices. In many cases, the stock can rise 10-20% in value overnight.

Of course, companies often disappoint. In fact, it doesn't even matter if a company reports a profit, if they fail to meet the expectations of the market, this can lead to a crash in the stock share price. Movements in price can be as large as movements due to positive earnings reports. If the reports are actually bad, that is, they not only fail to meet expectations but also report a loss or some other negative news. This can lead to massive losses on the stock. This happened to Netflix and Tesla in recent earnings calls. Netflix reported a loss of subscribers, which caused a plunge in their stock price.

A strangle is a two-leg strategy, which is just another way of saying that we will use two different options to create the trade. Strangles are speculative trades, and therefore, we will buy to open these positions.

You might be asking how we can profit no matter which way the stock moves. The answer is that a strangle involves buying a call option and a put option simultaneously on the same stock. They will have the same expiration dates but different strike prices. The movement of the stock has to be large enough to exceed the cost of buying both options. If the stock price rises, this means that the Put Option which is a part of our trade, is going to expire worthless. If the stock price crashes, on the other hand, that means that the call option is going to expire worthless.

For our breakeven price, we need to take into account the total cost of entering into the position, so it will be the cost of the call option + the cost of the put option. So, if the stock were to break to the upside, the price would have to rise above the strike price of the call option + total cost of buying both options. If the strike price were $100 and we paid $3 for the call option and $2 for the put option, then the price of the stock would have to go above $100 + $3 + 2 = $105 before we can make a profit.

To figure out the breakeven point for the put option, we start with the strike price used for the put option and then subtract the total cost for entering the position. Therefore, if our strike price for the put option on this hypothetical trade were $90, the breakeven point to the downside would just be $90 - $3 - $2 = $85.

In this hypothetical setup, we would not make any profit if the share price were to stay within the two strike prices. Specifically, this means that if the share price stayed between $90 and $100, we would lose on the trade. The total loss would be equal to the cost of the two options, or $3 + 42 = $5. Since there are 100 shares underlying the option, the total loss would be $5 x 100 = $500. The maximum loss occurs if the share price stays the same. Of course, the probability of a share price staying the same after an earnings call is practically nil. The stock is going to move somewhat, so the question is: will the stock price move enough so that you make a profit? If it doesn't, any movement in the share price will at least reduce your losses.

So how much can you make? To the upside, in theory, the maximum gain is unlimited. It depends on how high the stock price rises. Share prices on big stocks can rise $30 or $40 after an earnings call, and so it is possible to make thousands of dollars in profit. Of course, that doesn't mean you should go into these types of trades expecting that kind of profit. However, it is possible to earn substantial profits.

To the downside, the maximum gain is equal to the share price when you enter the position multiplied by 100. To earn the maximum gain to the downside, the share price would have to drop all the way down to zero. Of course, that is something that rarely happens, so don't expect it. But it is not uncommon to see share prices on big stocks drop $20, $30, or $40 a share after a bad earnings call. So, to the downside, very large profits are also possible.

How to Implement the Strategy

When there are big events like earnings calls, stock prices can even change dramatically after hours before the markets open the next morning. Therefore, it is important to plan ahead for using this type of strategy.

The first step is to identify an event that is coming up where the strategy might be appropriate. For stocks, the earnings call is the primary event to look for. Therefore, find stocks you are interested in and look up the dates of their upcoming earnings calls. These occur on a quarterly basis; therefore, we have four opportunities per year for each stock to employ the strategy.

Another opportunity might be the upcoming company announcements. For example, Apple has regular presentations it gives every year. They have a developer conference where the new operating system for the iPhone and iPad devices is unveiled to the public for the first time. This may or may not have a big impact on the viewpoint of major market analysts, and so it could cause a large shift in share prices of Apple if the changes to the operating system are viewed as having a possible impact on Apple's future bottom line. In the fall, Apple has presentations where they reveal their latest iPhones and changes to their computer line. If there are major changes and announcements by Apple, this can have a big impact on stock prices as well.

Apple is the quintessential example for using the strategy in this manner, but you can look up and follow different companies to see when and if they are going to make major announcements about their product line, or if there are going to be upcoming announcements on things that might impact the company's fortunes. For example, a pharmaceutical company might be seeking FDA approval for a major drug. If the drug is approved, the stock of the company could shoot up significantly. If the drug is rejected, the stock could decline by a large amount. This possibility suggests that a strangle might be an appropriate technique to use in order to earn profits from these events.

Index funds are also possible targets for the strategy. Any index fund on the blue-chip companies can be considered, most notably the S & P 500. You can also consider index funds on the Dow Jones Industrial Average, the NASDAQ 100, or the total market. In this case, major news events and releases of economic data will be important to consider. Of course, it is hard, if not impossible, to plan for unexpected events. But there are major scheduled events that occur on a monthly and quarterly basis. These include announcements of interest rate changes by the federal reserve, announcements on jobs and the unemployment rate, and announcements of the GDP growth rate.

Just like with stocks, the actual nature of the announcements may not be what drives changes in the share prices of index funds. Rather, it will be how the announcement compares to the expectations held by the market. For example, if the market expects the creation of 170,000 jobs, but it's announced that there were 190,000 jobs created, the market will be jubilant. This would mean that index funds like SPY would see large spikes in share price.

Once you have an event identified, you can buy one or more strangle contracts on the stock or index fund in question. A strangle is entered into as a single transaction, and so you will buy the call and put option simultaneously. Remember that options have time decay. This can mean that buying a strangle far ahead of time can be overly expensive. This can mean that some balance is going to be necessary. It is advisable that you get some experience trading straight call and put options for a few months before attempting this. As you are doing so, you should be studying the market behaviors and look at the prices of strangles on your trading platform to see how they change with time. In particular, look for earnings calls and see what happens.

The balance is going to come from the anticipation of the markets. Since people know that big movements in share price are possible when earnings calls are approaching, although the options have time decay, prices are going to be rising from increasing demand.

So, it is a matter of balance, is there enough increasing demand to wipe out the time decay. The longer you wait to get into a position the more it is going to cost if there is a lot of interest swirling around the stock. This can happen with major stocks like Tesla, Facebook, Apple, and so on.

Once you've gotten in your position, you have to be ready to sell it at the right moment. Typically (but not always), what happens in these situations is that stock prices are going to rise very quickly. Companies may have a late afternoon earnings call. They often schedule these such that they take place after the markets close. Even though the markets are closed, there will be after-hours trading. Under normal circumstances, after-hours trading doesn't have significant impacts, but after earnings call, the impacts can be dramatic. Prices on a stock might rise or fall 20-30% even before the next market open.

What happens next is hard to say, as the market is inherently unpredictable. If there is going to be more movement, it is likely to occur in the first 30 minutes after the market open. At some point, the stock may stabilize at new levels of support and resistance. How quickly it does this will depend on the intensity of the earnings call. If the earnings call only mildly exceeded or failed to meet expectations, then the stock price might settle at a new level fairly quickly. If the announcement was dramatic, then a sell off or rush to buy the stock might last for a longer time period.

If you decide to implement the strategy, you should be prepared to be paying close attention to the market the morning after the earnings call or other announcement. Be ready to sell your position so that you can take an acceptable level of profit before the market stabilizes, and the demand for strangles on the stock starts to decline. The key here is to take advantage of latecomers to the marketplace. There are always people that come in late, but they eventually fizzle. However, buyers will come in late after noticing the large shift in share prices for the stock, and they will be interested in buying up strangles so that they can profit from any late hour movements in share price. But the key to being a successful options trader is to not be one of those late arrivals. You should plan these trades out and already be in your position before the earnings call. Remember, with a strangle you are going to be earning profit no matter which direction the stock moves, so if it goes up or down is not going to be your concern. The chart below graphically illustrates the way a strangle works.

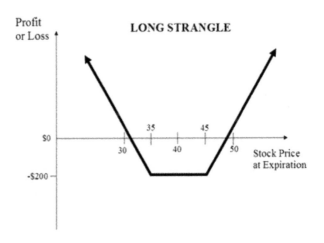

In the center of the chart, you see a flat line. This is the range in between the strike prices where you will have maximum loss. From here, on both sides, the line slopes upward to the breakeven point, which remember is the strike price + cost to enter the position on the upside, and the strike price minus the cost to enter the position on the downside. From there, the more the price moves past the strike prices of the options used to set up the position, the more profit that is earned. In the graph above, we see a hypothetical example with strike prices of $35 and $45, with a total cost to enter the position of around $5. The chart is for illustration purposes only and does not represent actual prices.

Let's look at a real example to see how much this would cost. Facebook is trading at $208 a share, and we can enter a strangle that expires in one week for a price of $2.10, or $210 in total. The strangle has strike prices of $212.50 for the call and $205 for the put.

The breakeven point for the upside is $214.60. This is computed by adding the cost to enter the position, which is $2.10, to the strike price of $212.50. To earn a profit with this trade, the share price of Facebook would have to rise above $214.50. If the share price rose to $216.50, you would earn a $190 profit. If it rose to $224, you could earn around $1,000 in profit.

Under normal conditions, you wouldn't expect the stock price of Facebook to rise to $224 a share. But if there was a very good earnings call, that is something that is definitely in the realm of possibility.

On the downside, the maximum possible profit on this trade is $20,200. To be profitable, it would have to drop below the strike price used for the put option, which is $205, less the cost of entering the position, which is $2.10, and so the breakeven point is $202.90. If there was a bad earnings call and the share price were to drop to $195 or so, you could earn a profit of $750.

Once the event has occurred, you can risk holding the position to expiration. If there are no other major movements in the share price, the options will expire, and you'll earn your profits. But a good strategy is to simply sell the position for a profit once the major movement in stock prices has occurred.

Straddle

Now we turn our attention to a related strategy that is called a straddle. This is also a two-legged strategy that is designed to take advantage of price breakouts of a stock, without regard to the direction that the breakout occurs. Like a strangle, a straddle will also involve buying a call option and a put option on the same stock, and with the same expiration date, simultaneously.

However, a straddle differs from a strangle in one key aspect. To set up a straddle, you will also set up the trade so that the call option and the put have the same expiration date. The chart for a straddle is shown below. This narrows down the range over which there are losses. Maximum loss on the trade would occur if the stock price were equal to the strike price at option expiration.

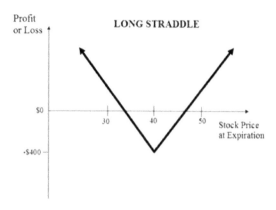

To summarize, both a strangle, and a straddle is set up in order to earn profit from large moves in the price of a stock. In either case, it doesn't matter if the stock moves up or down in price. No matter what direction the stock moves, they will earn a profit provided that the price move is large enough to overcome the breakeven points. Like a strangle, you can use straddles when there are big events or announcements coming up, such as earnings calls.

The same type of strategies should be employed when using straddles rather than strangles. This means that you want to enter your position over a time frame of a week up to maybe three or four weeks prior to a big event like an earnings call. Over the time period between your purchase and the earnings call, the straddle will gain in value from stock movements, regardless of whether or not the price of the stock moves up or it moves down. If the price of the stock increases, the value of the straddle will increase because of the call option that is a part of the trade. However, it could also lose value as a result of the put option that is a part of the trade. The price has to move one way or the other so that the share price is higher than the strike price + cost of the position, or lower than the strike price minus the cost of the position. Remember that for a straddle, the call option and the put option both have the same strike prices.

Let's say that the price of some stock is $234 per share. We create a straddle with a strike price of $235 a share. Although maximum loss occurs when the strike price is equal to the share price, we want to pick a strike price that meets that condition when entering the trade, because we are doing so expecting the share price to move off the strike price in one direction or the other at a later date before the options expire.

For our example, we are entering the trade 21 days before expiration. At this point, the call is $6.93, and the put is $7.89, and so the total cost to enter the position would be $14.92. Let's say that there is an earnings call when the option is five days to expiration.

Now, by 15 days to expiration, in anticipation of the upcoming earnings call, the share price might have moved a bit. Let's suppose that the market is expecting a good earnings call, and so share prices are going up. If the share price went up to $237, this is a modest gain that, despite time decay, will help the value of the call option. It has risen from $6.93 to $7.36. However, the put option has lost some value due to time decay combined with the modestly higher stock price, and it's now going for $5.33.

Our plan, however, is to hold the position until the earnings call. Remember that earnings call also impact volatility. We are setting the implied volatility at 33% for this exercise, but as we get closer to the earnings call, that value will rise.

Now 10 days to expiration, which would be five days to the earnings call in our scenario. The share price has risen to $240 share since the markets are expecting good news. Implied volatility has also increased to 37%. At this point, the call has jumped to $8.37, but the put is now down to $3.63.

Moving forward to just 7 days to expiration, there are only two days left until the earnings call. Now implied volatility has risen to 45%. The share price has increased steadily with the passing days and now stands at $245. Under these conditions, the call is $12.26, and the put is $2.25. The total value now is $14.51, and it cost $14.92 to enter the position, so we have a mild loss at this point – but it should be ignored. We need to hold the position until the earnings call.

Later that day, the stock is at $247, and the implied volatility has risen to 50%. The call is now $14.32, and the put is $2.30, so our position is now worth $16.62. Since it cost $14.92 to enter the position, we are now at a point of profitability to the tune of $16.62 - $14.92 = $1.70. If you wanted to, you could sell it now for a profit of $170. You'd find an eager buyer without a doubt because most traders would be anxious to get in on the trade prior to the actual earnings call.

Finally, we reach the earnings call. It beats expectations by a surprising margin, and the price of the stock jumps $23 a share in after-hours trading. At market open, the call option is worth $36.01, and the and the put is worth pennies on the dollar. At this point, the put option is worthless, but the call option has gone up so much in value that we are looking at a profit of $36.01 - $14.92 = $21.09 per share, putting us in a position where we can sell for a total profit of $2,109.

If the stock continued climbing the morning after the earnings call, which sometimes happens, we could earn even more profits. If it went to $280 a share by the afternoon, the call option would be worth $45. In that case, we'd have another $900 in total profits on the trade. Of course, you are taking some risk. The longer you hold the position. The stock might start declining a bit or stop rising. And if you hold it overnight, you are going to get hit with time decay. The put option is entirely worthless at this point, but it really doesn't matter.

Suppose that instead, the price had plummeted. Our hypothetical company might have missed expectations by a large margin, and rather than rising by a huge amount, it could drop to $210 a share instead. The beauty of the straddle is that in this scenario, we make a profit as well. This time, the call option would be completely worthless on the trading day after the earnings call, but the put option would be worth $24.99, giving us about a $1,000 profit. The more the stock drops, the more profit we would earn. The same holds true for a strangle but remember with the strangle the call and put options have different strike prices, and there might be a wider range over which the stock needs to move in order to earn profits. But in either case, the goals are the same.

Tips and Things to Watch Out For

There are a few things to watch out for with the strangle and straddle. For a strangle, you probably want to bracket the strike prices of your call and put such that the current share price is in the middle. For a straddle, you can use the current share price as your strike or pick a strike price that is very close to the current share price.

You can enter the position at any time, but depending on market conditions, costs might go up a lot in the days coming up to the earnings call. Prior to making your first trade, it is a good idea to simply watch from the sidelines and wait until the next quarter before actually doing trades. In fact, many trading platforms have demo accounts that let you go through the process of making trades, but without spending any money. In other words, they are pretending, simulated trades, but using the real data going on in the marketplace. New traders are often quite anxious and want to get in on the action, but it is worth spending one quarter going through the practice trades to get some experience doing it without risking real money. Since you are just observing, you can also keep an eye on multiple stocks to see how they and options prices are changing as their earnings date approaches, since all the major stocks are going to be doing earnings calls within a couple of weeks of each other.

Another thing to consider is liquidity, an issue that we've raised before. The bottom line here is that once the large shift in share price has occurred, you want to be able to get out of your position quickly. For this reason, you really need to focus on high volume, popular stocks if you are going to employ this strategy. So, you'll be checking the open interest and volume. It's good to focus on the big-name movers such as Amazon, Netflix, Facebook, Google, and Apple, the so-called FAANGS, at least as a beginner. These are not cheap stocks, of course, and that cuts both ways. It is more expensive to enter a position, but the potential profits are also quite large. These are the stocks that will experience very big moves in share price based on earnings calls, and they are also highly liquid and so you will have no problem selling a position when you need to.

For practice without risking money, you can try the technique out on lower priced stocks like AMD, which is trading at around $45 a share. We can enter a straddle on AMD for about $345. Apple is trading at $297 a share. A straddle choosing the closest strike price to the share price would cost $1,448. The Apple straddle is likely to earn far higher profits if the stocks moved a given percentage, so there are tradeoffs that have to be made. Of course, in the beginning, you are probably not going to want to risk large amounts of capital.

Chapter 7: Call and Put Spreads (Vertical Spreads)

In this chapter, we are going to discuss an advanced technique that can be used to speculate on stock price movements or as a method of generating regular income selling options. These techniques are called vertical spreads because they involve trading two options simultaneously of the same type which have a spread in strike prices, but the same expiration dates. There are two ways that you can set these trades up. They are going to involve two options of the same type. The trades also involving buying one option and selling another option with a different strike price, but the same expiration date, and of course, on the same underlying stock.

If you spend more on the option that you buy than you do on the option that you sell, this is going to create a net debit. The purpose of a debit spread is to trade on speculation as you would trading a single option. So, for example, if you thought that the stock price would go up, you'd buy a call option and sell a call option. This procedure will actually reduce your risk as opposed to buying a single call option. But the tradeoff of reducing your risk in this fashion is that you will cap the amount of profit you can make. For a single call option, the amount of possible profit you can earn is theoretically unlimited.

Keep in mind the jargon used in spreads by the industry. An option that you sell is short, while an option that you buy is long.

Debit Spreads

A debit spread is the purchase of one option and the sale of another option of the same type and with the same expiration date with different strike prices, such that the complete transaction results in a net debit. There are two types of debit spreads. You can do a call debit spread, which means buying a call and selling a call, or you can do a put debit spread, which means buying a put and selling a put simultaneously. The purpose of a debit spread is to reduce the amount of risk you face if the trade does not work, but this comes at the expense of capping profits below what you would get with an equivalent winning trade just buying a call or a put.

Let's consider the situation involving calls first. A call debit spread is also known as a bull debit spread or a bull call spread. The reason for the terminology is that this is a trade that you would enter into if you were bullish on the stock. In other words, you're expecting the share price of the stock to increase by the time the options expire.

This is a two-legged trade, meaning that we are going to trade two options simultaneously. The two options will have different strike prices, but the same expiration dates. This makes the trade a vertical spread, the vertical being along the strike prices. For a call debit spread, you are going to buy a call option with a lower strike price and sell an out of the money call option with a higher strike price.

Entering into this type of spread is going to change the Greeks associated with a position, as compared to simply buying a call option at a given strike price. It will reduce the delta and theta for the trade. This means that with a smaller delta, your position is going to be impacted less by changes in the underlying stock price. But that really isn't a concern. There is still enough delta that the trade can be profitable. Our position is also less sensitive to theta, which means it will be a little less sensitive to time decay as far as losing value. But don't rest on your laurels, any option position that you enter with a net debt (aka buying to enter the position) is impacted by time decay, and a call debit spread is no exception.

In order to make a profit, we need the underlying stock price to appreciate in value. The maximum profit that you can earn on a call debit spread is as follows:

Max profit = difference in strike prices − premium paid to enter the position

Looking at Apple, here are a couple of examples. We could enter into a call debit spread using two out of the money options by buying the $302.50 strike price and selling the $307.50 strike price. The cost to enter this position with one week to expiration is $1.19. The width of the strike prices is:

$307.50 - $302.50 = $5

Therefore, the maximum profit is found by subtracting the cost to enter the position from this value:

$5 - $1.19 = $3.81

Once again, there are 100 underlying shares, so it would cost $119 to enter the position and we could earn $381. Again, this is a capped amount. Maximum profit occurs if the share price goes above the strike price of the call option that we sell (the short call) in order to enter the position. If you had only bought a put option, your possible profits could be much higher. No matter how much higher the stock price goes above the strike price of the short option, your profit stays the same at a fixed amount. So, any time you enter into a call debit spread, if the share price of the underlying stock goes above the short strike price, sell the position to get out of it with your profits. If conditions warrant it, you can just let the options expire.

Maximum losses for a call debit spread are capped. The maximum loss that you can incur with a call debit spread is when the underlying stock price drops below the long strike price (that is the strike price of the option that you buy to enter into the position). Again, this is a fixed value. So, no matter how low the price of the underlying stock drops, even if it were to drop all the way to zero, the number of losses that you could incur would be limited to the premium paid to enter the position.

The breakeven point occurs at the strike price of the long call plus the premium paid to enter the position. Using the Apple example, the premium paid was $1.19, and the lower strike price (or the strike price of the long call) was $302.50. So, the breakeven point is $302.50 + $1.19 = $303.69. Let's summarize this for our example, and this will help you understand how these trades work:

- If the stock drops below $302.50, even by a penny, we incur the maximum loss. That is the premium paid to enter the position, which in this case would be $1.19 per share or $119 for the 100 shares in total.

- The breakeven point is $302.50 + $1.19 = $303.69. If the stock is between $302.50 and $303.69, we incur losses, but they will be less than the total premium paid. If it reaches $303.69, we neither lose nor earn money.

- In between $303.69 and the short strike price of $307.50, we would earn a small profit.

- If the underlying share price were to go above $307.50, then we'd earn a maximum profit of $381. Even if the share price were to go up to $500, it wouldn't matter, our profit is strictly capped in this trade.

A call debit spread is a smarter way to play rising stock prices as opposed to buying call options. You actually cut your risk, because when you sell a call option, you get paid premium for that call option. Since the strike price is higher than the strike price for the long call in this trade, the amount you get paid is lower than the amount spent to buy the long call. However, it reduces the amount you have to pay, as compared to buying the long call by itself.

Put Debit Spreads

Now let's consider a put debit spread. This trade also goes by the name of bear debit spread or bear put spread. The purpose of this trade is the same goal as you would have to buy a single put option; you are anticipating that the share price of the underlying stock is going to go down. The basic setup is the same as it is with a call debit spread. However, since we are looking at put options, we are going to be doing the reverse in our thinking. We will belong on a higher strike price and short on a lower strike price. Both put options that are a part of the trade are going to have the same expiration date.

Once again, the maximum profit will be the width of the strike prices minus the cost to enter the position. The maximum loss you can incur on the trade is the premium paid to enter the position.

From here, things are just reversed in the sense that we are looking for declining prices in the share price of the underlying stock. Therefore, the maximum profit is going to occur if the share price of the underlying stock goes below the strike price of the short put option. The breakeven point will be the strike price of the long-put option minus the premium paid to enter the position. Again, the long-put option will have a higher strike price than the short put option in this case. This is a strategy that can be employed to minimize risk when you believe that the share price of the underlying stock is going to decline.

Debit spreads are limited risk, limited reward strategies. They are set up in order to reduce the amount of risk (the amount of money you can lose) associated with a trade. The cost of doing this is that you also have a reduced profit potential for the trade. However, a lesson you should learn is that very few professional options traders just do straight trading of call and put options. That type of strategy is a high-risk strategy. But you can do the same type of speculating using debit spreads.

Put Credit Spreads

Now let's continue our investigation of vertical spreads but shift gears. This time we are going to talk about using options in order to generate income, rather than speculating on the direction of the stock. Of course, there is always a little bit of speculation, but in this case, we are only hoping that the price stays above a certain value, and not worry about what it is doing otherwise.

A put credit spread is created by trading two put options simultaneously. It can be said that this is set up just like the put debit spread, but we reverse the roles of which option is bought or sold. In this case, we are going to sell a put option with a higher strike price. The purpose of doing so is to generate a credit to our account that earns income. In order to reduce our overall risk of the trade, we are going to sell a put option with a lower strike price. A put option with a higher strike price is going to cost more than a put option with a lower strike price; therefore, there is a net credit on the trade.

There is only one rule to use when deciding to trade put credit spreads. You want to trade put credit spreads in good markets. It doesn't have to be a particularly strong bull market; it just has to be a market where prices are not declining. This applies to the individual stock as well, so you want to trade put credit spreads when the stock is doing well. A good rule of thumb is to avoid trading put credit spreads during the week of an earnings call when stock prices might suddenly plummet.

The main thing to learn about put credit spreads is that this is a selling position. You are going to sell to open, and therefore you will have the obligations of a seller associated with the short put with the higher strike price. That is, you could be "assigned". When a put option is exercised, the buyer will sell you 100 shares of stock at the strike price, no matter what the market price is. And theoretically, you need to have the cash on hand to cover the transaction. When you are assigned, you are required by law to buy the 100 shares.

But the good news about the put credit spread is you don't actually have to buy the shares, and your liability is capped. The reason is that you have covered yourself by purchasing a put option with a lower strike price. What happens is you are able to exercise the put option with the lower strike price. It works like this – you have to buy the 100 shares at the higher strike price. But you can turn around and sell them at the lower strike price by exercising the other put option. So, with a credit spread, you are assigned on one option and can exercise the other option. You would lose money in this situation; it would be the difference between the strike prices minus the net credit received. But at least it is a fixed amount of money.

In practice, you aren't going to have to do anything at all, because your broker takes care of all this automatically in the event the option expires in a situation where it could be exercised. As a trader, you won't know all this happened, the stocks will be bought and sold on your behalf, and you will only see the end result.

In order to sell put options, you are going to need some collateral. This is done by putting a cash deposit into your account. The purpose of doing so is to cover the theoretical loss that can occur if the trade does not work out for you. To see how this works, let's look at an example.

Consider a put credit spread on Apple that expires in one week. The strike prices are $297.50 and $295. The breakeven price is the strike price of the short put option, $297.50, less the net credit received. It is important to remember that with a credit spread, you don't actually pay anything to enter the position. You are actually receiving credit for it. But you won't actually see the credit materialize until the options expire or you buy it back.

In this case, the credit received is $1.12 per share, or $100. So, the breakeven point is $296.38. As long as the stock price stays above $296.38, you will make a profit (at the time of writing, it's $297.35). Maximum gain happens if the stock price stays or goes above the upper strike price. So, if it stays at or goes above $297.50 per share, a real possibility in this case, then you would earn the maximum credit of $112. Maximum loss is computed by taking the difference between the strike prices and subtracting the credit received. In this case, we have ($297.50 - $295) - $1.12 = $1.38, or $138.

In order to actually enter the trade, you would have to deposit some cash to cover that potential loss.

Put credit spreads are popular for generating regular income. Many professional options traders earn a living by selling put credit spreads at regular intervals. You can sell as many as you can back with collateral and can mix it up by using different stocks. The higher the share price on a stock, the more you can earn by selling put credit spreads. And at all times, the possible losses you can incur are known and fixed.

Call Credit Spreads

Put credit spreads sound great, but of course, the stock market is not going up and up all the time, even though it seems that way right now because we've been in a long-time bull market. What to do then? The answer is simple – you switch to selling call credit spreads in a bear market or when a stock is crashing. A call credit spread is designed to earn money when stock prices are dropping or staying below the lower strike price used in the spread.

In the call debit spread, we trade two call options with the same expiration date, and that is what we are going to be doing in this case. With the call debit spread, we bought a call option with a lower strike price and sold a call option with a higher strike price. Since call options with lower strike prices are worth more money, this results in a net debit to our account.

Now, we are going to do the reverse. So, we are going to sell a call option with a low strike price, and then buy one with a high strike price to reduce our risk. This will result in a net credit to our account. Other than the differences in the relationships of the strike prices and the fact these are calls rather than puts, the principles are exactly the same as a put credit spread.

In this case, the risk of assignment is that we would have to sell shares. But when using a credit spread, you don't actually have to own the shares. When a call option is exercised, the seller/writer of the option is required to sell 100 shares of stock at the strike price. In this case, if that were to happen to you with a spread, you don't have to do anything other than cry when you get your losses. The broker will sell the shares on your behalf and exercise the long option to recoup some of the losses.

If you decide to be an options seller, you can make a good living switching between call and put credit spreads as market conditions warrant. This is completely different than stock trading, as you will never have to worry about whether the stock market is bearish or bullish, you can earn money under any circumstances using these methods.

Time Decay and Buy Backs

Two things work in your favor as an options seller. For options buyers, time decay works against them because the option is losing value. As an options seller, that doesn't affect you – in fact, it helps you a great deal if you are selling out of the money options (and they stay out of the money). As a seller, time decay works in your favor as the options become less valuable to buyers. That makes it less likely they are going to be exercised as time passes.

The second key strategy is to buy your positions back either close to expiration, or in the event, they go in the money. If the options are not close to expiration, but they go in the money, there is a chance that they would be exercised. However, that is generally less likely. But if you feel there is a risk that the options are not going to go out of the money again prior to expiration, you can simply buy the contract back. When you buy an options contract back, you are freed of all obligations associated with that contract.

Chapter 8: Selling Options

In the last chapter, we actually touched on selling options, doing it by mitigating risk using credit spreads. In this case, we are going to talk about selling options without mitigating the risk, which is simply selling them alone. If the options are backed, we have covered calls and cash covered puts. If the options are not backed by anything, they are called "naked". Although it sounds crazy to sell naked options at first glance, the truth is many professional options traders make $500,000 and up per year selling naked options. Let's investigate each of these in turn in this chapter.

Covered Calls

The least risky option strategy is to sell covered calls. In order to sell a covered call, you must own 100 shares of stock. Many investors earn income from dividends, and covered calls provide an alternative and often more lucrative way to earn money from stock ownership. However, it does carry some risk in that your stock may be "called away". That is, if the stock price moves above the strike price of any option you sell + the premium received for the option, the buyer of the option may choose to exercise it, which means they have the legal right to buy 100 shares of stock from you at the strike price.

But, if you own 1,000 shares in Apple (actually any number of a specific stock of 100 shares or more), or some other good company that can fetch a good options premium, and you are willing to assume the risk of having your stock called away, this can be used to generate regular income from your stocks. Each option that you sell must be backed by 100 shares of stock.

When you sell an option, you get to keep the premium that is paid for the option. In fact, you can keep it no matter what happens. So that is cash in your pocket even if you have to sell the shares. And in many cases, you aren't going to lose anything in a fundamental sense. If you had purchased the shares in the past at a lower price, this means that you will actually be selling them at a profit, although the amount of profit you earn will be lower than what you could have earned on the stock market. That is because you will have to sell them at the strike price, no matter how high the stock price rises. But there is the possibility that you can still "lose" in the trade and come out financially ahead.

Different people have different risk tolerance, and for some people, this is going to be too much. They aren't going to be willing to risk losing their stock. But if you are willing to take on that risk, there are ways to minimize it. Although you will make less money, you can sell out of the money call options that have a low probability of being exercised. Suppose that we had 300 shares of Tesla stock. It is currently trading at $441.91 per share. We could sell a call option with a $450 strike price to receive a premium of $14.93 per share. This option is listed by the broker as having a 70% chance of profit. For 100 shares, that would be $1,493. If we did that for all 300 shares, the total premium received would be $4,479. So, you could make big money doing this.

Like with credit spreads, you can always buy your options back. In the situation where you sell a covered call and then buy it back later, you are freed of the obligation of having to sell your shares, and you get to keep your shares. So generally speaking, unless you are careless, it is a low-risk strategy. Keep in mind that if the option goes in the money, there is a chance that a buyer can exercise it and require you to sell the shares. But most options are not exercised until expiration. So, you can avoid the situation by selling in the money options prior to expiration.

Cash Protected Puts

Another way to sell single options is by selling cash protected puts. A cash protected put means that you deposit the money in your brokerage account that would be necessary to buy 100 shares of stock. This is a less popular strategy for a few reasons. If you have that kind of money lying around, there are better ways to utilize it in stock and options trading. Another reason is that you can sell put credit spreads and only tie up a small fraction of the capital.

This can be an expensive proposition. To sell the $437.50 put on Tesla expiring in one week, you would need to deposit $42,982.34 into your brokerage account. For the trouble, you would make $750. That would only be a 1.7% return on your money. If you have $42k to invest, I am sure you don't want to tie it up to make $750, especially when you could sell put credit spreads and make $750 tying up, maybe $1,200 or so.

The bottom line is that cash protected puts are not a favored strategy. In fact, they might be called pointless.

Naked Put Options

Finally, we come to the holy grail of income generation using options, which is selling naked options. This is a simpler strategy than selling vertical spreads, but the goals are the same. We have simply removed the risk mitigating factor. When you sell naked put options, you are selling one option in each trade. You receive the premium credit, and that's it.

In order to sell naked options, you are required to have a margin account and to deposit a certain amount of money to cover a trade. The amount of money is a fraction of the amount of money that you have to put in in order to sell a cash protected put. So, while you might be required to deposit $180,000 to sell cash protected puts against Amazon, you'd only have to deposit around $11,000 to sell naked Amazon puts.

The biggest risk of naked put options is assignment. That is, you are not paying attention, and the share price drops well below your strike price, and someone exercises the option. That would put you in a position of having to buy the shares. Then you could resell them on the market at the lower share price and take the loss.

This is why a margin account is necessary. A margin account is a type of account that lets you borrow money and shares from the broker. So, the required capital you must deposit helps cover your losses to some extent. You are going to have to borrow from the broker to buy the shares, and then after you sell them on the market the collateral you put up will cover the net loss.

You can also sell naked call options when stock market prices are declining. These are well-known winning strategies used by professionals. In the event that it looks like it is a losing trade, you use the same techniques you would use for credit spreads, that is you simply buy back the contracts.

Chapter 9: Tips for Successful Trading

In this chapter, we are going to run through some tips for successful options trading. These tips are based on years of experience trading options and come from many different people.

Set Stops on Your Trades

The biggest risk for an options trader is that they will get emotional during a trade. This can result in selling too early because of panic about declining options prices or staying in a trade too long because of greed. To avoid these problems, you can set a rule on the amount of loss you are willing to accept and the amount of profit you are willing to take on a trade. Many brokers allow you to hard code this with the trading software so that it gets implemented automatically. Then you don't have to worry about your trades. You just accept the end results. Another way to say this is to have a defined exit plan.

Letting Options Expire

Never let options expire, unless specific conditions are met. If you are buying call options and want to actually own the stock, then you can let an in the money option expire. If you are trading out of the money options, you should never let them expire. Sell them even it would mean a losing trade, a day or two before expiration. That way you can at least cut your losses.

Consider Rolling Out Trades That Aren't Working

Rolling out an option means closing the position and then entering the position again, but with a longer expiration date. This gives you more time to work the trade by pushing the expiration date to the future.

Avoid Options with Low Volume

Remember, you always want to look for liquidity. One of the biggest mistakes made by novice options traders is to trade options that are illiquid. Remember the rule for open interest, only trade options that have an open interest of 100 or higher. That will save you from getting into trouble trading options with low volume where you could get stuck in a trade.

Attempting to Make up for Past Failures

Don't try to trade using a higher volume in order to make up for past mistakes.

Conclusion

Thank you for making it through to the end of *Options Trading Crash Course*, let's hope it was informative and able to provide you with all of the tools you need to achieve your goals whatever they may be.

Options trading is a very exciting part of the stock market. With options trading, you can control large amounts of stock without actually owning it. This means that you can earn profits from movements in the stock price without risking huge amounts of capital. The return on investment on options is simply much better than the possible return on investment that you can earn trading options.

In this book, I have attempted to demystify options trading for you. We have explained what an option is, the difference between call and put options, and the strategies used by professional options traders when investing in options.

My hope is that rather than join the scare chorus that surrounds options from "financial advisors", I have shown you that options are actually a rational investment that can help you build your own successful trading business. Whether you engage in "speculation" or trading for investment income, options can help you read a six or even seven-figure income from your trading business, provided that you make careful trades and stick to the fundamental principles that are guaranteed to lead to success.

Your next steps are to actually get your feet wet with some trades. Start slowly, and spend some time trading small numbers of call and put options to build up some experience. Be sure to do both. Many novice traders are scared away from put options because they are not used to thinking in terms of earning money from declining stock prices. So, it's important to get over that and actually go through the experience of earning money while the company is having losses.

From there, you can start to employ options strategies after you've got a few months of experience making some trades. Before settling on a favorite, try the different strategies to see what you like best. Some people will end up focusing on only one trade. For example, many professional traders only trade iron condors, while others only sell put options. Others have a lot of variety and will engage in whatever trades suit them at the moment and what the market conditions are. This is a matter of personal taste, so you will have to figure out what works best for you.

I want to wish my readers good luck in the trading business!

Finally, if you found this book useful in any way, a review is always appreciated!